Scriptology™

FileMaker® Pro Demystified

by Matt Petrowsky and John Mark Osborne

www.scriptology.com

Scriptology© "FileMaker Pro Demystified" with Companion CD ROM

ISO Production's Scriptology "FileMaker Pro Demystified", First Edition
Published by ISO Productions, Inc.
Copyright ©1998 ISO Productions, Inc.

ISO Productions, Inc.
4049 First Street, Suite 215
Livermore, CA 94550
http://www.isoproductions.com/
<iso@isoproductions.com>

Published in the United States by ISO Productions, Inc.

ISBN: 0-9660876-0-7

Composed and produced by ISO Productions, Inc.
Manufactured in the United States of America

10 9 8 7 6 5 4 3 2 1

Limit of Liability/Disclaimer of Warranty: The authors and publisher have used their best efforts in preparing this book, the CD ROM accompanying this book, and the programs and data contained herein. However, the authors and publisher make no warranties of any kind, expressed or implied, with regard to the documentation, programs or data contained in this book or CD ROM, and specifically disclaim, without limitation, any implied warranties of merchantability and fitness for a particular purpose with respect to the CD ROM, the programs and/or techniques described in the book. In no event shall the authors or publisher be responsible or liable for any loss of profit or any other commercial damages, including but not limited to special, incidental, consequential, or any other damages in connection with or arising out of furnishing, performance, or use of this book or the programs or data.

Trademarks: A number of entered words in which we have reason to believe trademark, service mark, or other proprietary rights may exist have been designated as such by use of initial capitalization. However, no attempt has been made to designate as trademarks or service marks all personal computer words or terms in which proprietary rights might exist. The inclusion, exclusion or definition of a word or terms is not intended to affect, or to express any judgment on, the validity or legal status of any proprietary right which may be claimed in that word or term.

Credits

Publisher
ISO Productions, Inc.

Managing Editor
Matt Petrowsky

Editorial Supervisors
John Mark Osborne and
Brian Ball

Production Director
Matt Petrowsky

Production Editors
Matt Petrowsky and
John Mark Osborne

Technical Editors
Matt Petrowsky and
John Mark Osborne

Layout Design
Matt Petrowsky

Cover Design
Matt Petrowsky

CD ROM Content Developer
John Mark Osborne

Interface Development
Matt Petrowsky

Director of Marketing
Brian Ball

Copy Editing
Jim Spelman, John Mark
Osborne, Barbara & Monte
Nichols, Brian Ball

Product Testing
Matt Petrowsky, John Mark
Osborne, Brian Ball, Marc
Norman, Bob Cusick, Marc
Sigel, Bill Swagerty, Barbara &
Monte Nichols and Glenn
Killam

Production Team
Matt Petrowsky, John Mark
Osborne, Brian Ball and Donna
Shaun Ferraro

Acknowledgments

When I was creating my first FileMaker Pro database, I never dreamed that I would someday be capable of doing what can be done today. One of the most overwhelming feelings you get from FileMaker Pro is that of empowerment. To be able to sit down, control and manipulate volumes of information is such a wonderful feeling.

On my path of growth with FileMaker Pro there have been many people who have helped me along the way. It would be impossible to mention them all. There are a few individuals who stand out in my mind as having had a significant part in the whole process. In no favorable order these would be Joel Bowers, Bill Swagerty, Bob Cusick, Eric Culver, Jeff Gagné and not to forget the wunderkind, John Mark Osborne, who has contributed to this project quite significantly and without whom it would not exist.

Surprisingly, the people I would like to thank most are those people who say "It can't be done." It was because of such defeatist statements that I sat down at my first FileMaker Pro database in 1990 and have been hacking out files ever since.

I would also like to express my sincere appreciation for all of the supporters of ISO FileMaker Magazine. Without their support, this product would never have been conceived.

Matt Petrowsky

About the Authors

Matt Petrowsky has been creating intriguing interfaces and developing in FileMaker Pro since 1990. Early excursions into computers and technology started with Texas Instruments and Commodore computers. After schooling, Matt worked as a consultant to the Interface Design Group at Claris Corp. He was commissioned to participate in the productions of both Claris Organizer and ClarisWorks 5.0. At the beginning of 1994 he started a digital publication for FileMaker Pro users named ISO FileMaker Magazine <http://www.filemakermagazine.com/>. He is now leading a group of motivated FileMaker Pro enthusiasts as President and CEO of ISO Productions, Inc., the leader in third party FileMaker Pro training and resource information.

John Mark Osborne got involved at an early age with computers using an Apple II at the family home. Throughout college, he worked with computers as a Teaching Assistant for a Pascal course, conducting training classes at the UC Santa Barbara computer laboratory, assisting sales representatives as an Apple Student Representative, forming a Macintosh Users Group and volunteering to teach computers to underprivileged children. John Mark earned his FileMaker degree while working at Claris in their Technical Support department. For the last two years of his five year employment, he held the position of FileMaker Technical Lead. His most significant accomplishment at Claris was the writing of a large portion of the articles in the Claris TechInfo library. John Mark also maintains a free web site for FileMaker Pro users with one of the largest collections of tips and tricks on the internet <http://www.best.com/~jmo/>.

Contact ISO Productions

ISO Productions, Inc. provides high quality services and products based on FileMaker Pro. Over the past few years, we've noticed an increase not only in the number of people using the software but also the quality of the solutions being produced. Every day there are more and more commercial FileMaker Pro solutions grabbing main stream media attention.

We'd like to hear from you regarding any comments, suggestions or ideas about Scriptology "FileMaker Pro Demystified" and the services that ISO Productions, Inc. provides. You can visit us any time on the web at:

http://www.isoproductions.com/

Or, send email to:

iso@isoproductions.com

We are constantly seeking top quality FileMaker Pro products, services and talent.

Contact ISO with your information.

ISO Productions, Inc.
4049 First Street, Suite 215
Livermore, CA 94550
United States

Phone: (925) 454-0187
Fax: (925) 454-9877

Other FileMaker Pro Products & Services

ISO Productions, Inc. produces other products related to the instruction and development of FileMaker Pro. For more information on these products visit their web sites or call (925) 454-0187.

ISO FileMaker Magazine

http://www.filemakermagazine.com/

The ISO FileMaker Magazine is the premier digital magazine. It takes the reader inside FileMaker Pro by providing in-depth articles covering techniques and methods for solving problems. One of many highlights of the publication is its monthly bonus FileMaker Pro files. These hands-on files provide examples of techniques discussed in the associated articles. Published twelve times a year, this product is a valuable addition to the beginning, intermediate and advanced FileMaker Pro user. Available for Windows 3.1/95/NT and Macintosh.
$50 US for annual subscription. (current price at date of publication)

Everything CD for FileMaker Pro

http://www.everythingcd.com/filemaker/

The Everything CD for FileMaker Pro is a huge collection of the best that the FileMaker Pro industry has to offer. It includes over 1 gigabyte of freeware, shareware, commercial demos, tips & tricks, online mailing list archives, learning resources, developer tools and other items related to FileMaker Pro. All these FileMaker Pro files are indexed in a FileMaker Pro database to make it as easy as possible to locate what you need. Available for both Macintosh and Windows 95/NT.
$49.99 US (current price at date of publication)

Training Courses for FileMaker Pro

http://www.isoproductions.com/training/

ISO retains one of the most educated pools of FileMaker Pro talent in the world. Please visit their web site or call (925) 454-0187 for training information.

Contents

Chapter 4: ScriptMaker Steps Defined   41

Chapter 5: ScriptMaker Fundamentals   143

Chapter 6: ScriptMaker Debugging   187

Chapter 7: Calculation Fundamentals 197

Chapter 8: Calculation Debugging 209

Chapter 9: Validations 227

Chapter 10: Value Lists 245

Chapter 11: Data Operations 261

Chapter 12: Understandable Relationships   281

Chapter 13: Portal Power   305

Chapter 14: Relationship Debugging   323

Chapter 15: Going Cross-Platform   331

Chapter 16: User Interface Issues   353

Chapter 17: Advice - Making it Easy   381

Appendixes   400

Introduction

Who this book is for: This book and CD are not intended to teach the fundamentals of using FileMaker Pro. If you picked it up thinking that it was, then you may want to peruse the FileMaker Pro user manual and one or two other books that do a great job with the basics.

Scriptology "FileMaker Pro Demystified" was created for individuals like yourself, whether beginner or advanced, who want to move to the next level – beyond the basics. Within this book, and especially on the CD, you will find more FileMaker Pro techniques and tips than you will find anywhere else. It is the presentation that makes Scriptology so powerful. If you take the time to go through the example material and practice what you learn, it won't be long before you are creating files that you previously could only dream of making.

As you read this book, keep in mind this question, "Can FileMaker Pro do that?" More often than not the answer is, "If I don't know now, I'm sure I can find a way!" If you keep this attitude, there is almost nothing stopping you from becoming a FileMaker Pro master!

How this product was developed: Scriptology was developed by combining the knowledge of the two authors and the pool of information available directly from the FileMaker Pro community. The CD ROM contains hands-on examples that would take many pages of code and syntax in the book. The book was written to provide the fundamentals of higher level design and approach when creating FileMaker Pro databases. There is no shortage of practical examples on the CD ROM, and throughout the book there are references to these examples contained on the CD ROM. When you find yourself wishing there were examples provided in the book, utilize the CD ROM and print out any instructional information that will help you learn the specific technique.

How the book is broken down: The book is broken down into four primary areas of interest to FileMaker Pro users. These cover some of the more complex issues related to using ScriptMaker, working with Calculations and understanding Relationships. The last area covers techniques the experts use to polish their solutions, like cross-platform considerations, interface design and templates.

Starting Out

1.0 Overview

Congratulations on purchasing one of the most powerful FileMaker Pro instructional products available. Though we put the words on paper and organized the ideas, what you will find in this book and CD did not come only from us. Whether a beginner or experienced FileMaker Pro user, it was you who contributed to this expansive base of FileMaker Pro knowledge. All this knowledge is now organized into a coherent learning environment so the information is easily accessible – we call it Scriptology.

A short history of FileMaker Pro

For years, FileMaker Pro has been the number-one rated database system for the Macintosh. In the past few years, FileMaker Pro has become increasingly well known in the Windows world and this trend will continue in the years to come. The seamless nature of its cross-platform compatibility is very appealing to system administrators, developers, small business owners and general users.

FileMaker Pro was developed in 1983 by Nashoba Systems of Concord, Massachusetts. It was acquired by Claris Corporation, a wholly owned subsidiary of Apple Computer, in July of 1988. Ironically, FileMaker Pro, at that time, was named FileMaker 4 and later called FileMaker II. Back then, under the distribution of a company named Forethought Inc., FileMaker captured 40% of the Macintosh market and the position has increased to over 70% since that time. To say that FileMaker Pro is a run-away success is an understatement. With its entry into the

FileMaker Pro 4.X

FileMaker Pro 3.X

FileMaker Pro 2.X

FileMaker Pro 1.X

FileMaker II

FileMaker 4

FileMaker Plus

FileMaker

Windows database market and its assault on the territory dominated by Microsoft Access, FileMaker Pro is already a significant player in the database market. Now sold through its own company, FileMaker, Inc., the software will continue to evolve into a powerful tool for information management.

The basics: an expectations disclaimer

Much of FileMaker Pro's difficulty lies in its nuances. Despite its stated "ease-of-use" there are parts of FileMaker Pro that are not readily understood or explained. It is the intent of this book and the companion CD to show you the ins and outs of FileMaker Pro rather than teach you the basic features found in the FileMaker Pro manual. *You should have already read the manual that came with FileMaker Pro, or at the very least, be familiar with FileMaker Pro fundamentals before working with Scriptology.*

Macintosh or Windows?

This book and CD were created using both Macintosh and Windows based computers. It is without bias that the screen shots were created using a Macintosh. The information provided is truly cross-platform, as is FileMaker Pro itself. If a feature specific to either version is pointed out, you can expect to see the respective icon for that OS next to the text.

1.1 How to use this book

This book is not designed to be a purely linear read. It is designed to be used as a learning reference. The best approach is to read the first chapter and then jump around to the areas that interest you. You will find complete areas that focus on the more elusive concepts of FileMaker Pro, such as scripting, calculations and relationships. Combining these powerful concepts with a solid understanding of the fundamentals will allow you to create very powerful database solutions.

1.2 Using the companion CD ROM

The CD ROM in the back of this book contains hundreds of hands-on examples covering specific FileMaker Pro techniques. Throughout this book you will find references to the Chapter, Technique and Reference files on the CD. The Chapter files supplement the concepts discussed in the book by giving working, FileMaker Pro examples. Technique files are similar to Chapter files, but rather than follow chapters in the book, the instructions for Technique files are included in the FileMaker Pro database titled INDEX.FP3 (see Picture 1.2). Make sure to use the help button in the INDEX.FP3 file to gain a complete understanding of the icons, buttons, and other interface elements in the techniques index.

You'll find CD file references (below) in the side bar throughout the book.

 17_A.FP3
Chapter File:
Moving Data Between Files

 XPLAT.FP3
Reference File:
Cross-Platform Considerations

 COND.FP3
Technique File:
Conditional Menus

Technique files on the CD ROM use FileMaker Pro files to guide you through the implementation of a solution or technique.

Use the help button found in the INDEX.FP3 file on the CD ROM for more information about the files contained on the CD.

Picture 1.2
Each of the 200 plus technique files are indexed on the CD ROM in the INDEX.FP3 file.

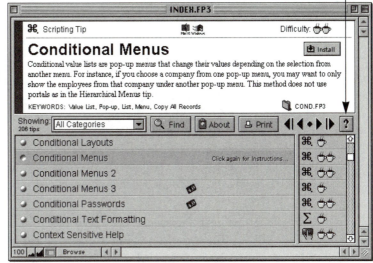

About the CD ROM files

File types and their function

Chapter files   FileMaker Pro files that correspond to the content discussed in the book.

Technique files   FileMaker Pro files that highlight a specific FileMaker Pro technique. These files are referenced throughout the book, but can be used separately.

Reference files   FileMaker Pro files that contain FileMaker Pro information useful when creating database systems.

List of Reference files:

On the CD ROM you'll find a set of files called reference files.

The 12 reference files on the CD include:

- ASCII Characters
- Native Palettes
- Error Codes
- Power Keys
- Calculation Functions
- A Graphics Library
- New FileMaker Pro 4.0 Features
- ScriptMaker Steps
- Technical Specifications
- Template Files
- Top FileMaker Pro Resources
- Cross-Platform Considerations

These Reference files help you to quickly and efficiently locate FileMaker Pro information. It is recommended that you install these files on your computer's hard drive. This allows you to customize any of these databases to your individual needs. For example, you may choose to add notes about a ScriptMaker feature that worked particularly well.

1.3 Conventions

The conventions in this book allow you to quickly identify ScriptMaker code and calculation functions. When a particular function or technique is specific to a version of FileMaker Pro, a tag will be used as seen below.

3.0/4.0   **4.0 Only**

Bullet, check and numbered lists emphasize procedures and highlight important information. Words found in **bold text** can be found in the glossary.

Scripting Example

4.0 Only

ScriptMaker script: "Example code"

Throughout the book you will find various instances of ScriptMaker or calculation code.

```
Comment ["READ ME..Be sure to comment your scripts"]
If ["Field X = "Contains Text""]
    Perform Script [Sub-scripts, "BUTTON: Go To Layout: Form View"]
End If
If ["Field Y = "Print Instructions""]
    Perform Script [Sub-scripts, "PAGESETUP: Comm 10 Envelope"]
    Perform Script [Sub-scripts, "PRINTFORM: Envelope"]
End If
```

Troubleshooting Example

ScriptMaker checklist

- ❑ Does the script use Copy, Paste, Paste Literal or any other script step that requires the script to be on a certain layout?
- ❑ Did you double-check that the field you need to access is on the layout?
- ❑ Is the Restore Criteria option checked when you don't want it to be?
- ❑ If the script is running slow, did you try using a Freeze Window step?
- ❑ Does your Status(CurrentMessageChoice) check for the correct result?

Power Tips are found in the sidebar throughout the book. They present additional insights about the subject being discussed.

1.4 What you won't find in Scriptology

No single book can cover every aspect of FileMaker Pro. The approach taken in Scriptology is to avoid reiterating the information detailed in the FileMaker Pro manual and other third party books. For this reason, Scriptology does not cover the following:

- Searching for records
- Importing and exporting
- How to create your first database
- Layout parts and how they work
- Relational theory and concepts
- ER Diagraming (making relational data charts)
- Complex print forms
- Security issues
- Networking optimization
- Interconnectivity with other applications
- Web enabling FileMaker Pro

1.5 What you should already know

Power Tip

When working with Scriptology, it's best to be at a computer with a CD ROM drive.

You should already be familiar with FileMaker Pro to make the best use of this book. While it's not necessary that you know FileMaker Pro in depth, it does help if you are familiar with the basics of how to set up a FileMaker Pro database. This book assumes that you wish to learn more about the intricacies of ScriptMaker, calculations and relational techniques. A solid understanding of the following concepts will allow you to take full advantage of this product.

- Creating and adjusting layouts
- Creating fields
- Making basic calculations
- Using Find mode
- Formatting fields and value lists
- Using merge fields
- Making a basic relationship
- Creating simple scripts
- Sorting

1.6 What you can expect to learn

We have included everything we know about FileMaker Pro calculation functions, scripts and relationships. Scriptology shows you how to combine them all to create sophisticated FileMaker Pro solutions. The level of understanding you can expect to achieve depends on the amount of time you spend practicing the techniques discussed. ***Reading alone will not enable you to master the material.***

Working through this book and the companion CD, while practicing what you learn, will allow you to acquire:

- A higher level of scripting ability
- More advanced calculation techniques
- Unique approaches to using FileMaker Pro
- A better understanding of logical and looping functions
- How to approach cross-platform issues
- Skills for troubleshooting calculations, scripts and relationships
- Knowledge of validation techniques
- Advanced relationship and portal techniques
- Interface enhancement skills

Practicing the techniques doesn't just mean implementing the solutions as presented. It's important to learn the concepts, rather than the sequence of steps. Almost every script, calculation and relationship technique shown will teach you something. Take what you learn and apply it to your own solutions.

The focus of the Scriptology product

The main areas covered by Scriptology

ScriptMaker scripting	The first area of Scriptology focuses on a deeper understanding of FileMaker Pro's ScriptMaker and how to use it more efficiently.
Complex calculations	The second area of Scriptology focuses on multi-function calculations and understanding how to implement them into your database solutions.
Mastering relationships	The third area of Scriptology deals with relationships and how they are used in FileMaker Pro.
Advanced methods	The fourth area of Scriptology is spread throughout the book and covers information specific to mastering FileMaker Pro. In some cases, the concepts discussed may seem abstract. Understanding the concepts will provide the ability to develop solutions to your own unique problems.

Chapter 2

ScriptMaker™: The Basics

2.0 ScriptMaker
A macro language

In this chapter, you'll learn the basics of ScriptMaker – how it's useful and why you should use it. Though much of FileMaker Pro's raw power lies in ScriptMaker, scripting is one of the last areas most users explore. If you've been working with FileMaker Pro without using ScriptMaker, hang on and buckle up for the ride of your life.

2.1 What is ScriptMaker?

ScriptMaker isn't a computer language like BASIC, Pascal or C/C++. ScriptMaker is basically a macro generator. What's a macro? It's a sequence of steps that run in a linear fashion to automate a process that would otherwise be performed manually. What you get with ScriptMaker, that you don't get with other macro languages, is a dynamic environment. Once finished, you can end up with many scripts (macros) that create a feature set. One script can call another script, which can, in turn, call yet another script. Scripts can also make logical decisions (If statements) and perform repetitive tasks (Looping statements).

INDEX.FP3

Technique File Index

Searching the INDEX.FP3 on the CD ROM for the keyword "Case" will result in 17 techniques dealing with If statements which are essentially the same as Case statements. Searching for the keyword "Loop" will provide you with 20 different techniques.

Scripting is what makes a database solution equivalent to a piece of software. So, in the truest sense, you are programming when creating functional scripts. You can even think of ScriptMaker as quasi object-oriented. While it could be argued that it is unlike object oriented programming (because it lacks aspects such as inheritance, classes and a few other technical features), you are still creating objects (scripts) that perform actions and can be referenced by other scripts. You needn't be scared off by these technical sounding terms. Developing a FileMaker Pro solution requires only a fraction of the time, yet the results are similar to developing with a programming language.

2.2 Understanding the Macro functionality of ScriptMaker

⊙ SCRPTNG.FP3

Reference File:
ScriptMaker Steps

The best approach to creating a script is to list out the steps of the procedure in plain English. A good example is finding and printing all delinquent payments for an invoicing system. The steps in a script are similar to those you would use if performing the task manually. You might find yourself doing the following:

Sending delinquent notices

In real life...

Steps you might take to send out notifications of delinquent payments.

Step 1. Find all the invoices that are past due.

Step 2. Print out each invoice, stopping when you reach the last delinquent invoice.

Step 3. Make a notation that a second invoice was sent to the customer.

Step 4. File the original invoices.

This four-step process is a simple task once the steps are broken down. These steps just need to be translated into the ScriptMaker language.

ScriptMaker uses a linear process much like you would. ScriptMaker starts at the beginning and steps through each script step until it comes to the end of the script or until something tells it to stop. (Either a Halt or Exit script step will stop a script prematurely; both will be covered in a later chapter.)

Sending delinquent notices

ScriptMaker script: "Delinquent Notice"

This is an example script, written in English, that finds all delinquent invoices and prints a notice for each one.

```
Step 1: Find [Restore] -- a find that locates all past due invoices
Step 2: Go to the first record
Step 3: Go to layout formatted to print invoices
Step 4: Begin Loop (Repeat the printing process until all invoices
        are printed. Steps 5,6, and 7 comprise the loop.)
Step 5: Print the invoice
Step 6: Make a note on the current invoice that this is the second
        notice
Step 7: Go to the next invoice (record) [Exit the loop if it is the
        last invoice, otherwise go to Step 5 and loop again]
Step 8: End Loop
Step 9: Go back to the original layout
```

2.3 How powerful is it?

You can do anything with FileMaker Pro that you can do with a calculator or even a paper and pencil. The advantages of using a database are speed and automation of repetitive tasks. Calculation fields, along with the Find and Sort mechanisms, provide the speed. They evaluate and arrange data more quickly and easily than by any other means. Using ScriptMaker adds a level of automation and sophistication to your database, making it significantly more useful. Sequencing the steps which perform Finds and Sorts, adding repetitive controls (looping) and incorporating the power of decision-making conditional statements (if-then-else), enable your database to do just about anything you can dream up. By attaching the script to a button, the whole process becomes a one-click operation.

2.4 The real learning curve

Mastering ScriptMaker is like learning to play a musical instrument. The more you practice, the more you will be able to determine when and how to use this new skill. When working with FileMaker Pro you should always ask yourself the following questions:

Key questions when using ScriptMaker

Things to ask about your database
- Would it be faster if the computer did this?
- Am I repeating steps that could be automated?
- Are there too many steps for another person to remember if I told them how to do it?
- Can I simplify the process?

With the information in this book, you set your own learning curve. This book, plus the companion CD, will give you everything that we've ever come across in the life of FileMaker Pro. Beyond that, it's a simple matter of taking the time to understand how ScriptMaker can work for you. Examine your own use of FileMaker Pro. If there is something you are doing manually on a routine basis, it can be automated. If it's taking too much time to step through a certain procedure, you can optimize it. The time invested up front in programming ScriptMaker will pay off handsomely in the long run.

What you should have learned
- What ScriptMaker is and does
- How breaking down the events of a process can lead to automation
- Working with ScriptMaker is the only way to learn

Intermediate/Advanced

Methods to ScriptMaker Madness

3.0 ScriptMaker and good practice

As a database project grows larger and more complex, you'll end up with a growing number of scripts. This is especially true if you adhere to a modular script design that divides complex scripts into smaller pieces (covered in Section 3.2). FileMaker Pro doesn't have a robust system for documenting scripts. For this reason, it's important to develop your own documentation style (see Picture 3.0). This practice will help later on when you need to understand what you did just a couple of months before. Once you find a system that fits how you work, you will be able to utilize ScriptMaker more efficiently.

Picture 3.0
The beginning of an efficient organization method for scripts.

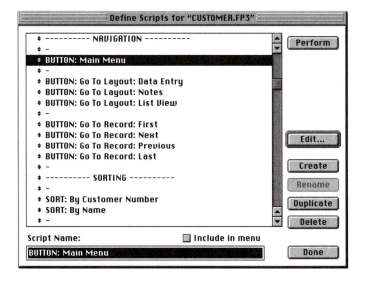

3.1 Good habits – standards

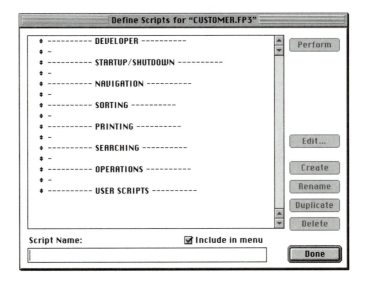

COMMENT.FP3

Technique File:
Commenting Files

FileMaker Pro has very few organizational tools within ScriptMaker. Navigating to the script you want to work with requires scrolling through a list of all of the scripts in the file. You can't organize your scripts into folders or categories. Because of this, a system for organization becomes imperative when a large number of scripts is involved. Separate your scripts however you wish; function, layout, use, etc., but be consistent.

Section Dividers

Section Dividers simulate a folder structure by allowing you to separate your scripts into categories. In Picture 3.1, you see an example of this technique. Scripts which contain no commands are used to organize the ScriptMaker list. The name of your empty script will act as the Section Divider.

Picture 3.1
Section dividers give you organizational control over your scripts.

Indenting

Indenting is another useful technique found in almost all coding environments. Although you're not really coding in ScriptMaker, you can take advantage of a proven system. Fortunately, ScriptMaker does not limit the naming of scripts. Extra spaces or characters in the name do not affect the running of the script. With that being the case, scripts can be indented to show their relationship to other scripts. By referring to scripts and sub-scripts as parent and child, any indented child script is related to the preceding unindented parent script. Sub-scripts perform very specific tasks and are usually called from the parent script. Indenting allows you to easily identify related scripts from a large list.

Picture 3.1.1
Indenting your sub-script names indicates that they are used in main scripts.

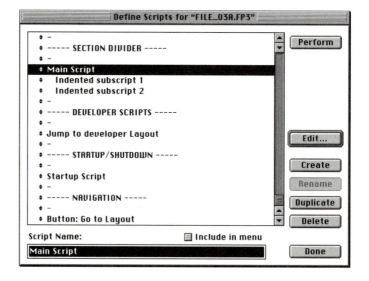

Naming Conventions and Script Identifiers

Naming your scripts should allow you to identify their function at a glance. Too often, the function of a poorly named script will be difficult to recognize a month later. A good practice when naming scripts is to attach identifiers. By attaching specific words to your script names, you can readily determine the function based on your own organizational style. There are many ways to name scripts. One method is the prefix and suffix model. In this system, you would use the word "Button:" as a prefix to all script names that are activated by buttons. Extending the name to describe the function is the purpose of the remaining part (e.g. Button: Perform Search). Identifiers can also indicate what a script will do when called from another script. For example, calling a find script named "No criteria found: HALT" from another script, identifies it as a script that halts the scripting

Power Tip

Unlike naming calculations and relationships, there are no limitations to the characters you can use in a script name.

Picture 3.1.2
Prefix and suffix identifiers make it easier to identify your script and its function.

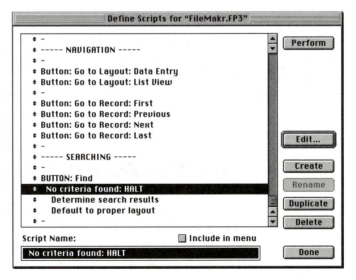

process when a find doesn't locate any records. For this naming system to function effectively, it is important to modify all script names whenever their function changes.

Suggested Naming Conventions

Different ways you can identify your scripts
- Use the prefixes "Button:" or "[BUTTON] =" on all scripts attached to buttons.
- Use "Layout:" or "[LAYOUT] =" as a prefix to all navigation scripts.
- Use "[ROUTINE] =" in any script that performs only a small part of a large multi-part script.
- Use "[TOOLBOX] =" on any script used as a development script.
- Use suffix identifiers on any script that will cause either the Halt or Exit of any calling script.

Example script names

[BUTTON] = Post Invoice
[LAYOUT] = Go To List View:Browse
[LAYOUT] = Go To List View:Find
[ROUTINE] = Loop Data Checksum
[TOOLBOX] = Developer layout & variables

3.2 Modular script design

If you think about anything you might accomplish in the real world, more than likely it's procedural and each part of the whole process can be broken down into smaller pieces. When you want to pick up a friend to go to the movies, you can break down the car trip to the friend's house as one part and the trip to the movies as another. The return trip would be yet another part. Combining the parts makes up the basic procedure of driving to the movies.

Open this file and follow along

◎ **03_A.FP3**

Chapter File:
Modular Script Design

Modular design with ScriptMaker is defined as breaking one larger script into many sub-scripts and linking them together. The linking is done with a single master script. The Perform Script step is used to "call" each sub-script. Creating a sub-script makes a typically static structure into something dynamic and capable of being reused multiple times. This allows a single sub-script to be called from many other scripts. If modifications become necessary, only that sub-script needs to be changed.

It is essential that you learn how to break down your scripts into smaller chunks and name them something representative of what they accomplish. The intention is to break up the script in a logical fashion, so the pieces represent distinct parts of the whole. Even if you have a sub-script that only performs the Go To Layout script step, you're better off. Let's say you have five scripts that perform different tasks, but all go to the same layout. If you decided you wanted to add a Zoom Window script step, you would have to modify each of those five scripts.

In modular script design, a single script called "Go to Layout: List View" would be called from each of the other five scripts using Perform Script. When you later decide to make the zooming window part of your interface, just add the Zoom Window script step to the "Go to Layout: List View" script. This makes the change universal. Modular design will save you the time of tracking down each one of the scripts and adding the Zoom Window script step, as well as keep the length of your scripts manageable.

Managing the length of a script is also part of the modular approach. One of the easiest ways to recognize when your script is getting too long, is to look at the number of steps you can see on the screen. If you can't see all the steps within the ScriptMaker dialog box without scrolling, you probably have a script that's too long. To break a script down into smaller subparts, select the script and click the Duplicate button. Making the duplicate will save time creating the sub-scripts and offer a way to revert to the original script if needed. After you have duplicated the script, open it and trim out the steps that will remain in the original script. Return to the original script and remove the steps that are being broken down into

Duplicate

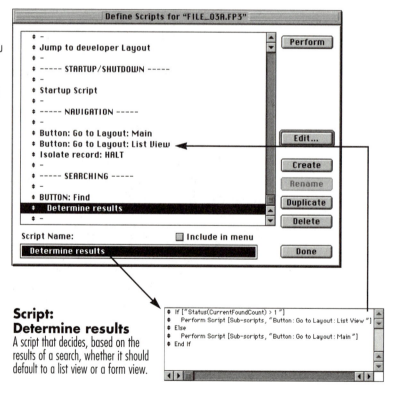

Picture 3.2
Modular script design allows you to add a simple Zoom Window script step to the Go to Layout script. The changes affect any script that call it.

Script:
Determine results
A script that decides, based on the results of a search, whether it should default to a list view or a form view.

sub-scripts. Now add the Perform Script step into the original script for each new sub-script that will be called (see Pictures 3.2.1, 3.2.2 & 3.2.3).

Breaking down larger scripts

Steps for creating sub-scripts out of larger scripts
1. Duplicate the larger script.
2. Open the duplicate script and trim out the parts to remain in the original script.
3. Open the original script and replace the script steps, now in the new duplicated script, with a Perform Script step.

Picture 3.2.1
A screen shot of an original script before it was duplicated and broken down.

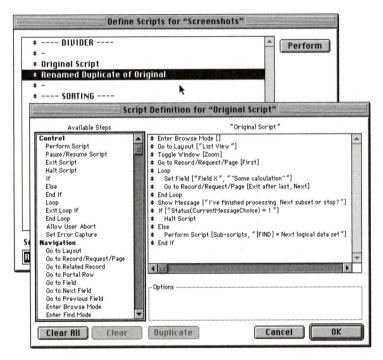

Being broken down
The loop in the above script could stand on its own, but is easier to follow if it's broken out as a sub-script.

Picture 3.2.2
This is the original script with the Loop removed. In its place is a Perform Script step.

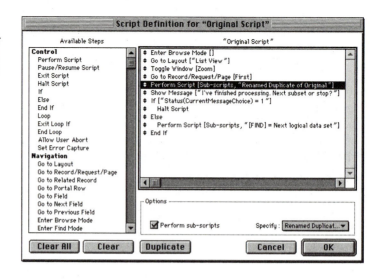

Picture 3.2.3
This is the duplicate of the original script. It contains only those steps that were removed from the original.

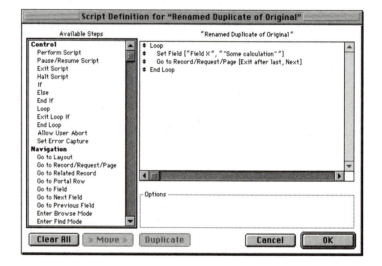

After being broken down

The new sub-script is a duplicate of the original script without the steps before and after the loop. In the original script, the loop is replaced with a Perform Script step. This is the modular approach to script design.

Example script (too long!)

ScriptMaker script: Find (from the database INDEX.FP3 on CD ROM)

While there may be cases where you can get away with a very lengthy script, it is usually not advisable to do so. This script can be found in the INDEX.FP3 file on the CD ROM and is a good example of a script that could be broken out into many different parts.

```
Allow User Abort [Off]
Set Error Capture [On]
Perform Script [Sub-scripts, "Trap Bad Find"]
If ["Find_Go Variable = 1"]
    Set Field ["Find_Go Variable", "2"]
    Set Field ["About_Cancel Variable", "4"]
    Go to Field [Select/perform, "Find Criteria"]
    Pause/Resume Script []
End If
If ["Find_Go Variable = 2"]
    If ["IsEmpty(Find Criteria) or Find Criteria = "Enter search criteria & click
GO""]
        Exit Record/Request
        Beep
        Set Field ["Find_Go Variable", "1"]
        Set Field ["About_Cancel Variable", "3"]
        Show Message ["No find criteria were entered!"]
        Exit Script
    End If
    Enter Find Mode []
    If ["PatternCount(Find Criteria, " or ")"]
        Set Field ["Counter", "1"]
        Set Field ["Exit Loop", "PatternCount(Find Criteria, " or ")"]
        Set Field ["Find Criteria", "" or " & Find Criteria & " or ""]
        Loop
            Set Field ["Find", "Middle(Find Criteria, Position(Find Crit…"]
            Exit Loop If ["Counter > Exit Loop"]
            New Record/Request
            Set Field ["Counter", "Counter + 1"]
        End Loop
    Else
            Set Field ["Find", "Find Criteria"]
    End If
    Perform Find []
    If ["Status(CurrentError) = 401"]
        Beep
        Set Field ["Find_Go Variable", "1"]
        Set Field ["About_Cancel Variable", "3"]
        Show Message ["No records were found!"]
        Find All
        Exit Script
    End If
Go to Layout ["Find"]
Copy All Records
Go to Layout ["List View"]
Paste [Select, No style, "Found Set"]
Set Field ["Show Categories", ""Found Set""]
```

> If statements make good logical breaks because they take care of a certain condition.

> Even embedded loops can be broken out

> More embedded If statements

```
Exit Record/Request
If ["Current Record <> Show Categories::Serial Number"]
   Perform Script [Sub-scripts, "Show Instructions"]
End If
Set Field ["Find_Go Variable", "1"]
Set Field ["About_Cancel Variable", "3"]
End If
```

Learning where to make the logical breaks in scripts is something that will come with time and may not yet feel natural. It will "click" at some point and designing modular systems will become second nature.

4.0 The many states of a script

A ScriptMaker script has three states; the running state, the not-running state and the paused state. When controlling these states with buttons, you have four options; Pause, Exit, Halt and Resume. Learning how to control script states with buttons is very powerful, yet often overlooked.

Picture 4.0
There are four options when assigning a Perform Script step to a button.

Options

HALT	Will stop **all** currently running scripts.
EXIT	Will stop **only the currently** running script. Sub-scripts will continue to run.
RESUME	Will **start** a **paused script**.
PAUSE	Will temporarily **suspend** the **running** of a **script**.

To better understand the different states of a script, compare executing a script to jogging. While jogging, you're most likely heading towards a planned destination. Along the way, many things can happen. Each time you hit an intersection you have the option of taking a different direction, basing your decision on the conditions. If you have to wait for traffic, you'll likely jog in place. This is much like a paused script. You're not at your destination, but you're still jogging. While on your normal route, you enter an area under construction. You can't continue so you decide to take another route. Taking the different route would be like exiting a sub-script since you are still jogging. At the next intersection, you hit another condition, a friend who invites you to lunch. Based on this condition you stop jogging. This would be considered a halt because you won't finish your daily mileage until you start the jog again. At this point your primary function is no longer jogging, it's eating lunch. In this scenario a condition prompted you to halt your jog, keeping you from completing the route you had planned, but you can always jog the route again later.

4.1   Pause/Exit/Halt/Resume

More than likely you know how to make a button and you know how to assign it a script. However, when assigning Perform Script to a button, you need to understand the Pause, Exit, Halt and Resume options. These are important only when other scripts might be running at the time the button is clicked. The default when creating a new button is Pause. Most of the time you won't change the default, but knowing when and why to change it is the key to powerful scripting.

How it affects buttons

When assigning a script to a button, you have to think about what other scripts could be running. Ask yourself:

- What other scripts could be running when the user clicks this button?
- What do I want to happen to any currently running scripts when the user clicks this button?
- What is the current state of ScriptMaker when the user has access to this button?
- If there are scripts running, what do I want to happen to those scripts?

ScriptMaker could be running a script, paused or idle. In most cases, the default Pause will work just fine. It will pause any currently running script, perform the script that is assigned to that button, and then resume the paused script.

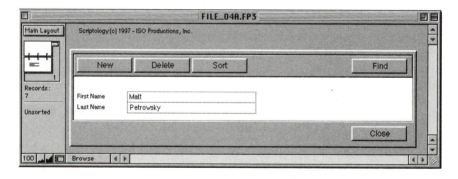

Picture 4.1
Clicking the Find button in the above file results in what is shown in Picture 4.1.1.

The confusion arises when you need to assign options other than the default to a button. This depends on how you want the currently running scripts to react to a button being clicked. A good example of when you might change the button option would be in the middle of a scripted find process.

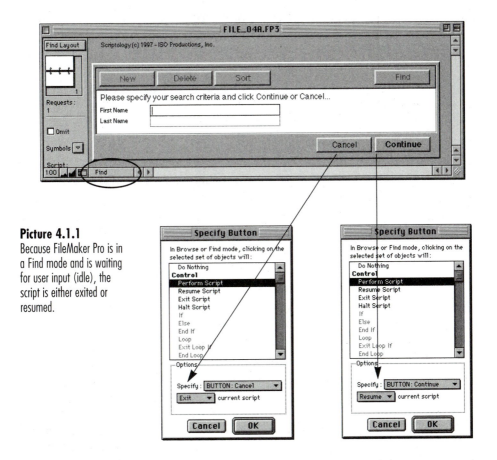

Picture 4.1.1
Because FileMaker Pro is in a Find mode and is waiting for user input (idle), the script is either exited or resumed.

Open this file and follow along

04_A.FP3
Chapter File:
Button States with Find

Let's assume, by way of example, that a Find button is provided in the user interface (see Picture 4.1). When clicked, a layout that looks like a find dialog box is presented, the mode is changed to find and the script pauses for user input. On this find layout, you have two buttons – a Continue button and a Cancel button (see Picture 4.1.1). If the user clicks the Cancel button, you want the paused Find script to be stopped. You can stop the script using the Exit or Halt option depending on what you want to happen. Using Halt stops all currently running scripts and sub-scripts. Exit only stops the currently running script, so if it had been called by another script, the calling script would continue. In file 04_A.FP3, the cancel button uses the Exit script step to exit the find script, enter Browse mode and switch back to the entry layout.

The Continue button from the Find example in Picture 4.1.1 implements the Resume option. The script attached to this button may or may not contain script steps. No script steps will be added if you want the Continue button to emulate a manual resume, i.e. hitting the Return key, typing the Enter key on the keypad or clicking on the Continue button in the status area. If steps are included in the script attached to the button, the Continue script will process its commands before resuming the paused Find script. In our example the Find script enters Find mode and pauses for the user to enter criteria. After the find criteria is entered, the Find script can then be resumed using the Continue button or any of the manual options. Since the main goal of providing a Continue button is to avoid confusion about how to resume the Find script, the Continue script doesn't require any steps.

How it affects scripts

Notice that at Step 4 in Sub-script #2, a decision is made. If no records are found, there is no reason to sort the records. Step 7 causes ScriptMaker to leave the sub-script without performing Step 9 "[SORT] = Sort by date". When it returns to the main script "Custom Find Script" at Step 4 it continues to perform the other script steps in that script. Had the Step 7 in Sub-script #2 been a Halt step, none of the other steps in the Main Script would have been performed.

Sub-script #1

Name: [LAYOUT] = Go to search layout
    Step 1: Go to Layout "Search Layout"
    Step 2: Zoom Window

Main Script

Name: Custom Find Script
    Step 1: Enter Find Mode
    Step 2: Perform Script "[LAYOUT] = Go to search layout"
    Step 3: Perform Script "[SEARCH] = Execute search"
    Step 4: Perform Script "[DECISION] = Determine display layout"
    Step 5: Another step...
    Step 6: Another step...

Sub-script #2

Name: [SEARCH] = Execute search
    Step 1: Go to Field "Search Field"
    Step 2: Pause script *(wait for user input)*
    Step 3: Perform find
    Step 4: If Status(CurrentFoundCount) = 0
        Step 5: Show Message "There were no records found"
        Step 6: Perform Script "[LAYOUT] = Return last layout"
        Step 7: **Exit Script**
    Step 8: End If
    Step 9: Perform Script "[SORT] = Sort by date"

Diagram 4.1.2
Understanding how and why you would use Exit versus Halt is important knowledge.

Sub-script #3

Name: [DECISION] = Determine display layout
    Step 1: If Status(CurrentFoundCount) = 1
        Step 2: Perform Script "[LAYOUT] = Single record view"
    Step 3: Else
        Step 4: Perform Script "[LAYOUT] = List view extended"
    Step 5: End If

Universal script updates

Diagram 4.1.2 is also a good example of modular script design. Using the Exit script step in one sub-script, which is a part of a larger script will allow the other sub-scripts in the main script to run. If you have a single script calling five sub-scripts, for example, exiting the third sub-script will allow the calling script to continue and proceed with the remaining two scripts. This is best described as "branching"(see Diagram 4.1.2).

5.0 Keep/Replace – the Script Settings dialog

One of the most confusing dialogs that you'll find in ScriptMaker is the Keep/Replace or Script Settings dialog (see Picture 5.0). This dialog can appear when including any one of the following steps in a script:

Page Setup
Import
Find
Sort
Export

Picture 5.0
The Keep/Replace dialog that "remembers" stored values.

The confusion occurs for two reasons: 1) The dialog box appears whether changes have been made or not, and 2) It appears whether or not the Restore option has been checked.

Picture 5.1
With the restore option checked FileMaker Pro "remembers" the last operation performed for that step.

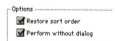

For example, consider a script that sorts in ascending order by Last Name. To create this script, do the following:

• Sort the database by Last Name in ascending order.
• Create a new script.
• Add the Sort script step, leaving the Restore option checked.

The attributes of the manual sort (by Last Name in ascending order) will be remembered by the script, because the Restore option is checked. The Script Settings dialog box is referring to these attributes. Each time you modify the script, you will be presented with the Script Settings dialog (Picture 5.0). The dialog is prompting you with this question, "Do you want to keep the settings that are stored in the script or do you want to replace the settings with the most recently performed manual settings?"

A good question to ask is, "What can this dialog do for me?" An even better question is, "What if this dialog didn't exist?" If this dialog didn't exist and you decided that sorting by First Name was better than by Last Name, you would have to write an entirely new script just to change to the new stored sort order. That would be simple if your script contained only a few script steps, but what if it contained many script steps?

Now that you understand the functions of the Script Settings dialog, keep these important points in mind:

- This dialog doesn't appear when a script is created, only when it is modified.
- Even if the Script Settings dialog appears, it is only relevant if a script step has the Restore option checked.
- Opening and closing a script causes this dialog to appear, even if no changes are made.

The original idea behind this feature was to enable easy modification of the attributes in a stored script. This, however, is not the only benefit.

5.1 Using the stored value steps productively

The Script Settings dialog saves tons of time when creating multiple scripts that use similar stored settings. Let's say you wanted to create two buttons; one that sorts ascending and another that sorts descending. Without the Script Settings feature, you would have to write two complete scripts. With this feature, it's a simple process of creating the first script, duplicating it and replacing the saved settings. This seven step process is covered below using sort scripts as an example.

Quick sorting scripts

ScriptMaker process: Duplicate sort

These steps duplicate a sorting script and then change the sort order it performs.

1. Sort the data in ascending order.
2. Create a new script, clear all steps, add the Sort step, then close ScriptMaker.
3. Sort the database in descending order.
4. Open ScriptMaker and select the script you created in step 2.
5. Duplicate the script, using the duplicate button, and give it a different name with the rename button.
6. Open the script and click OK to close it.
7. When FileMaker Pro asks you to keep or replace the sort order, select replace and close the script (this is where the saved settings from the original script change).

The first sort script you create is a template for your subsequent scripts. All you have to do is instruct FileMaker Pro to sort in a different order, open the duplicate script and use the Script Settings dialog to replace the previous sort with the new sort. The example given is a very simple sorting script, but imagine the time it will save with complex scripts.

Chapter 3 Overview & Quiz

Test yourself to see what you've learned.

1. **A section divider in ScriptMaker is what?**
   - ○ A line that divides sections of scripts
   - ○ An empty script used for organization
   - ○ A script that splits the found set
   - ○ All of the above

2. **Methods for improving ScriptMaker efficiency include?**
   - ○ Prefix and Suffix naming
   - ○ Modular sub-script functions
   - ○ Indenting
   - ○ All of the above

3. **Advantages of modular scripting systems are?**
   - ○ Universal updates
   - ○ Script repurposing
   - ○ Efficient troubleshooting
   - ○ All of the above

4. **The three states of ScriptMaker are?**
   - ○ Running, Paused, Not Running
   - ○ Idle, Running, Waiting
   - ○ Running, Watching, Stopped
   - ○ All of the above

5. **Pause/Exit/Halt/Resume applies to?**
   - ○ Buttons only
   - ○ Buttons and scripts
   - ○ Scripts only
   - ○ All of the above

6. **The difference between Halt and Exit is...**
   - ○ Exit only stops the current script
   - ○ Exit halts all scripts
   - ○ Exit quits FileMaker Pro
   - ○ All of the above

7. **The Keep/Replace dialog remembers what?**
   - ○ Field definitions
   - ○ Replace script step calculations
   - ○ The last manual action performed for those steps that have the Restore option
   - ○ All of the above

Answers:

Answers: 1. An empty script used for organization 2. All of the above 3. All of the above 4. Running, Paused, Non Running 5. Buttons and scripts 6. Exit only stops the current script 7. The last manual action performed for those steps that have the Restore option

Chapter 3 Highlights

What you should have learned
- The importance of developing your own modular style with ScriptMaker
- The three script states and four button options
- When and how to keep or replace the information used in a script
- Documenting and organizing your scripts

Technique files that relate to this chapter

DIALOG.FP3
Custom Dialogs

Demonstrates how to create custom dialogs using layouts. This technique uses the Exit button option.

INDEX.FP3
Technique File Index

While this isn't a technique file, there are examples of the Halt and Resume button options throughout the file.

COMMENT.FP3
Always Validate False

Shows how to comment and organize a file, including scripts, calculations, fields and relationships.

ALL CD FILES
All CD ROM Files

Look at all the files on the CD ROM for techniques on how to effectively organize scripts.

Chapter 4

ScriptMaker Steps Defined

6.0 ScriptMaker script steps

One of the keys to understanding any computer language or software environment is understanding the basic tools. Without a strong foundation, more complex operations are frustrating. The same is true for FileMaker Pro. You need to learn how to use each ScriptMaker step well enough to define it off the top of your head and use it in an example. This chapter breaks down the individual ScriptMaker script steps with examples of how to use them. Work through every example to start learning, refresh your memory and possibly learn a new trick about a familiar script step.

6.1 Individual steps defined

The individual steps in this section are organized in alphabetical order.

Allow User Abort   Control

What it does: Prevents or enables the cancellation of a script with Command-Period (Macintosh) or ESC (Windows).

Options: [1] Turn On or Off

When to use: Use this script step any time you don't want users to exit your scripts prematurely.

ABORT.FP3
Technique File:
Never Abort

Application: By default, Allow User Abort is turned on for the entire script. In order to prevent a user from exiting a script prematurely, you must add the Allow User Abort script step and turn it off. Script Maker will automatically turn Allow User Abort on once the script is completed. If there are multiple scripts connected via Perform Script, you only need to turn Allow User Abort off in the initial script. A common use of this step is to prevent users from canceling out of a find script. Most find scripts are used in conjunction with a specially designed layout. You don't want the user to be able to cancel prematurely and end up stuck in the find layout.

Script Examples (Allow User Abort)

1. Don't allow a script or sub-script to be cancelled
Placing Allow User Abort [Off] before a script is run prevents all sub-scripts from being exited.

```
Allow User Abort [Off]
If ["Field X = "Special Operation""]
    Perform Script [Sub-scripts, "Power Script"]
End If
```

2. Must complete a scripted find
Adding this script step will force a scripted find to complete its operation.

```
Allow User Abort [Off]
Go to Layout ["Find"]
Enter Find Mode [Pause]
Perform Find []
Go to Layout ["Data Entry"]
```

Beep   Miscellaneous

What it does: Plays the system beep sound.

Options: [1] None

When to use: Use this script step when you want to get the user's attention.

Script Examples (Beep)

1. Get the user's attention
A common place to use the beep step is just before a dialog is presented.

```
If ["Warning Field = "Bad Record""]
    Beep
    Show Message ["Attention! The data you just entered is incorrect."]
End If
```

Change Password   Files

What it does: Allows users of your solution to change their password.

Options: [1] None

When to use: When users need to change their passwords on a regular basis due to security issues.

Considerations: If the same password is used by many people, you shouldn't allow users to change their password. A password changed by one user will lock other users out of the file unless they are informed of the new password. This step is often misunderstood, thinking that it allows a user to switch to a different password with different access rights. Instead, this script step allows the user to change the password they are currently using (e.g. from "123" to "abc").

Script Examples (Change Password)

4.0 Only

1. Change group password
Uses a FileMaker Pro 4.0 feature to check the group that is being used to access the database.

```
If ["Status(CurrentGroups) = "Accounting""]
    Change Password
Else
    Show Message ["You do not have access to change passwords."]
End If
```

Check Found Set
Spelling

What it does: Spell checks all the fields on the current layout for the entire found set of records.

Options: [1] None

Script Examples (Check Found Set)

1. Check Found Set
Spell checks the found set of records.

```
Check Found Set
```

Check Record
Spelling

 SPELL.FP3

Technique File:
Spell Checking
Specific Fields

What it does: Spell checks all of the fields on the current layout for the current record.

Options: [1] None

Script Examples (Check Record)

1. Check Record
Spell checks the current record.

```
Check Record
```

What it does: Allows you to spell check only the currently selected text.

Options: [1] Select entire contents of field
[2] Specify a target field

This is the best spell check script step to use for most situations.

Script Examples (Check Selection)

1. Check Selection

Spell checks selected text within a field.

```
Check Selection
```

What it does: Clear performs the same action as Cut, but doesn't replace the clipboard with the object or text that is removed.

Options: [1] Select entire contents of field
[2] Specify a target field

If you don't specify a field, the currently active field will be used. If you don't select the option for select entire contents, the currently selected text will be cleared.

When to use: When you need to remove information from a field, but don't wish for the clipboard contents to be replaced.

Script Examples (Clear)

1. Clear all fields on current record
A script that clears all fields on the current layout for the current record.

```
Comment ["A script that clears all fields on the current record."]
Exit Record/Request
Go to Next Field
Set Field ["First Field", "Status(CurrentFieldName)"]
Loop
    Clear [Select]
    Go to Next Field
    Exit Loop If ["First Field = Status(CurrentFieldName)"]
End Loop
Exit Record/Request
```

Close   Files

What it does: Closes a specified file. If a file is not specified, the currently active file will be closed.

Options: [1] Specify a file

When to use: The best use for this step is a script that runs when a file is closed. The script would close the rest of the files in the solution. By closing all of the files together, it appears that all the files are part of a whole, rather than a series of individual files.

Script Examples (Close)

1. Close all files in a solution
A closing script, as specified in the document preferences, performs whenever a file is closed.

```
Comment ["Set this script, in preferences, to run whenever the file
          is closed."]
Close ["Invoice.FP3"]
```

```
Close ["Items.FP3"]
Close ["Customer.FP3"]
Close ["Prefs.FP3"]
```

Comment Miscellaneous

What it does: Enables you to document your scripts. The standard practice is to place the comment before the script step(s) it describes.

Options: [1] Specify comment text

COMMENT.FP3

Technique File:
Commenting Files

When to use: Use a comment step as a reminder of the function of any script longer than five steps.

Special note: You can use comment script steps as dividing lines in your longer and more complex scripts (see example below).

Script Examples (Comment)

1. Commenting Scripts Well

Use the comment script step to document your scripts.

```
Comment ["Leave yourself a reminder as to what the script does
         using the Comment script step."]
Comment ["You can also use Comment steps to create divisions
         within scripts. The divisions below mark the beginning and
         ending of an If statement."]
Comment ["_____"]
If ["Field X <> Field Y"]
    Perform Script [Sub-scripts, "Another Script"]
End If
Comment ["_____"]
```

What it does: Copies the selected text, number, time, picture or date to the system clipboard.

Options: [1] Select entire contents of field
[2] Specify a target field

If you don't specify a field, the currently active field will be used. If you don't select the option for select entire contents, the currently selected text will be used.

When to use: Use this step to move data from one field to another or one file to another, only if Set Field is not an option.

Considerations: If you must use the cut, copy or paste steps, make sure you are on a layout containing the target field. To understand why the field needs to be available, try manually copying from a field that is not available on the current layout. In contrast, Set Field does not require the field to be on the layout.

Script Examples (Copy)

1. A simple copy and paste between layouts
A script that copies a field from one layout and pastes the text into another layout.

```
Comment ["Make sure you are on the layout that has the fields
         if you use cut, copy or paste."]
Go to Layout ["Layout #1"]
Copy [Select, "Field X"]
Go to Layout ["Layout #2"]
Paste [Select, "Field Y"]
```

2. Find similar records in the database
A script that will copy a value from a field and find similar records based on that value.

```
Comment ["This script copies a value from the current record
         so it can find all similar records."]
Copy [Select, "Last Name"]
Enter Find Mode []
Paste [Select, "Last Name"]
Perform Find []
```

Copy All Records Records

MATCHES.FP3
Technique File:
Match List

SAVE.FP3
Technique File:
Save a Found Set

What it does: Copies all the fields on the current layout for the entire found set of records. Fields are separated by tabs and records are separated by carriage returns.

Options: [1] None

When to use: This is an excellent feature which is best demonstrated with a technique called Match List. This technique uses the Copy All Records step to make a many-to-many relationship work without a join file. Another technique named Save a Found Set also utilizes the Copy All Records script step.

Script Examples (Copy All Records)

1. Saving a found set of records
A script that will create a list of values for a found set relationship.

```
Comment ["Grab all the customer IDs and paste them into a
         single field"]
Freeze Window
Go to Layout ["Customer ID Field ONLY"]
Copy All Records
Go to Layout ["Main Screen Layout"]
Paste [Select, "Group Customer ID"]
```

What it does: Copies all the fields on the current layout for the current record. Fields are separated by tabs and records are separated by carriage returns.

Options: [1] None

When to use: This script is not widely used like the Copy All Records step, but could be helpful in allowing a user to transfer data from FileMaker Pro to another application, such as a spreadsheet or a word processor. The format is ideal for a spreadsheet since a spreadsheet will interpret the pasting of tabs as column dividers. Transferring the data to a word processor doesn't work as well unless it is a data file for a merge document.

Script Examples (Copy Record)

1. Copy a whole record
A script that will copy the current record and place it into the clipboard.

```
Comment ["Copy data from the current record for placement in a
         spreadsheet"]
Go to Layout ["Layout #1"]
Copy Record
```

What it does: This script step works in conjunction with the spell as you type feature. Spell as you type beeps when you type a word that is not spelled correctly. This script step simply allows you to display the spelling dialog to correct the last word that was typed incorrectly.

Script Examples (Correct Word)

1. Spellcheck as you type
A script that works with the spell as you type feature, found in preferences.

```
Comment ["Spell as you type must be turned on in preferences
          for this script step to work."]
Correct Word
```

Cut

What it does: Cuts the selected text, number, time, picture or date to the system clipboard.

Options: [1] Select entire contents of field
[2] Specify a target field

If you don't specify a field, the currently active field will be used. If you don't check the option to select the entire contents, the currently selected text will be used. Cut will replace what is currently on the clipboard.

Considerations: If you must use the cut, copy or paste steps, make sure you are on a layout containing the target field. To understand why the field needs to be available, try manually cutting from a field that is not available on the current layout. In contrast, Set Field does not require the field to be on the layout.

Script Examples (Cut)

1. Cut & Paste text
A basic script that cuts from one field and pastes into a field on another layout.

```
Comment ["Make sure you are on the layout that has the fields
          if you use cut, copy or paste."]
Go to Layout ["Layout #1"]
```

```
Cut [Select, "Field X"]
Go to Layout ["Layout #2"]
Paste [Select, "Field Y"]
```

Delete All Records Records

What it does: Deletes all the records in the found set.

Options: [1] Perform without dialog

When to use: The best place to use the Delete All Records step is when you create a set of records for a temporary function and then need to delete that found set of records. The Printing Multiple Labels technique uses the Delete All Records script step in this way. It deletes all the records in the found set, but only in a temporary database where no harm can be done to important data.

LABEL.FP3

Technique File:
Printing Multiple
Labels

Another good use is to move records into an archiving database and delete the records in the original database. This works well for environments that maintain and store lots of data.

Considerations: Making a button available to users that deletes all records is dangerous, since they are likely at some point to delete the entire database. Deleted records cannot be recovered.

Script Examples (Delete All Records)

1. Delete archived records

You can archive records by importing them into an ARCHIVE.FP3 database. After the records are archived, they can be deleted. It is a good idea to keep a backup of your database in case something goes wrong with this procedure.

```
Perform Script [Sub-scripts, "Find Last Month"]
Perform Script [Sub-scripts, "Archive Records"]
Delete All Records []
```

Delete Portal Row   Records

What it does: Deletes the currently selected Portal Row. Make sure you have the portal defined to allow deletion of portal records or this script step will do nothing.

Options: [1] Perform without dialog

 **PORTPORT.FP3**

Technique File:
Portal Row Movement

When to use: The most common usage of this script step is as a single step to delete portal rows. Add a button to the first portal row in layout mode and attach a script that uses Delete Portal Row. If the button is not in the portal it will not work correctly. A more advanced example is demonstrated in the Portal Row Movement technique file.

Script Examples (Delete Portal Row)

1. Delete Portal Row
A basic script that deletes the currently selected portal row. The button must be in the portal.

```
Delete Portal Row []
```

Delete Record/Request   Records

What it does: Deletes the current record when the mode is Browse and the current request when the mode is Find.

Options: [1] Perform without dialog

SORTPORT.FP3

Technique File:
Sorting Portals

When to use: The most basic use of this script step is to allow users the ability to delete records via a button, rather than using the menus. A more advanced usage of this feature is implemented in a technique called Sorting Portals.

Script Examples (Delete Record/Request)

`4.0 Only`

1. Delete Record/Request

By using the Status(CurrentModifierKeys), it is possible to incorporate power user features into the database.

```
Comment ["Give power users the option to delete without a
          warning dialog when holding down the Shift key."]
If ["Status(CurrentModifierKeys) = 1"]
    Delete Record/Request [No dialog]
Else
    Delete Record/Request []
End If
```

Dial Phone   Miscellaneous

What it does: Dials a phone number via a modem or the computer speaker. The phone number can come from a field value or a dialog entry. FileMaker preferences contain dialing options that are used by this script. If you don't use the dialing options, the prefixes can be specified by a calculation. To switch so that the computer speaker is used, you must change the Modem options in the FileMaker Pro preferences.

Options: [1] Perform without dialog
[2] Use value from target field or
[3] Use statically assigned number
[4] Use dialing preferences

When to use: If the person using the database has a modem, the Dial Phone step can dial the phone without them typing the numbers. All they need to do is pick up the telephone and start speaking. If the preferences are to use the computer speaker, holding the receiver close to the computer speaker will dial the number using the tones generated.

Script Examples (Dial Phone)

1. Dial a phone number
Any field that contains numbers can be specified to be dialed.

```
Dial Phone [No dialog, "Work Phone Number"]
```

Duplicate Record/Request   Records

What it does: Duplicates the current record when in browse mode and the current request in find mode.

Options: [1] None

DUP_PORT.FP3
Technique File:
Duplicating Portals

When to use: The most basic use of this script step is to offer a button that allows duplication of a record. A more advanced technique is discussed in the file called Duplicating Portals.

Considerations: Records duplicate to a different position within the found set of records, depending on whether the database is sorted or not. When unsorted, records duplicate to the end of the found set and when sorted, they duplicate to a position just after the current record. This can cause problems with looping scripts that duplicate multiple records. Therefore, it is important to always use the Unsort step before looping the duplication of records. Also, auto-enter data will override the data in a field when a record is duplicated.

Script Examples (Duplicate Record/Request)

1. Simple duplicate script
Just the duplicate step by itself can be a useful feature for most databases.

```
Duplicate Record/Request
```

2. Duplicate found set
A script that duplicates the found set of records.

```
Comment ["Duplicates all the records in the current found set."]
Unsort
Go to Record/Request/Page [First]
Loop
    Exit Loop If ["Status(CurrentFoundCount) = 0"]
    Duplicate Record/Request
    Omit
    Go to Record/Request/Page [First]
    Omit
End Loop
```

Edit User Dictionary   Spelling

What it does: Allows you to add words to the user dictionary.

When to use: If your database users spell check often, this is a useful script step to attach to a button.

Script Examples (Edit User Dictionary)

1. Editing the user dictionary
This script step aids solutions that rely on the spelling capabilities of FileMaker Pro.

```
Edit User Dictionary
```

What it does: Else speeds up nested If statements by exiting the statement once a condition is satisfied. Normally, when a conditional If statement is satisfied, successive If statements still need to be evaluated. With an Else step, embedded If statements will be ignored once the first condition has been met.

When to use: One way to use an Else statement is inside a conditional startup script. Let's say you want to determine which layout is presented depending on the user name entered into a field. A large number of user names could take a long time to process. To speed up the script, use the Else statement along with the If statement. Once a user is identified, the following conditions will be ignored. Even if the script is short, it is important to save processing time wherever possible.

Script Examples (Else)

1. Check for User Name
A script that checks the Status(CurrentUserName) to make sure that the right user is running the database.

```
If ["Status(CurrentHostName) = "FileMaker Server" and
    Status(CurrentUserName) = "Administrator""]
    Go to Layout ["Admin Layout"]
Else
    If ["IsEmpty(Status(CurrentUserName))"]
        Show Message ["You must have a user name for access."]
    Else
        Go to Layout ["Main User Layout"]
    End If
End If
```

End If

What it does: End If always accompanies the If statement. End If tells FileMaker Pro where the conditional statement ends. When adding the If statement into a script, the End If step is also moved. The only time you'll need to add an End If is when you are modifying a script and the closing End If has been accidentally removed.

(See the If script step for an example.)

End Loop

What it does: This is the closing portion of a Loop script step. An End Loop step always accompanies each Loop step. In fact, the End Loop step is moved into your script every time you use the Loop step. The only reason you would double-click on the End Loop statement is if you have been modifying your script and removed it by mistake.

(See Loop for an example of how to use End Loop.)

Enter Browse Mode

What it does: Changes the current mode to Browse.

Options: [1] Pause

When to use: Anytime a script should only run while in Browse mode. If this is the first step in any script, it will ensure that the user is in an editing mode for data entry rather than in Find mode.

Considerations: A common problem with scripts is not anticipating that a user may have entered into Find mode. It is good practice to include an Enter Browse Mode script step into all scripts that are expected to function in Browse mode. Otherwise, your user may enter data into Find mode and lose all the data when the file is closed.

Script Examples (Enter Browse Mode)

1. Only enter Browse if mode is Find or Preview
Use the Status(CurrentMode) function to determine the current mode. It is not necessary to check the current mode if you always want the script to run in Browse mode.

```
Comment ["Status Current Mode allows you to check the current
         mode and set it to Browse if needed."]
If ["Status(CurrentMode) <> 0"]
    Enter Browse Mode []
End If
```

Enter Find Mode   Navigation

What it does: Takes the user into Find mode. The Restore option remembers the find criteria used in the manual find prior to creating the find script. To change the find criteria stored with this script step, perform a manual find. Next, open the script as if you are going to edit it and click the "Okay" button without making any edits. A message will appear asking if you want to Keep or Replace the find requests. Choose Replace and the most recent manual find requests will be attached to the script (see Chapter 3 Section 5).

Power Tip

The Set Field script step can manipulate values stored in global fields, even while in Find mode. This enables you to transfer data from Browse to Find mode without using Copy and Paste.

Options: [1] Restore find requests
         [2] Pause

FOUND.FP3

Technique File:
Avoiding
"No Records Found"

RESTORE.FP3

Technique File:
Mixing Finds

When to use: Anytime you need to script a find and allow criteria entry by the user.

Application: The Restore option can be used to set predefined search criteria on a manual find. For example, you might want to use a button to search for all records containing "California", but still allow the user to designate additional search criteria. You don't need to include the State field on the Find layout, since the requests will be restored whether the field is present or not. This technique is outlined in the Mixing Finds file.

Script Examples (Enter Find Mode)

1. Basic scripted Find
Entering into Find mode and pausing for a user to enter search criteria is a common way to script a find.

```
Comment ["This is a basic find script that allows users to
        enter criteria in a find layout."]
Go to Layout ["Search Layout"]
Enter Find Mode [Pause]
Perform Find []
Go to Layout ["Data Entry Layout"]
```

Enter Preview Mode   Navigation

What it does: Changes the current mode to Preview. When you enter Preview mode, the first record in the found set will be shown, rather than the currently selected record from Browse mode.

Options: [1] Pause

When to use: When a printed form needs to be reviewed before printing. It is also useful for displaying a sub-summary report without printing.

Application: When you first enter Preview mode, the number of pages is shown as a question mark. Calculating the number of pages requires FileMaker Pro to layout all of the records on pages and perform operations like sliding objects. This process may be short or long depending on the number of records and the design of the layout. If you don't mind the wait, use a script to enter Preview mode, go to the last page and then go to the first page. This will show the number of pages in the status area instead of the question mark. There is also a technique named Previewing the Current Record that teaches how to preview the current record in Browse mode.

PREVIEW.FP3

Technique File:
Previewing the
Current Record

Script Examples (Enter Preview Mode)

1. Creating page totals

FileMaker Pro does not have a feature for showing page X of Y at the bottom of printed pages. This feature can be scripted with the addition of a global field.

```
Comment ["This script places the total number of pages into a global
         field for printing page totals (e.g. page 4 of 10)"]
Enter Preview Mode []
Go to Record/Request/Page [Last]
Set Field ["Total Pages", "Status(CurrentPageNumber)"]
Print [No dialog]
Enter Browse Mode []
```

2. Showing total number of pages

When previewing layouts, the status area has a question mark indicating the number of pages. This script will go to the last page in order to generate the total number of pages.

```
Comment ["This script shows the total pages in the status
         area rather than the question mark."]
Enter Preview Mode []
Go to Record/Request/Page [Last]
Go to Record/Request/Page [First]
```

What it does: This script step is used in conjunction with the Loop script step to exit the loop when a condition is met. Placement of the Exit Loop If script step is crucial. If you place it too early within the loop, certain actions may not be performed. For instance, let's say you're looping through records. If the Exit Loop If script step occurs too early, the last record may not be manipulated by the other steps within the loop. For this reason, Exit Loop If is often the last step in a loop.

Options: [1] Specify calculated exit criteria

When to use: Whenever it's needed to exit a loop based on a condition. Exit Loop If is often used with a Counter field as seen in the example below. Another step that exits loops is the Go to Record/Request/Page [Exit after last, Next]. The option, "Exit after last", stops the loop when the last record in the found set is reached.

 **COUNTER.FP3**

Technique File:
Better Counter

Script Examples (Exit Loop If)

1. Exit loop when counter is zero
Most loops use some sort of control value to determine when they should exit. The most common control value is a global counter field.

```
Comment ["This script cycles through the loop ten times and
          then exits."]
Set Field ["Counter", "10"]
Loop
    Delete Record/Request [No dialog]
    Set Field ["Counter", "Counter - 1"]
    Exit Loop If ["Counter = 0"]
End Loop
```

What it does: Exits the current record or request depending on whether the user is in Browse mode or Find mode. Exiting a record or request means that any active fields will become deselected. This script step is equivalent to typing the Enter key on the keypad or clicking on a record outside any fields. An alternate method to accomplish what Exit Record does is to use a Go to Field without specifying a target field.

Options: [1] None

When to use: A record is updated when it is exited. This will force the record to formulate all calculations, update relationships and send changed data for the current record to the host in a multi-user scenario.

Script Examples (Exit Record/Request)

1. Portal loop within a record loop
The portal must be refreshed so the loop cycles through the correct related records.

```
Comment ["This script has a loop within a loop. The outside loop
        cycles through the records and the inside loop moves
        through the portal rows."]
Loop
    Set Field ["Invoice Date", "Past Due"]
    Comment ["First you must target a field in the portal."]
    Go to Field ["Items::Item ID"]
    Loop
        Set Field ["Items::Shipping", "Sent"]
        Go to Portal Row [Exit after last, Next]
    End Loop
    Exit Record/Request
    Go to Record/Request/Page [Exit after last, Next]
End Loop
```

What it does: Exits the current running script only. If the Exit Script step is used within a sub-script, only that sub-script will stop running. Any calling script will still continue with its remaining script steps. Compare the Exit Script script step with Halt Script which aborts all running scripts.

Options: [1] None

When to use: This script step is most commonly used in conjunction with nested If statements to determine if the script should continue running or exit.

Script Examples (Exit Script)

1. Exit script when criteria are met
This script exits when a condition is met.

```
Comment ["Use IF statements to watch for conditions and exit
        the script if they are true."]
If ["Database Mode = "Demo Mode""]
    Show Message ["This database is in demo mode."]
    Exit Script
End If
Perform Script [Sub-scripts, "Set User Prefs"]
Perform Script [Sub-scripts, "Layout: Main"]
```

Export Records
Import/Export

What it does: Exports the found set of records using any of the file formats supported by FileMaker Pro. To restore an export order, export manually and then create your script. The export option on the Export step will remember the field order.

Options: [1] Specifying destination file
[2] Export file type
[3] Export field order
[4] Present dialog [Yes/No]

When to use: This script step is quite useful when exporting to a word processing merge file. The whole process of merging FileMaker Pro data with a word processor can be automated using ScriptMaker and AppleScript or WinBatch.

Application: The CD ROM contains a technique file called Deleting Duplicates. Records are exported using the Summarize by feature and then imported back in without duplicates. The Summarize by feature is seldom used, but is a powerful tool that allows you to export your data like you would see it presented in a sub-summary report.

(◎) **DUP2.FP3**

Technique File:
Deleting Duplicates

Script Examples (Export Records)

1. Deleting duplicates using export

Deleting duplicates is as simple as exporting using the Summarize by feature, deleting all the records and then importing the exported text file. Make a backup before running this script.

```
Comment ["Be sure to use the export option of Summarize by."]
Export Records [Restore, No dialog, "FMPXPRT.TXT"]
Delete All Records [No dialog]
Import Records [Restore, No dialog, "FMPXPRT.TXT"]
```

Find All   Sort/Find/Print

(◎) **ISOLATE.FP3**

Technique File:
Isolating a Record

What it does: Shows all the records in the database, thus breaking the current found set of records. The current record remains selected after the Find All script step is performed.

Options: [1] None

When to use: The most common usage of the Find All script step is to attach it alone to a button, so a user can easily show all the records in the database. Another common usage is to show all the records in a database before performing a looping script. Quite often, you will want all the records to be cycled through, rather than just the current found set.

Script Examples (Find All)

1. Looping through all records in a database
The Find All script step is useful when loops need to cycle through the entire database to perform maintenance.

```
Enter Browse Mode []
Find All
Go to Record/Request/Page [First]
Loop
    Comment ["Perform script steps here."]
    Go to Record/Request/Page [Exit after last, Next]
End Loop
```

Find Omitted

ISOLATE.FP3

Technique File:
Isolating a Record

What it does: Finds all the records not in the current found set. In other words it finds the inverse set of records currently being viewed. For instance, if you have four records found in a database of ten, performing this script step will create a found set of six.

Options: [1] None

When to use: This step is great when you want to isolate a certain record. To do this you combine the Omit and Find All script step. The script would look like the following example.

Script Examples (Find Omitted)

1. Isolate a single record
Since the record position is retained in FileMaker Pro when a Find All is performed, only two more steps need to be added to isolate the record so that it is the only one showing.

```
Find All
Omit
Find Omitted
```

Flush Cache to Disk   Miscellaneous

What it does: FileMaker Pro saves during idle times (but not more than every 5 seconds) unless otherwise specified via Preferences. The Flush Cache to Disk script step allows you to force FileMaker Pro to save the cache to disk at your command.

Options: [1] None

When to use: FileMaker Pro caches data to RAM in between saves. In a multi-user scenario, FileMaker Pro Server can get busy and not have time to save to disk. If there is both a huge amount of activity and a large amount of RAM available, data loss could occur if the system crashes. Your best defense is to force FileMaker Pro to flush the cache to disk.

Script Examples (Flush Cache to Disk)

1. Flush cache when high usage
One of the best places to use Flush Cache to Disk is either in a multi-user environment or when serving with FileMaker Pro over the web. In some instances FileMaker Pro is dealing with so many requests for information, updates to records and new record creations, that it doesn't have time to write to disk. While this is rare, it is a good practice in environments with high usage.

```
If ["Status(CurrentUserCount) > 20"]
    Flush Cache to Disk
End If
Perform Script [Sub-scripts, "Another Script"]
```

What it does: Prevents the window from being updated.

Options: [1] None

When to use: The typical usage for the Freeze Window script step is at the beginning of a script to make your solutions look more professional.

Application: Use it when you don't want users to see the changing of layouts, records or files. Freeze Window does not prevent dialogs or process information from appearing (e.g. the export records process window). The screen is automatically unfrozen when the end of the script is reached or a dialog or process is activated.

FREEZE.FP3

Technique File:
Freeze Window

Special note: A little known fact is that Freeze Window can speed up your scripts. You may be surprised at the difference in speed between a script that loops through your records when a Freeze Window step is added. The resulting speed can be as much as four times faster, since the redraw of advancing records is eliminated.

Considerations: Adding a Freeze Window step to a script that doesn't need it will cause unnecessary screen refreshes when the script ends. This makes a solution look unprofessional.

Script Examples (Freeze Window)

1. Quicker looping records
The Freeze Window script step will actually increase the speed of a looping script.

```
Comment ["A freeze window will actually speed up some operations that
         attempt to draw to the computer screen. A looping script is
         the most common example."]
Freeze Window
Loop
    Comment ["Whatever scripts steps you want here."]
    Go to Record/Request/Page [Exit after last, Next]
End Loop
```

Go to Field   Navigation

What it does: Goes to the specified target field.

Options: [1] Select/perform
[2] Specify target field

If the option for Select/Perform is checked, the entire contents of the field will be selected (if the field stores a sound, the sound will be played). If the option is not checked, the cursor will be placed after the last character contained within the field. The Go to Field script step can enter a field even if it is set to not allow data entry or when it is not in the current tab order.

When to use: The most common use of this script step is to select a particular field. This allows you to direct user input when entering a new layout. It's also useful when entering Find mode. The field that was selected in Browse is the same that is selected when entering Find mode. If needed, a different field can be targeted when a Find button is clicked.

Another way to use this script step is to control what a user does. If you don't want the user to enter a field by clicking or tabbing into it, you can turn off access to that field via Field Format by unchecking Allow entry into field. Whenever you want to allow the user access to the field, run a script that enters the locked field.

A user interface technique that utilizes the Go to Field script step is on the CD ROM (POPUP.FP3). It allows you to click into a field and enter custom data or click a button next to the field and get a pop-up list.

POPUP.FP3

Technique File:
Pop-up menus

Advanced technique: If multiple portals are on a layout, the Go To Portal Row script step will select the portal placed first on the layout. The most secure way of targeting a portal is to use the Go to Field script step. Just target a related field in the portal before using the Go to Portal Row step.

Script Examples (Go to Field)

1. Waiting for user search criteria
Using the Go to Field script step, it's possible to put the user into the field that will most likely be searched.

```
Go to Layout ["Find Layout"]
Enter Find Mode []
Go to Field ["Search Field"]
Pause/Resume Script []
Perform Find []
Go to Layout ["Data Entry Layout"]
```

What it does: Switches to a specified layout.

Options: [1] Refresh (check box)
[2] Specify Layout
[3] Layout number from field...
[4] Original Layout

When to use: Whenever you need to take the user to another layout.

Application: There is a technique called Next/Previous Layout (LAYOUT.FP3) that demonstrates how to go from layout to layout using Status(CurrentLayoutNumber) and the Go to Layout script step. This technique demonstrates how to grab a layout number from a field. Layouts are numbered sequentially as displayed in the layout menu while in Layout mode.

The option to go to a layout based on a value found in a field can be used to remember the previous layout. The trick is to use the Set Field script to set a global field to the current layout using the Status(CurrentLayoutNumber) before leaving the layout. This technique is discussed in a technique called Remember Layout (REMEMBER.FP3).

(◎) LAYOUT.FP3

Technique File:
Next/Previous Layout

(◎) FOUND.FP3

Technique File:
Avoiding "No Records Found"

(◎) REMEMBER.FP3

Technique File:
Remember Layout

Script Examples (Go to Layout)

1. Go to next layout
This script cycles through all of the available layouts in a database, hidden or not. In order to modify this script to go to the previous layout instead of the next, subtract one rather than add in the Set Field step.

```
Comment ["This script increments the layout ID so you can cycle
        through them."]
Set Field ["Stored Layout ID", "Stored Layout ID + 1"]
Go to Layout ["Stored Layout ID"]
```

2. Displaying the appropriate layout
Combining an If statement along with the Go to Layout script step, makes it possible to display a form or list view layout.

```
Comment ["This script performs a find and then goes to a list or
        form layout depending on the number of records in the
        found set."]
Set Error Capture [On]
Go to Layout ["Find Layout"]
Enter Find Mode [Pause]
Perform Find []
If ["Status(CurrentFoundCount) = 1"]
    Comment ["If the found set is 1 record then
    go to the single record layout."]
    Go to Layout ["Single Record: Standard Form View"]
Else
    Comment ["Otherwise, go to the multiple record layout."]
    Go to Layout ["Multiple Records: Extended Columnar List View"]
End If
```

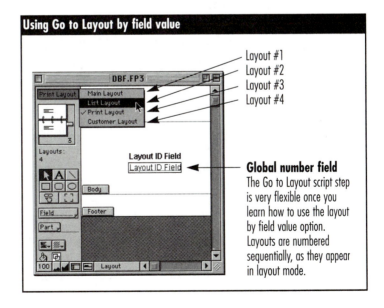

Using Go to Layout by field value

Layout #1
Layout #2
Layout #3
Layout #4

Global number field
The Go to Layout script step is very flexible once you learn how to use the layout by field value option. Layouts are numbered sequentially, as they appear in layout mode.

Visible Layouts

The check box in the Layout Setup dialog box controls whether a layout is visible in the layout selection menu in the status area. Because a layout is not visible in Browse mode does not mean it can't be referred to by the Go to Layout script step.

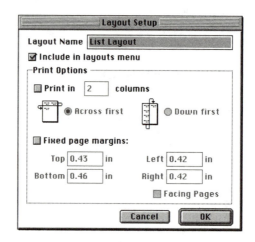

Go to Next Field

What it does: Moves to the next field in the tab order on the current layout.

Options: [1] None

When to use: When you want a script to navigate to the next field.

Applications: The Exit Record/Request script step is often used just before a Go to Next Field script step. This enables you to select the first field in the tab order, no matter what field is selected before the script is run. It is also a very useful script step for selecting the correct field when entering a find layout.

◎ EMAIL.FP3

Technique File: Parsing Email

Parsing Email (EMAIL.FP3) shows how to cycle through an email, extract data and put it into the appropriate fields. This technique is portable to any database or layout without modification.

Script Examples (Go to Next Field)

1. Parse a return separated list into separate fields

The following script grabs the first value in a return separated list, places it into a field and then removes that item from the list.

```
Comment ["This script grabs the values from the ListField field and
         places each line in a separate field. Returns designate
         the next line."]
Exit Record/Request
Set Field ["ListField", "ListField & "¶""]
Loop
    Go to Next Field
    Set Field ["Left(ListField,Position(ListField,"¶", 1, 1) - 1)"]
    Set Field ["ListField", "Middle(ListField,Position(ListField,
    "¶", 1, 1) + 1, 999999999)"]
    Exit Loop If ["IsEmpty(ListField)"]
End Loop
```

NOTE: There are two special circumstances to notice about the above script. 1) The first Set Field does not have a target field specified. It is not necessary to specify a target field if you know that you are in the field that you want the Set Field to affect and 2) the Middle function in the second set field uses a really high number as the size parameter. This will cause the function to grab text well beyond the maximum size of the 64K allowable in a text field.

Go to Portal Row   Navigation

What it does: Navigates to the next, previous, first or last portal row. Also goes to a portal row by field specification.

Options: [1] Select entire contents (check box)
[2] First Portal Row
[3] Last Portal Row
[4] Previous Portal Row
[5] Next Portal Row
[6] By Number...
[7] By Field Value...

The select entire contents check box option highlights a portal row. The Previous and Next options allow you to exit after the last portal row, if used within a looping script. This is similar to the Go to Record/Request/Page script step, except it works with portals and not records.

When to use: When it's necessary to take the user to a specific portal row.

Considerations: If there are two portals on the same layout, FileMaker Pro will use the portal that was placed on the layout first or the portal that is farthest back in the object layer. You can push an object forward or backward in the object layer by using the Send Backward and Bring Forward menu choices under the Arrange menu. In order to target a portal that is not the first on the layout, you must use a Go to Field script step. The CD example technique named Go to Portal (GO_PORT.FP3) explains this.

(○) GO_PORT.FP3

Technique File:
Go to Portal

Application: If you leave a portal by typing the Enter key, clicking in a field outside the portal, changing records, changing layouts or changing files, then the current portal row is deselected. You can use Set Field to place the Status(CurrentPortalRow) value into a global field to remember the portal row. The By Field Value option on the Go to Portal Row script step can then be used to come back to the same portal row. This example is outlined in the technique file, Return to Portal Row (RETURN.FP3).

(○) RETURN.FP3

Technique File:
Return to Portal Row

Script Examples (Go to Portal Row)

1. Targeting the proper portal

The Go to Portal Row will target the first portal on the layout based on the layer order. The portal that is farthest back in the layout order will be targeted unless you use this technique.

```
Comment ["How to target a portal row on a layout with more
          than one portal."]
Go to Field [Select/perform, "Relationship::Field"]
Go to Portal Row [Select, "Portal ID Value"]
```

NOTE: The Portal ID Value field contains a numerical value from the last portal row that was edited. It was acquired by a Set Field in another script. See the technique titled Return to Portal Row for details.

Go to Previous Field   Navigation

What it does: Moves to the previous field in the tab order on the current layout.

When to use: When you want a script to take a user to the previous field.

Note: This script step is not used often. See the Go to Next Field script step for ideas.

Go to Record/Request/Page   Navigation

What it does: This script step will navigate to a specific record in the current found set in Browse mode, a request in Find mode or page in Preview mode.

Options: [1] First Record/Request/Page
             [2] Last Record/Request/Page
             [3] Previous Record/Request/Page
                 Exit after last (check box)

[4] Next Record/Request/Page
Exit after last (check box)
[5] By Number...
[6] By Field Value...

The options for going to a record or request based on a number or a field value are rarely used, but can provide a unique fix to situations where a specific record must be targeted.

When to use: When you need to take the user of the database to a specific find request, record or page.

Application: This script step is used so often, it is difficult to come up with a few examples that demonstrate the significance of this tool. It is used in tasks that range from looping scripts that cycle through records to single line scripts that navigate a database. Following are a few of examples.

If you are going to enter Preview mode, you may want to display the total number of pages. To do this, enter Preview mode, go to the last page and then return to the first page. This will show the total number of pages in the status area instead of a question mark.

If you want to loop through all the records in the current found set, this script step gets used twice, but with different options. First, it is used to display the first record in the found set. Second, it is used to go from record to record.

Advanced technique: In cases with very advanced queries (searches), you may want to create a number of preset requests. For example, you may want request data to automatically be input when the user clicks a find or search button, in addition to custom

MARK.FP3

Technique File:
Marking Records by
Category

entered criteria. If you have three requests and you need to have the user input more data in the second request, you could take the user to that request by going to the request by number.

Script Examples (Go to Record/Request/Page)

1. Mark/Tag all records in found set
A script that uses a loop to cycle through all of the found records and sets a field value of 1 to the field named "Mark". Note, however, that the Replace script step could be better suited to this task.

```
Comment ["Marks all the records in the current found set."]
Go to Record/Request/Page [First]
Loop
    Set Field ["Mark", "1"]
    Go to Record/Request/Page [Exit after last, Next]
End Loop
```

1. Preview page totals
A script that prompts the user whether they would like to preview the total number of pages before printing.

```
Enter Preview Mode []
Go to Layout ["Print Layout"]
Show Message ["Would you like to total the pages? This may take a
              little longer depending on the number of records
              showing."]
If ["Status(CurrentMessageChoice) = 1"]
    Go to Record/Request/Page [Last]
    Go to Record/Request/Page [First]
End If
Pause/Resume Script []
Print []
Enter Browse Mode []
Go to Layout ["Main"]
```

Go to Related Record   Navigation

What it does: Navigates to a record in a related database corresponding to the match field used for the relationship. The related database becomes active.

Options: [1] Show only related records (check box)
[2] Specify: Relationship

The show only related records option creates a found set of records in the related database based on the match value from the current record. If more than one record is related to the current record, the first of those records will be the active record.

When to use: Whenever navigation from one database to another through a relationship is required. For example, to show the respective record in a Company database from a record in a Contact database.

Application: If you place a button within a portal with this script step attached, it will show the record related to the portal row, even though all the records have the same match or key value.

Advanced technique: One of the most commonly overlooked facts, is that FileMaker Pro can maintain multiple keys in one field. As long as the values are separated by a return, each value is considered separate from the next. Using the Go to Related Record script step will not only take you to the first value in the list, but also to all the values found in the list. This technique is used in quite a few technique files on the CD ROM.

SAVE.FP3

Technique File:
Save a Found Set

See the example of saving found sets of records for future retrieval in a file named Save a Found Set (SAVE.FP3). This technique utilizes the Go to Related Record script step to retrieve found sets of records.

Script Examples (Go to Related Record)

1. Go to Related if valid
Using the IsValid function within an If script step allows FileMaker to check if the relationship is valid before going to the related database. If no relationship exists, a message can be provided.

```
If ["IsValid(Company Relationship::Contact)"]
    Go to Related Record [Show, "Company Relationship"]
Else
    Show Message ["There isn't a company for this contact."]
End If
```

NOTE: The IsValid function will return true if there are related records and false if there are none.

Halt Script Control

What it does: Forces all scripts to halt including sub-scripts and external scripts.

Options: [1] None

When to use: When it is necessary to stop all scripts from running.

Considerations: Understanding the difference between Exit and Halt is important. Halt stops all scripts that are running or paused. Exit stops the currently running script, but will continue with any scripts that called it.

Script Examples (Halt Script)

1. Halt based on a condition
Combined with an If script step, a FileMaker Pro script can be stopped at any time. In this example, a database loops through the records in the found set and checks the State field. As soon as the loop encounters a record containing "California", it stops the script.

```
Loop
    Go to Next Record/Request/Page [Exit after last, Next]
    If ["PatternCount(State, "California") >= 1"]
        Halt Script
    End If
End Loop
```

NOTE: The PatternCount function serves as a "contains" operator to search within text strings.

What it does: Determines the direction of a script based on a condition. The condition is tested by a calculation formula.

Options: [1] Specify conditions via calculation

The result of the If statement must be a Boolean true (1) or false (0). If the calculation result is zero, the calculation evaluates as false and the subsequent script steps are not executed. If the calculation result is any value other than zero, the calculation evaluates as true and the script steps are performed.

When to use: Whenever a script needs to take one of two paths.

Advanced technique: Nested If statements can be created using the Else script step. They allow you to test more than one condition which branch to different sets of script steps. See the Else script step for more information.

Script Examples (If)

1. Determining the version of FileMaker Pro
This script uses the Status(CurrentVersion) function in order to determine which version of FileMaker Pro is being used.

```
Comment ["Demonstrates how to go to different layouts based on
         the version of FileMaker Pro being used."]
If ["Left(RightWords(Status(CurrentAppVersion), 1), 1) = "4""]
   Perform Script [Sub-scripts, "Go to Layout 4.0"]
Else
   Perform Script [Sub-scripts, "Go to Layout 3.0"]
End If
```

2. Database in "demo" mode
If the database has the word "Demo Mode" in a field, perform certain script steps.

```
Comment ["Use IF statements to watch for conditions and if they
         are determined true then exit the script."]
If ["Database Mode = "Demo Mode""]
   Show Message ["This database is in demo mode."]
   Exit Script
Else
   Perform Script [Sub-scripts, "Set User Prefs"]
   Perform Script [Sub-scripts, "Layout: Main"]
End If
```

Import Movie/QuickTime   Import/Export

What it does: Imports a QuickTime movie into the currently selected container field.

Options: [1] Specify file...

The only option is to specify a target file. This option is not very useful since the file must always be named the same and reside in the same location. This limitation can be avoided with a scripting language like AppleScript or WinBatch, but requires a good knowledge of how to use these languages. The scripting program can move a file into the proper location and change the name. Using this information, it is possible to move any movie into the correct location, change the name and import in a dynamic fashion.

When to use: There may be situations where a user needs the ability to import QuickTime movies into each record. This script step will save users from going to the menus all the time.

Import Picture Import/Export

What it does: Imports a picture from a file.

Options: [1] Specify file...

The only option is to specify a target file. This option is not very useful since the file must always be named the same and reside in the same location. This limitation can be avoided with a scripting language like AppleScript or WinBatch, but requires a good knowledge of how to use these languages. The scripting program can move a file into the proper location and change the name. Using this information, it is possible to move any picture into the correct location, change the name and import in a dynamic fashion.

When to use: When you want to prompt the user with a dialog box for importing a picture into a container field.

Special note: When the import picture dialog is showing, there is an option to store the picture as a reference or to import it into the FileMaker Pro file. Importing pictures as a reference will reduce the size of your database, but will not work in a multi-user scenario unless the pictures are on a network shared volume.

1. Import only if empty

Checking to see if a container field is empty or not can prevent a user from accidentally deleting data.

```
If ["not IsEmpty(my data)"]
    Show Message ["There is already a picture in this record. Should I
                  replace it?"]
    If ["Status(CurrentMessageChoice) = 1"]
        Go to Field ["Picture Field"]
        Import Picture []
    End If
End If
```

NOTE: The Go to Field step is needed since the Import Picture step cannot specify a field.

Import Records   Import/Export

What it does: Imports records from another source. File formats supported use the XTND translation system.

Options: [1] Restore import order
[2] Perform without dialog
[3] Specify file...

Restoring the import order is probably the most important feature. Import records manually and then create the script. The restore option will remember the order of the fields when last imported.

When to use: When you want to import records from another source or file.

Application: By using a global field formatted as a pop-up menu, it is possible to provide multiple import options to the user. When an option is selected from the pop-up, a conditional script can determine which import to use.

SYNCH.FP3

Technique File:
Synchronization

Advanced technique: Importing can be used to support synchronization between two FileMaker Pro files. There is an example of this feature in the Synchronization (SYNCH.FP3) technique.

Script Examples (Import Records)

1. Pop-up import script

Using a global field formatted as a pop-up menu allows users to make selections of what to import, rather than having one button for each import script.

```
If ["Import Popup = "Employee data""]
    Import Records [Restore, No dialog]
Else
    If ["Import Popup = "Monthly Receipts""]
        Perform Script [Sub-scripts, "IMPORT: Monthly Receipts"]
    Else
        Import Records []
    End If
End If
```

Insert Object	Fields

Windows only

What it does: Embeds or links an OLE object.

Options: [1] Specify Object

When to use: Use this script step when it is desired to link an object to a FileMaker Pro field. This is useful for product shots which might be updated. Since the object is linked, it can be updated without importing or copying and pasting again.

---

1. Link logo image

OLE linking and embedding allows live links to objects. Whenever the graphic is updated, so is the FileMaker Pro field that contains the object.

```
Insert Object ["Bitmap Image"]
```

Loop   Control

What it does: Repeats a sequence of steps between the Loop and End Loop statements.

Options: [1] None

When to use: When a repetitive sequence of steps needs to occur.

Application: A loop cycles until a step within the loop stops the process. There are many ways to exit a loop. One of the most common methods is to use the Go to Record/Request/Page step with the exit after last option. The script loops through the records in the found set. When it reaches the last record, it exits the loop. A good example of looping is a technique file called Marking Records by Category (MARK.FP3). It marks duplicate records by visiting each record in the found set.

MARK.FP3

Technique File:
Marking Records by
Category

A common script step to use with a loop is the Exit Loop If step. A Set Field script step increments a global counter field by setting itself plus or minus one. The Exit Loop If script step condition will exit the loop when the global counter field equals a certain value.

COUNTER.FP3

Technique File:
Better Counter

Another way to exit a loop is adding an If statement within the loop. If the If statement condition is met, an Exit or Halt Script is performed. This technique is not as common, but is necessary in some scenarios.

Script Examples (Loop)

1. Basic record loop

Because FileMaker Pro has a built in feature for going to the next record, the script can watch to see if it is on the last record and exit the loop automatically.

```
Loop
    Comment ["Do more script steps here."]
    Go to Record/Request/Page [Exit after last, Next]
End Loop
```

2. Exit Loop If conditional exit

Another common control for exiting a loop is the Exit Loop If script step.

```
Loop
    Comment ["Do more script steps here."]
    Exit Loop If ["If(My Field = "Expected Data",1,0)"]
End Loop
```

3. Embedded conditional loop exit

When the Exit Loop If script step will not work well for the type of loop that is being used, a regular If script step along with the Exit or Halt script step can be used. The most common example of this type of exit is when script steps after the loop should not be performed.

```
Loop
    Comment ["Do more script steps here."]
    If ["Status(CurrentRecordNumber) > 20"]
        Exit Script
    End If
    Go to Record/Request/Page [Exit after last, Next]
End Loop
Comment ["Do more script steps here, only if the found set is less
         than 20 records."]
```

What it does: Enters Find mode and restores the last set of search criteria used.

Options: [1] None

When to use: When the last set of search criteria did not provide the desired results the most recent find needs to be expanded.

Application: One of the instances in which this script step can be used is for a complex find that builds on itself. The user might perform a find for a certain state, such as "CA". After the search was performed a button could be used that would read "Find More". Clicking this button would use the Modify Last Find to bring up the previously searched for "CA" and add a new request, so the user could add another state to the search criteria.

Script Examples (Modify Last Find)

1. Expand search requests
A script that determines if the current mode is browse. If so, the script modifies the last find and adds a search request.

```
Comment ["This script adds new find requests. It checks
         to make sure the mode is Browse before it
         executes the steps."]
If ["Status(CurrentMode) = 0"]
    Modify Last Find
    New Record/Request
End If
```

What it does: Creates a new FileMaker Pro file.

Options: [1] None

Application: This script is hardly ever used because there are hardly any scenarios where a solution would need to create a new file.

What it does: Creates a new record when in Browse mode and a new request in Find mode.

Options: [1] None

When to use: Whenever a new record is needed in browse mode or a new request in find mode.

Considerations: A common mistake for newer users is clicking a New Record button while in find mode. Data entered into find mode will be lost. Your best defense is to always add the script step Enter Browse Mode before every New Record/Request. Another approach is to use the Status(CurrentMode) function to determine the current mode and then enter Browse if necessary.

FIND.FP3

Technique File:
Find Window

Application: The most common use of this script step, while in Browse mode, is to create a new record. Other uses include looping scripts that create several new records at once. An advanced technique uses a looping script while in Find mode to create multiple find criteria (FIND.FP3).

Script Examples (New Record/Request)

1. Create multiple records
A script that creates a number of records according to a value entered into a field.

```
Enter Browse Mode []
Show Message ["How many records do you want to create?
               Click continue, enter the value and click ok."]
Go to Field [Select/perform, "Global"]
Pause/Resume Script []
Loop
    New Record/Request
    Set Field ["Global", "Global - 1"]
    Exit Loop If ["Global = 0"]
End Loop
```

Omit   Sort/Find/Print

What it does: Removes the current record from the found set. When in Find mode, it checks the omit check box in the Status Area.

Options: [1] None

When to use: Whenever it is necessary to remove a record from the current found set or facilitate a find with the omit option.

(◎) FINDOMIT.FP3

Technique File:
Scripting the Omit
Box

Application: This feature is very useful if you want to construct custom finds with multiple requests with the Omit option checked. This creates a NOT search request.

A looping script can use the Omit step to remove records from the found set once they have been processed. It is essential to remember that by omitting a record you automatically go to the next record

 **SORTPORT.FP3**

Technique File:
Sorting Portals

in the found set and not the previous. An example of this can be found in the techniques section of the CD called Sorting Portals (SORTPORT.FP3). When you open the technique file, find the Duplicate/Delete sorting portals script.

Script Examples (Omit)

1. Duplicate a found set of records

Duplicating a found set of records is useful for many situations. For instance, you might want to duplicate an invoice that contains a portal. The following script would be able to duplicate all the related records for the portal.

```
Comment ["This script duplicates an entire found set of records.
         Notice that the first step is to unsort the database.
         Records duplicate differently when sorted. See the
         Duplicate Record/Request step for more information."]
Unsort
Set Field ["Global", "Status(CurrentFoundCount)"]
Loop
    Exit Loop If ["Global = 0"]
    Duplicate Record/Request
    Set Field ["Data Field", ""Duplicate""]
    Go to Record/Request/Page [First]
    Omit
    Set Field ["Global", "Global - 1"]
End Loop
```

NOTE: When records are duplicated, auto-enter values override any values stored in a field with auto-enter options.

Omit Multiple   Sort/Find/Print

What it does: This step is the same as the Omit script step, except it allows you to remove multiple records starting from the currently selected record.

Options: [1] Perform without dialog
[2] Specify starting record

When to use: When a large number of records need to be removed from the found set. Omit Multiple is much more efficient than a looping script that uses an Omit script step.

Considerations: The biggest limitation of the Omit Multiple script step is that it can't use a value from a field. As a work around, you can specify a very large number with the no dialog option checked and FileMaker Pro will omit all the records that are available starting from the current record. If you are on record 50 and have 100 records in your found set, a script that omits 999,999 records will only omit records 50 through 100.

RANDPICK.FP3

Technique File:
Randomly Picking
Records

Application: There is a good example of using this script step in a technique called Randomly Picking Records (RANDPICK.FP3). The Omit Multiple script step comes in handy for taking all but the selected records out of the found set.

Script Examples (Omit Multiple)

1. Omit a range of records
This script goes to a record number based on a value stored in a global field and omits all the records after it. If the global field contained the number 50 and the database contained 500 records, the last 450 records would be omitted.

```
Go to Record/Request/Page ["Global"]
Omit Multiple [No dialog, 999999]
```

Open   Files

What it does: Opens another FileMaker Pro file.

Options: [1] Open hidden
[2] Specify file

When to use: When a large number of files are opened at startup or a specific file needs to be launched.

Considerations: The option for specifying a file allows you to indicate which file to open, rather than presenting the user with the Open dialog. Open as hidden allows a file to be opened, but can only be accessed from the Window menu. If you want to open a file created by another program, use the Send Apple Event (Macintosh) or Send Message (Windows). There is a technique called Opening a Path (OPEN.FP3) that covers the specifics.

OPEN.FP3

Technique File:
Opening a Path

Application: The best use of this script step is as a single step. For instance, it could be used on a main menu layout to open particular files. However, other script steps, such as the Perform Script step, will automatically open a file if it is not already available.

The most common use is to open a file on startup, before a relationship opens the file. This is desirable because files opened via relationships do not perform their startup scripts.

Script Examples (Open)

1. Startup opening script
Files that are opened with a relationship will not run startup scripts. Your best solution is to open all the files on startup. It is also a good idea to open the files as hidden, so users don't accidentally click on a window behind the active one.

```
Comment ["Opening startup script"]
Open ["Customers.FP3"]
Open [Open hidden, "Company.FP3"]
Open [Open hidden, "Invoices.FP3"]
Open [Open hidden, "Inventory.FP3"]
Open [Open hidden, "Shipping.FP3"]
```

What it does: Opens the Define Fields dialog.

Options: [1] None

When to use: This script step is rarely made available to end users, but can be helpful for developers to more easily access Define Fields.

Considerations: Be careful who you allow access to this script. If someone doesn't already know how to access Define Fields manually, they probably shouldn't have access via a script.

Open Define Relationships   Open Menu Item

What it does: Opens the Define Relationships dialog.

Options: [1] None

When to use: This script step is rarely made available to end users, but can be helpful for developers to more easily access Define Relationships.

Considerations: Be careful who you allow access to this script. If someone doesn't already know how to access Define Relationships manually, they probably shouldn't have access via a script.

What it does: Opens the Define Value Lists dialog.

Options: [1] None

When to use: This script step is rarely made available to end users, but can be helpful for developers to more easily access Define Value Lists.

Considerations: Be careful who you allow access to this script. The best method for giving value list modification capabilities is through adding the Edit option to a pop-up list.

Open Help   Open Menu Item

What it does: Opens the FileMaker Pro online help.

Options: [1] None

HELP.FP3

Technique File:
Context Sensitive
Help

When to use: When the user needs to be presented with help documentation applicable to FileMaker Pro.

Applications: If your solution is designed well, users may not even realize they are using FileMaker Pro. Designing your own help system can make your solution seamless. Three examples are provided in the technique section of the CD with the names Context Sensitive Help (HELP.FP3), Context Sensitive Help 2 (HELP2.FP3) and Context Sensitive Help 3 (HELP3.FP3).

HELP2.FP3

Technique File:
Context Sensitive
Help 2

HELP3.FP3

Technique File:
Context Sensitive
Help 3

What it does: Opens the Preferences dialog.

Options: [1] None

When to use: When general FileMaker Pro preferences need to be accessed by the user of the database.

Considerations: Be careful who you allow access to this script. If someone doesn't already know how to access Preferences manually, they probably shouldn't have access via a script.

4.0 Only

Application: This script step has been separated into two steps to reflect the changes in FileMaker Pro 4.0; Open Application Preferences and Open Document Preferences. In addition, these items have been moved in ScriptMaker from the Miscellaneous category to a new category called Open Menu Item. One of the reasons you might open the Application preferences is so that the user can change the user name to a custom name. It is possible with the Status(CurrentUserName) function to check for who logs into a shared database.

Script Examples (Open Preferences)

1. Startup user check
It is possible to check that the user name in preferences matches a user name stored in a file within your solution to prevent unauthorized login. This script can be expanded to track login dates and times or require users to enter a password in order to use the database.

```
Set Field ["Global", "Status(CurrentUserName)"]
If ["not IsValid(Users::User Name)"]
```

```
    Show Message ["The user name you are using is not a valid
    user. Please adjust your user name in preferences or contact
    the administrator."]
    If ["Status(CurrentMessageChoice) = 1"]
        Open Application Preferences
    End If
End If
```

NOTE: Placing the two different Preferences script steps right after each other is okay. FileMaker Pro is smart enough to wait until the Done button is clicked before continuing the rest of the script.

```
Open Application Preferences
Open Document Preferences
```

Open ScriptMaker™   Open Menu Item

What it does: Opens the ScriptMaker dialog.

Options: [1] None

When to use: When it is desirable for a user to add, delete or modify scripts in ScriptMaker.

Considerations: Be careful who you allow access to this script. If someone doesn't already know how to access ScriptMaker manually, they probably shouldn't have access via a script.

Open Sharing   Open Menu Item

4.0 Only

What it does: This is a new script step in FileMaker Pro 4.0 that displays the new networking dialog for changing between multi-user and single-user.

Options: [1] None

When to use: When it is desirable for a user to have access to the network sharing settings of a database.

Application: Could be useful to help people turn on FileMaker Pro networking. For instance, if someone purchases a site license from a commercial solution a script could be used to prompt for a password. With the correct password entered, the network sharing dialog would be shown.

4.0 Only

What it does: Allows you to open a URL in Windows 95/NT or Macintosh by passing the value in a field to your web browser, ftp or mail program.

Options: [1] Perform without dialog
[2] Specify URL
[3] Static text
[4] From field...

When to use: Whenever a web browser needs to open a URL from a FileMaker Pro record.

Considerations: On the Macintosh you must have Internet Config 1.1 or higher installed. If the URL begins with "http" then the web browser designated in Internet Config is used. The other protocols that are recognized are "ftp", "file" and "mailto". This script step is available for Windows 95 and NT but not Windows 3.1. FileMaker uses the information stored in the URL.DLL to determine which application will handle the URL.

OPEN_URL.FP3
Technique File:
Open URL

Application: Useful for creating a URL tracking program that replaces the bookmark feature of your web browser. The advantages of a database make it possible for you to track notes and other information about Internet URLs.

1. Open URL

The Open URL script step is useful if your system is setup correctly. On the Macintosh, the Open URL script step requires Internet Config to be installed. Under Windows, the URL.DLL must be configured properly. The Macintosh has an alternative if Internet Config is not installed, which is to use the Send AppleEvent script step. The Apple Event ID codes of GURL and GURL can be used to pass a value stored in a field.

```
Open URL [No dialog, "URL Field"]
```

Page Setup/Print Setup   Sort/Find/Print

What it does: This script step displays the Page Setup (Macintosh) or Print Setup (Windows) dialog.

Options: [1] Restore setup options
[2] Perform without dialog

The restore option will only restore the FileMaker Pro specific options from the Print dialog such as records being browsed vs. current record and all of the options from the Page or Print Setup dialog. Set your dialogs the way you want them, create the script and it will remember the settings.

When to use: Whenever the Page Setup/Print Setup needs to be restored to a script that prints out a form.

Considerations: Print drivers on the Macintosh differ greatly from those in Windows, so page settings need to be stored separately. A little known fact about Page/Print Setup is that it can store two sets of page settings. This is used for cross-platform databases. Just create a script on one platform with the restore option. Next, edit the script on the other platform and click the Okay button. You will get a dialog asking you to Keep or Replace. FileMaker Pro will store the new settings for the two platforms separately when you choose Replace (see Chapter 3 Section 5).

Application: This step is useful when broken out on its own. You can create a Page/Print Setup for each of the various outputs you will want to support. Create an Envelope Page/Print Setup script, a Letter Page/Print Setup script and so on. All you have to do in your Print script is use the Perform Script step to call the Page/Print Setup script that you want to restore.

Script Examples (Page Setup/Print Setup)

1. Standard Preview script

Previewing a layout also requires Page/Print Setup to be restored in order for it to display properly. The best example of this is previewing an envelope layout.

```
Go to Layout ["Envelope Layout"]
Page Setup [Restore, No dialog]
Enter Preview Mode [Pause]
Enter Browse Mode []
Go to Layout [original layout]
```

Paste   Editing

What it does: Pastes data from the system clipboard.

Options: [1] Select entire contents
[2] Paste without style
[3] Specify field...
[4] Link if available

If you don't specify a field, the script will paste into the currently selected field. If you don't check the option for selecting the entire contents, the script will paste where the cursor is currently located.

When to use: When data from the clipboard needs to be pasted into a field or if a field based operation requires that a value be pasted into the field.

Considerations: Cut, copy and paste are the older methods of moving data from one place to another (FileMaker Pro 2.x). They used to be the only way to get information from one place to another. With the advent of Set Field, you should rarely use cut, copy and paste to move data, because moving information onto the clipboard will remove what the user may have manually stored there.

Important info ▶ If you need to use the cut, copy or paste steps, make sure you are on a layout containing the target field. The reason for this behavior is explained by an example. If you try to manually paste into a field, it needs to be visible. The same is true for scripts. In contrast, Set Field does not require the field to be on the layout.

RANGE.FP3

Technique File:
Date Range Finds

Application: There may be some cases where you want to automatically perform a find that requires special characters. Set Field will not set a less than sign "<" to a number field. You can use the Paste or Paste Literal script step to paste in the character and then paste the values that you want to search for. This technique is covered in the technique section of this CD and is called Date Range Finds (RANGE.FP3).

Script Examples (Paste)

1. Find similar records

A common scripting task is locating all of the records related to the current one. Copy a value from the current record, enter find mode and paste the value.

```
Comment ["Copies a value from the current record, enters it into
         Find mode and performs the find."]
Copy [Select, "Any Field"]
Go to Layout ["Search Layout"]
Enter Find Mode []
Paste [Select, No style, "Search Field"]
Perform Find []
```

NOTE: For a more powerful version of this script, see the Paste from Last Record script step.

Paste Current Date   Fields

What it does: Pastes the current date from the system.

Options: [1] Select entire contents
             [2] Specify field...

⊚ **NOTES.FP3**

Technique File:
Notes

When to use: It's more advisable to use Set Field with Status(CurrentDate), since it does not require the field to be on the current layout. This script step is a holdover from FileMaker Pro 2.x. Removing it would break converted FileMaker Pro 2.x scripts.

Script Examples (Paste Current Date)

1. Paste Current Date
Pasting the current date is useful for tracking a notes field in a chronological order.

```
Paste Current Date [Select, "Date Field"]
```

Paste Current Time   Fields

What it does: Pastes the current time from the System.

Options: [1] Select entire contents
[2] Specify field...

When to use: It is more advisable to use Set Field with the Status(CurrentTime) function, since it does not require the field to be on the current layout. This step is a holdover from FileMaker Pro 2.x. Removing it would break converted FileMaker Pro 2.x scripts.

Script Examples (Paste Current Time)

1. Paste Current Time
Pasting the current time is useful for tracking a notes field in a chronological order.

```
Paste Current Time [Select, "Time Field"]
```

Paste Current User Name   Fields

What it does: Pastes the current user name from the System.

Options: [1] Select entire contents
[2] Specify field...

When to use: It is more advisable to use Set Field and Status(CurrentUserName) since it does not require the field to be on the current layout. This script step is a holdover from FileMaker Pro 2.x since removing it would break converted FileMaker Pro 2.x scripts. The current user name comes from the system software unless otherwise specified in the FileMaker Application Preferences.

Script Examples (Paste Current User Name)

1. Paste Current User Name
Pasting the current user name can be used to keep a user log of who is using the database.

```
New Record/Request  (so each name can be stored on a separate record)
Paste Current User Name [Select, "Text Field"]
```

Paste from Index   Fields

View Index dialog box.

What it does: Displays the View Index dialog.

Options: [1] Select entire contents
[2] Specify field...

When to use: When the user needs to be presented with a list of all the words or values entered into a field's index.

Considerations: The View Index dialog is best used as a developer tool to check the index and not as a script step to aid data entry. The better option is using the Field Format options to set up a pop-up menu based on values from a field.

Application: When used in Find mode, it presents the user with all of the available options for searching within a specific field.

Script Examples (Paste from Index)

1. Use index for find
This script step can be used to display the values that can be used for a search. However, you are better off using a pop-up menu.

```
Enter Find Mode []
Paste from Index [Select, "Data Field"]
Perform Find []
```

NOTE: The script will automatically pause when the Paste from Index dialog shows.

What it does: Pastes information from the previously browsed record into the current field.

Options: [1] Select entire contents
[2] Specify field...

When to use: When trying to duplicate specific field information from the previous record, rather than the entire record.

Considerations: The most recently browsed record is specified when you activate one or more fields on the layout. Simply viewing that record does not activate it. The field also needs to be present on the layout in order for this script step to work.

Application: A good example for this script step is a feature that allows a user to locate all similar records. Create a script that goes to the last name field, enters find mode and then copies from the last record. This will copy the last name value and place it into find mode, allowing you to locate all records containing the same last name. You could use copy and paste, but that changes the contents of the clipboard. See the example below.

Script Examples (Paste from Last Record)

1. Find records based on field value(s)

When using the Paste from Last Record script step, it is important for a field to be selected before entering Find mode. Otherwise, nothing will be pasted. Use the Go to Field script step to select a field.

```
Go to Field ["Last Name"]
Enter Find Mode []
Paste from Last Record [Select, "Data Field"]
Perform Find []
```

NOTE: The above script can be modified to go to any number of fields in the current record and paste from the last record. For example, a find could be performed for last name "Smith" and state "CA".

What it does: Pastes a predefined value into a specified field.

Options: [1] Select entire contents
[2] Specify field...
[3] Specify value to paste

When to use: When other steps such as Paste Result and Set Field will not accomplish the desired results.

Application: This feature is not of much use in FileMaker Pro 3.0/4.0, since you can accomplish the same task with so many other script steps (e.g. Set Field). Removing this script step would break files converted from FileMaker Pro 2.X.

Script Examples (Paste Literal)

1. Paste special characters
One of the limitations of Set Field, while in Find mode, is that you cannot set the special find characters. While the Paste Result script step can be used, there may be instances where the Paste Literal is needed.

```
Enter Find Mode []
Paste Literal [Select, "Date Field", ">="]
Paste Current Date ["Date Field"]
Perform Find []
```

What it does: Pastes the result of a calculation into a field.

Options: [1] Select entire contents
[2] Specify field...
[3] Specify calculation value

With the advent of Set Field, you should rarely use Paste Result to move data, simply because Set Field does not require the field to be on the layout.

When to use: Whenever Set Field will not work to place the desired result into a field.

Considerations: When using a script that pastes, you must be on a layout where the field is present. The reason for this behavior is explained by an example. If you try to manually paste into a field, it needs to be visible. The same is true for scripts.

Application: There may be some cases where you want to perform a find that requires special characters. Since the Set Field step will not set a less than sign "<" to a number or date field, you can use the Paste Result or Paste Literal to paste in the character and then paste the values that you want to search for. This technique is covered in the technique section of the CD and is called Date Range Finds (RANGE.FP3).

 **RANGE.FP3**

Technique File:
Date Range Finds

Script Examples (Paste Result)

1. Perform special find

Set Field cannot be used to place special characters into fields because it attempts to coerce the data to the field type. Paste Result will accomplish the same task but will not coerce the data.

```
Comment ["Finds all the records from today to 30 days ago.
         Set Field cannot be used to accomplish this task."]
Set Error Capture [On]
Enter Find Mode []
```

```
Paste Result [Select, "Data Field", "DateToText(Status(CurrentDate) -
            30) & "..."  & DateToText(Status(CurrentDate))"]
            Perform Find []
```

Pause/Resume Script Control

What it does: Pauses or resumes a script.

Options: [1] Select settings
Pause Indefinitely until Resume
For duration given by field value
For specified hours, minutes & seconds

Manually resuming a paused script can be done by clicking the Continue button in the status area, typing the Enter key on the keypad or using another script to resume.

When to use: When a script needs to pause for user action or resume a script that has been paused for input.

Considerations: When you use the option to specify a duration given by a field, make sure to use a time field rather than a number field.

Application: There are many uses for the Pause/Resume script step. You can use it to pause a database on a layout during startup to simulate a splash screen. Another use is to pause after entering find mode. This allows find criteria to be entered by a user. An entirely different usage is for debugging your scripts. If a script is not running as conceptualized, placing pauses at key locations in the script allow you to stop the action while you check the state of your file.

Script Examples (Pause/Resume Script)

1. Splash screen
One of the most common startup scripts is pausing at the splash screen. It is especially common in commercial solutions. It is a good way to let users know who created the product.

```
Comment ["Startup script for showing splash screen."]
Go to Layout ["Splash Screen"]
Pause/Resume Script ["0:00:03"]
Go to Layout ["Main Data Entry"]
```

Perform AppleScript   Miscellaneous

Macintosh only

What it does: Sends AppleScript commands to other Macintosh applications. With FileMaker Pro 4.0, AppleScripts can now target FileMaker Pro itself.

Options: [1] Select settings
　　　　　　　AppleScript from a field
　　　　　　　Static AppleScript

The option of performing an AppleScript from a field adds the ability to merge in data from the database. Use a calculation field to combine AppleScript code with fields from the database.

When to use: Whenever inter-application communication is necessary under the Macintosh OS.

Considerations: One of the limitations of this script step is that the name of the target application needs to be exactly the same in the AppleScript as it is named in the user's system. Even though a prompt will try to locate the program, the name of the program will not be remembered after the file is closed.

This is different from an AppleScript applet, since it will remember the name of the user's application.

Using FileMaker Pro 3.0, you cannot send an AppleScript from FileMaker to itself. To accomplish this task you will need to use an AppleScript applet. FileMaker Pro will send an Apple Event to the applet and the applet will communicate back to FileMaker Pro.

Application: This script step can be used to accomplish anything that FileMaker Pro cannot do by itself. By communicating with other programs, it is possible to add features to FileMaker Pro. For example, you can link FileMaker Pro and Excel, enabling FileMaker Pro to do charting. FileMaker Pro would export the data to a text file and an AppleScript would make Excel import it and chart it. The chart could even be copied and pasted into a FileMaker container field.

OPEN.FP3

Technique File:
Opening a Path

Script Examples (Perform AppleScript)

1. Perform AppleScript from Field

One of the most powerful uses of the Perform AppleScript script step is to reference a calculation field that contains custom created AppleScript syntax. The calculation combines AppleScript syntax with field references from the database to vary the AppleScript from record to record.

```
If ["not IsEmpty(Application Name)"]
    Perform AppleScript ["AppleScript Syntax Field"]
End If
```

2. Capture input

FileMaker Pro 4.0 can capture data and send itself AppleEvents. The script below, which is actually just two lines of AppleScript, will ask for user input and then set the result provided into the field named "Data Field". Be sure to change the name of the field if you duplicate this script.

```
Perform AppleScript ["
    display dialog "You can use AppleScript to capture input."
    buttons {"OK"} default button "OK" default answer
    "Enter this into a field"
    set data of cell named "Data Field" of current record
    to text returned of result"]
```

Perform Find

What it does: Initiates a find. It is usually accompanied by the Enter Find Mode step, so that you can enter Find mode, pause for user entry and perform the find. If the Restore option is used, it can be used as a lone script step to perform restored finds.

Options: [1] Restore find requests

When to use: To continue a find when the current mode is Find or as a stand-alone step with the restore option to perform a find with predefined criteria.

Application: There are two main uses for this script step. One is when creating a find script that just finds by the same criteria every time (Perform Find [Restore]). The other place where Perform Find is used is when taking the user into a find where they can specify custom search parameters. This is done by entering Find mode, waiting for user input and then performing the find.

Key information: Set Field can be used to manipulate data within global fields while in Find Mode. This allows you to pass information from Browse to Find. There is a technique on how to do this called Find Window (FIND.FP3).

FIND.FP3

Technique File:
Find Window

1. Completing a find

A standard find script will enter Find mode and pause for user input. The user can either click a button with an assigned Resume action, click the Continue button in the Status area (if showing) or use the Enter key.

```
Enter Find Mode [Pause]
Perform Find []
```

Perform Script   Control

What it does: Allows you to nest or connect scripts.

Options: [1] Perform sub-scripts
[2] Specify script
Internal script
External script...

An external script allows you to link two FileMaker Pro files. A sub-script is a script which is called from within another script.

When to use: Whenever it is necessary to break down larger scripts into smaller ones and link the smaller scripts to create a more manageable structure. Can also be used to connect two databases together using the External option.

Application: Let's say you want to connect two databases so that they can communicate. You could have a script in file A open file B using the Open script step. What if you also want to perform some scripts while in file B? The answer is to have the script in file A call a script in file B (e.g. Perform Script [External: "File B Script"]). File B will open automatically and run the specified script.

1. Conditional Scripting

Combined with an If statement, it is possible to run a script based on a condition. When a condition is met, a Perform Script script step will tell ScriptMaker™ to run the other script.

```
If ["My Field = "xyz""]
    Perform Script [Sub-scripts, "Script A"]
Else
    Perform Script [Sub-scripts, "Script B"]
End If
```

Print   Sort/Find/Print

What it does: Prints from the current layout.

Options: [1] Perform without dialog

If the option for no dialog is selected, the script will print without showing the print dialog. This script step is commonly used with Page Setup (Macintosh) or Print Setup (Windows).

When to use: Whenever you need to print.

Considerations: The Page Setup or Print Setup script step only restores some of the options in the Print dialog. When no print dialog option is checked, the last Page Setup or Print Setup options will be used. Given these limitations, it's better to present the print dialog so the user can change options if necessary.

1. Printing a layout

Using a global field formatted as a pop-up menu allows the user to choose whether or not to be presented with a dialog box. You could also implement this feature using the Status(CurrentModifierKeys) function to bypass the print dialog when the Shift key is held down while clicking the print button.

```
If ["Print Popup Field = "Print with dialog""]
    Print []
Else
    Print [No dialog]
End If
```

Quit/Exit Application   Miscellaneous

What it does: Quits or Exits FileMaker Pro and all the files that are running.

Options: [1] None

When to use: Whenever quitting FileMaker Pro or the runtime version of FileMaker Pro is desired.

Considerations: It is advisable to rarely, if ever, use the Quit Application script step on solutions unless they are runtime. While you want to quit the runtime engine, you don't want to shutdown FileMaker since the user may be running other solutions.

Application: This script step is useful for runtime solutions instead of relying on the Quit item under the File menu. If a Kiosk solution built with the Solutions Development Kit (SDK) of FileMaker Pro is used, the quit option has to be included since there is no menu bar.

⚠ Power Tip

The SDK (Solutions Development Kit, also known as the Developer's Edition) is a runtime version of FileMaker Pro. It allows you to distribute a copy of FileMaker Pro bound to your files. For more information about the SDK visit the FileMaker Inc. web site at http://www.filemaker.com

---

1. Present Quit confirmation

It may be a better solution to offer the user the option to confirm their choice to quit or not.

```
Show Message ["Are you sure you want to quit FileMaker Pro?"]
If ["Status(CurrentMessageChoice) = 1"]
    Quit Application
End If
```

Recover   Files

What it does: Allows you to repair damaged files.

Options: [1] Perform without dialog
[2] Specify file...

When to use: Only in situations of technical support. This is not a common function and is rarely used.

Considerations: The improper shutdown of a FileMaker Pro file is the most common cause of file damage (e.g. your computer crashes). Frequent back-ups are the best defense against file corruption.

Application: This feature is for developers only. If a file becomes damaged, users can be taken through a manual recovery process. Recovery changes file names, so they need to be renamed in order to work with relationships and external scripts. There is no reason to make users of your solution feel insecure about their files by including a Recover button. If it is convenient for users to send in files for recovery, you could hide the Recover button where the user wouldn't see it unless you told them how to access it. You can have a recover button for each of the database files that are provided in the solution.

Script Examples (Recover)

1. Recover a file

Recover is not used often and may only be suitable as a technical support tool. If you provide a Recover button, hide it from your users. If they need it, you can instruct them on how to access the layout containing the button.

```
Recover [No dialog, "My solution file"]
```

Refresh Window Windows

What it does: This script step will cause the monitor or display hardware to refresh the computer screen.

Options: [1] Bring to front

The Bring to front option is used when sub-scripts are involved. This option makes the current database active.

When to use: When the user interface of your database solution needs to cause a window refresh.

Application: This script step is not commonly used since most scripts require the window to be frozen the entire length of the script. When a script completes, it will automatically refresh the window. If you pause a script, it automatically refreshes the screen as well. The value of this script is refreshing the window in the middle of a script.

1. Refreshing in the middle of a script

The Refresh Window script step is not used often because the window automatically refreshes itself when the script is done. However, it is possible that a script will need to be refreshed somewhere in the middle.

```
Comment ["This refresh window step makes sure the information in
         the global field is visible after it is updated."]
Go to Record/Request/Page [First]
Loop
    Comment ["Perform other scripts here."]
    Set Field ["Global", "Global + 1 & " Records have
    been processed.""]
    Refresh Window []
    Go to Record/Request/Page [Exit after last, Next]
End Loop
```

Relookup   Records

What it does: Triggers a lookup to relookup for all of the records in the current found set.

Options: [1] Perform without dialog
[2] Specify field...

When to use: When the data in lookup fields needs to be updated.

Important info ▶

Considerations: Lookups that use a calculation as the match or trigger field cannot have the relookup specified on the calculation field. You must select one of the fields the calculation is based upon in order to perform the relookup.

SYNCH.FP3

Technique File:
Synchronization

Application: There is an excellent implementation of this script step in a technique called Synchronization (SYNCH.FP3). This technique shows you how to synchronize two database files using relookups and imports. Before synchronizing, it is important to first make a backup.

Script Examples (Relookup)

1. Archive then relookup
The relookup script can be useful for replacing historical data with current data. However, you may want to archive the older data before performing the relookup.

```
Perform Script [Sub-scripts, "Archive Records"]
Comment ["Archive the records with the archive script then reset
         all data with new values."]
Replace [No dialog, "Date Field", "Status(CurrentDate)"]
Relookup [No dialog, "Match Field"]
```

Replace   Records

What it does: Replaces the values in a field, for the found set of records, with the field value from the current record. You can also replace the found set with serial numbers or a calculated result.

Options: [1] Perform without dialog
[2] Specify field...
[3] Specify replace settings
Use current value
Serial number values
Custom calculation value

When to use: When the values for an entire set of records need to be changed.

Considerations: Using the Replace script step can be catastrophic to an important database. Make sure to test the script out many times on duplicate copies of a database before putting it into general use. The field being replaced also needs to be present on the layout. If the field isn't present, the script will appear to work but no values will be replaced.

Key information: Replace is much faster than a looping script that cycles through each record and uses the Set Field step to place a value in a field.

Application: The Replace script step has many uses. One technique allows you to mark all the records in the current found set. This would allow you to retrieve that set of records in the future using a find.

SORTPRT2.FP3

Technique File:
Sorting Portals 2

Another basic technique is to reserialize your records. This can be useful if you want to renumber all of your records. A good example of how to use this in a real life solution is to look at the Sorting Portals 2 (SORTPRT2.FP3) technique.

Yet another technique allows you to place a calculated value on every record. One example would be to place the result of a GetSummary calculation into a number field so that it can be searched. GetSummary calculation fields do not store their results. Attempting to search the calculation field will return the message that no records match this request.

Script Examples (Replace)

1. Calculated replace
One of the most powerful uses of the Replace script step is a calculated replace. It is much faster than a looping script and easier to construct.

```
Replace [No dialog, "Customer Type", "
    Case(
    Units Ordered = 500, "Small Customer",
```

```
Units Ordered = 2500, "Large Customer",
Units Ordered = 500000, "Best Customer",
"Insufficient data"
)
"]
```

Revert Record/Request

What it does: Returns the record or request to the way it was before you made any changes.

Options: [1] Perform without dialog

When to use: When an undo feature for record modifications is desired.

Considerations: This script step only works if you haven't exited the record in any way, which includes typing the Enter key on the keypad or moving to another record or file. The difference between this feature and Undo is that this script step will undo everything that has been changed on a record instead of just the currently active field.

Application: This script is not widely used, but could be a helpful data entry aid for anyone who has accidentally modified a record and then realized the mistake before the modifications are accepted.

Script Examples (Revert Record/Request)

1. Revert Record
Not a frequently used script step, but could be useful for people who do a large amount of data entry.

```
Revert Record/Request [No dialog]
```

What it does: Saves a copy of the current file in compressed, clone or regular copy format.

Options: [1] Specify file...
Specify save type

When to use: When a feature for providing backup copies of a database is desirable.

Considerations: A compressed copy is a copy that is optimized for space and consistency, almost like defragmenting a hard drive. A clone is a copy of your file with no records in it.

Script Examples (Save a Copy as)

1. Backup this database

A good use of the Save a Copy in a script is to create a backup every time the database is closed. This script monitors a date field that tracks the last date the database was backed up so it only saves a copy once a day.

```
Comment ["This closing script will save a backup based on a
        specified interval."]
If ["Status(CurrentDate) - Backup Interval > Backup Date"]
    Show Message ["This database has not been backed up for a while.
    Would you like to save a backup copy now?"]
    If ["Status(CurrentMessageChoice) = 1"]
        Save a Copy as ["MyDatabase.FP3"]
        Set Field ["Backup Date", "Status(CurrentDate)"]
    End If
End If
```

What it does: Scrolls a window up or down.

Options: [1] Scroll to...
Home
End
Page Up
Page Down
To selection

The option called To Selection brings the currently selected field into view.

When to use: When layout specific navigation is desired.

Applications: If a screen size is smaller than the layout size, it's useful to use Page Up and Page Down to navigate around a layout.

Script Examples (Scroll Window)

1. Navigate large layouts
With larger layouts, it's convenient for users to have buttons for navigating the window.

```
Scroll Window [Page Up]
```

Select All   Editing

What it does: Selects all of the text, number, date or time data in the active field.

Options: [1] None

When to use: When the select option is not available for a particular script step being used.

Application: This script step is not very useful since most of the script steps that would require it, such as Copy, have an option for selecting all the data.

Script Examples (Select All)

1. Select All of next field
In some cases, the Select All script step may be helpful for highlighting the information in a field.

```
Go to Next Field
Select All
```

Select Dictionaries   Spelling

What it does: Allows you to choose a different dictionary.

Options: [1] None

When to use: When it is necessary to switch between dictionaries.

Application: Useful if a user needs to jump between two dictionaries when spell checking bilingual files.

Send Apple Event/Send Message   Miscellaneous

What it does: Sends an Apple Event to other programs that support Apple Events under the Macintosh operating system. Sends a message to another program under the Windows operating system.

Options: [1] Specify settings

An Apple Event requires two different codes, each four characters in length. When the Send AppleEvent script step is seen on another platform, it is shown as the Send Message script step.

(◎) OPEN.FP3
Technique File:
Opening a Path

Application: There is an example of using Send Apple Event and Send Message demonstrating how to use a path to open files. The technique is called Opening a Path (OPEN.FP3).

Script Examples (Send Apple Event/Send Message)

1. Open URL in Netscape Navigator
Using Apple Events in the Macintosh version of FileMaker Pro allows for inter-application communication. Apple Events is the standard set by Apple Computer and is what AppleScript uses to communicate between applications.

```
Comment ["Opens a URL from a FileMaker Pro database in Netscape
         Navigator."]
Send Apple Event ["Netscape Communicator™", "GURL", "GURL"]
```

2. Open Application in Windows
The Send Message script step allows a FileMaker Pro file to open any target application or document.

```
Send Message ["INSTAPP.EXE", "aevt", "odoc"]
```

Send DDE Execute   Miscellaneous

Windows only

What it does: Sends a DDE (Dynamic Data Exchange) command to another application. FileMaker Pro can send but not receive DDE commands.

Options: [1] Specify settings

Options include service name, topic, commands and specify field. This is a Windows only script step.

Application: Dynamic Data Exchange (DDE) is Microsoft's inter-application protocol to allow different Windows programs to send and receive information. An application can be a client, a server, or both. Client applications send information or issue commands to other applications. An application that receives information or commands is a DDE server.

FileMaker Pro 3.0 and 4.0 for Windows are DDE clients. They allow you to manipulate an open file using another application through ScriptMaker's DDE Execute script step. FileMaker Pro cannot receive DDE commands, nor does it support DDE data linking.

An example would be to use DDE to send a FileMaker Pro field value that contained a URL to a web browser, such as Netscape Navigator, and have it connect to that web site.

Script Examples (Send DDE Execute)

1. Open URL in Netscape Navigator
While not always a perfect solution, the DDE support in FileMaker Pro allows for limited communication between applications.

```
Send DDE Execute ["Netscape Communicator™"]
```

Send Mail   Miscellaneous

4.0 Mac Only

3.0/4.0 Win

What it does: Sends an email to the mail program your system is configured to use.

Options: [1] Specify settings

Options include the ability to specify the recipient, copy recipients and the subject and the message. All of these options also have the additional capability of specifying a field value for the email address. Other options include attaching a file and performing without a dialog.

When to use: When email services are desired in conjunction with a database file.

Considerations: This is a Windows only script step unless you have FileMaker Pro 4.0. If you have FileMaker Pro 4.0 for the Macintosh, you must have Internet Config 1.1 or higher installed to use this feature with Claris Emailer or Qualcomm Eudora Light or Pro. For Windows, you must have a [Mail] section in the WIN.INI file. Windows for Workgroups users must have the entry MAPI = I in the [Mail] section. Works with Microsoft Exchange or any other email program that is MAPI compliant. If you are using FileMaker Pro 3.0 on Windows, the only email program that is supported is Microsoft Mail.

(◎)) **MASSMAIL.FP3**
Technique File:
Mass Email

Application: An email could be sent any time a new record was entered into a technical reference database, so subscribers could be alerted of changes.

Script Examples (Send Mail)

1. Send email message
The send mail script step will send mail to the respective email application as specified in your system settings.

```
Send Mail [No dialog, "Message Subject"]
```

What it does: Suppresses normal FileMaker Pro error messages (called error "trapping") and stores the error number in memory temporarily.

Options: [1] Set capture [On/Off]

When to use: Whenever you want to capture a FileMaker Pro generated error and perform your own sequence of steps.

Application: Custom actions can be performed based on the error number. Presenting a custom message instead of the normal FileMaker Pro error message is a common implementation of this script step. Testing of the captured error must be done immediately after the error occurs since it is only stored in memory temporarily.

ERROR.FP3

Technique File:
Identifying Error
Messages

The most heavily used script step in conjunction with Set Error Capture is the If statement. The If statement tests for an error with the Status(CurrentError) function. If the error has occurred, the steps within the If statement will be performed.

ERROR.FP3

Reference File:
FileMaker Pro Errors

Novice users are often confused when the default error message for no records found is shown (error 401). Capturing this error allows you to present a more friendly error message. The technique showing how to capture a no found set is called Avoiding No Records Found (FOUND.FP3).

FOUND.FP3

Technique File:
Avoiding "No Records
Found"

1. Trap for no records found

The internal FileMaker error code for no records found is 401. This error can be captured and a custom dialog presented.

```
Set Error Capture [On]
Perform Find [Restore]
If ["Status(CurrentError) = 401"]
    Show Message ["No records were found."]
End If
```

Set Field   Fields

What it does: Replaces the specified field with the result of a calculation.

Options: [1] Specify field...
[2] Specify calculation

Fields don't need to be present on the current layout in order to be Set, as is the case with Cut, Copy and Paste.

When to use: When data in a field needs to be manipulated or moved.

Application: This is one of the most widely used script steps. Coming up with a few examples that demonstrate the capabilities won't do it justice. Almost every example in the techniques section of the CD uses Set Field. Here are a few ideas that showcase how to avoid Copy and Paste.

Set Field can be used to set values from global fields to fields in Find mode. If you place the values from regular fields into global fields just before entering Find mode, you can construct find requests. There is

FIND.FP3

Technique File:
Find Window

an example of this in the techniques area on the CD called Find Window (FIND.FP3).

Another cool application of Set Field is the ability to add to a field. For instance, you may want to append a value to the end of a specific field. A Set Field calculation can take the contents of a field and add anything to it. There are many examples of how to apply this append capability in real scenarios within the techniques section of the CD.

SCROLL.FP3

Technique File:
Scroll Through

Another ability of Set Field is to grab a portion of what is contained within a field. For instance, you could be trying to grab the second value in a return delimited list. Use Set Field with a calculation based on the Middle and Position functions. For an example of this, see the technique file titled, Scroll Through (SCROLL.FP3).

Advanced techniques: Set Field can be used to set a related field to a value. This means you don't need to activate a file to change a value in it.

If you don't specify a field, the Set Field script step will return the calculation result to the currently selected field.

Script Examples (Set Field)

1. Set Field to a related field

One of the advantages of Set Field, over copy and paste, is that it can be used across files using a relationship. The following script is a simple example of pushing data to another file.

```
Set Field ["Related File::Related Field", "Text Field"]
```

2. Self referencing append

The Set Field script step can set a field to itself. This allows you to append values to the end of a field. This is probably one of the more common Set Field techniques.

```
Comment ["Appending a value with Set Field."]
Set Field ["Field 1", "Field 1 & Field 2"]
```

3. Global setting while in Find mode

A lesser known fact is that Set Field can access a field no matter what the mode. Even while in Find mode, a global field can be manipulated to produce find requests. The following script finds all the records with the same last name as the current record

```
Comment ["Moving data to find mode."]
Set Field ["Global", "Last Name"]
Enter Find []
Set Field ["Last Name", "Global"]
Perform Find []
```

Set Multi-User   Files

What it does: Allows you to toggle between single-user and multi-user network access.

Options: [1] Set Multi-User [On/Off]

When to use: When you need to switch a database from single-user to multi-user.

Application: This script step is seldom used because most files are either used as multi-user or single user. It could be used to change a solution when a site license is purchased.

Set Use System Formats   Files

What it does: This script step allows you to set the file to the system formats of the current system. This does not change the original formats stored in the file.

Options: [1] Set Use System Formats [On/Off]

When to use: When creating a solution for world-wide distribution.

Considerations: FileMaker Pro saves the default date, time and number settings when a database is created.

Application: Use this script step in a startup script to update the system settings for the current operating system.

Script Examples (Set Use System Formats)

1. Default to proper formats
If the database is going to be used internationally, it is a good idea to include Set Use System Formats as one of the script steps in a startup script.

```
Set Use System Formats [On]
```

Set Zoom Level   Windows

What it does: Enlarges or reduces the zoom level.

Options: [1] Specify Percentage
[2] Lock (check box)

The zoom level is controlled manually by the mountains icons in the lower left hand corner. The zoom in and zoom out options change the zoom by one level using the following order: 25, 50, 75, 100, 150, 200, 300 and 400 percent. One last option is the ability to lock the manual toggle for zooming.

When to use: When a user interface is better viewed at larger or smaller percentage.

Considerations: Stick with even zoom levels like 200, 300 and 400 percent. A zoom of 150 percent does not accurately represent text and graphics.

Application: Any time a form with small type needs to be read. Zooming out can help when getting a bird's eye view of a previewed page.

Show Message | Miscellaneous

What it does: Displays a message box using predefined message content.

Options: [1] Specify Message

You can also specify the text of up to three buttons.

When to use: Whenever it is necessary to present the user with some type of message.

Application: There are many examples where the Show Message script can be used. For instance, most of the files on the CD ROM include an About script under the Script menu. It provides the contact information for ISO Productions, Inc.

SHOWMESS.FP3

Technique File:
Show Message
Buttons

A more advanced usage of this feature would be to offer a message with two choices when a find does not locate any records. The user would be able to show all the records or redefine the find parameters. There is a technique called Show Message Buttons (SHOWMESS.FP3) that covers this concept.

Considerations: In Windows, there is a close box in the upper right corner of the message dialog. Clicking there will dismiss the dialog, which will allow users to bypass a message. This can be avoided if you know that Status(CurrentMessageChoice) will return a 1 if the close box is clicked.

Script Examples (Show Message)

1. Testing Show Message

To get the hang of using Show Message, you must become familiar with the function Status(CurrentMessageChoice). When used together, you can capture the results of a button choice from a Show Message dialog.

```
Show Message ["Click a button to see a result."]
If ["Status(CurrentMessageChoice) = 1"]
    Show Message ["You clicked button # 1"]
Else
    Show Message ["You clicked button # 2"]
End If
```

Sort   Sort/Find/Print

What it does: Allows you to sort a database.

Options: [1] Restore sort order
              [2] Perform without dialog

The Restore option allows you to have the script remember specific sort orders.

When to use: When the data in the found set needs to be sorted in a particular order.

(o) SORTSTAY.FP3

Technique File:
Sorting and Staying

Considerations: When sorting, the currently selected record is lost and the first record in the sorted order becomes active. There is a technique on the CD, called Sorting and Staying (SORTSTAY.FP3),

that shows you a simple script to return you to the
record that was selected before sorting.

Script Examples (Sort)

1. Find and sort records
The sort script step is one of the most straight forward of all the steps available. By incorporating it with a user defined
find, it creates a found set that is sorted.

```
Enter Find Mode [Pause]
Perform Find []
Sort [Restore, No dialog]
```

Speak	(Macintosh only) Miscellaneous

Macintosh only

What it does: A Macintosh only feature that takes
advantage of PlainTalk™ text-to-speech.

Options: [1] Specify settings

You can specify the field to speak, the text to speak,
wait for speech completion before continuing and use
voice. The Speak script step brings up a dialog asking
you to type in the text you want spoken. The "use
voice pop-up menu" allows you to specify which voice
to use.

When to use: For enhancing the user interface by
speaking text.

Application: This can be a very valuable feature for
anyone who wants to have text read to them. You can
even have FileMaker Pro read the name of a button
when it is clicked.

Script Examples (Speak)

1. Speak email field
One of the many solutions that fit the text-to-speech feature of the Macintosh, is the ability to speak a field that stores incoming email.

```
Speak ["Email Content Field"]
```

Spelling Options   Spelling

What it does: Shows the Spelling Options dialog, which allows you to turn spell as you type on and off. It also allows the user to define the placement of the spelling dialog.

When to use: Whenever the spelling options need to be changed.

Application: This script step could be used on a database that has a high dependency on spell checking documents.

Toggle Status Area   Windows

What it does: Toggles the Status Area from visible to hidden. The status area is the gray column at the left side of the FileMaker Pro window that contains the book, layout menu and other information. An additional option allows you to lock this area, so users cannot show it by clicking on the toggle button in the lower left hand corner.

Options: [1] Show/Hide/Toggle
                    Lock

When to use: When it's unnecessary for users to see the Status Area.

STATAREA.FP3

Technique File:
Recreating the Status Area

Application: This script is almost exclusively used in startup scripts. Once you lock the Status Area with a script, it remains locked even after the script is completed. The only way to unlock it is to run another script or close and open the file without running the startup script. This script step is used in a technique called Never Abort (ABORT.FP3).

ABORT.FP3

Technique File:
Never Abort

The Toggle option is not used very often since most of the time you know what state you want the Status Area to be in.

Script Examples (Toggle Status Area)

1. Lock Status Area on Startup

When a database is designed to have a commercial look, the Status Area is often hidden. To prevent access to the Status Area, lock it on startup.

```
Comment ["Startup script"]
Enter Browse Mode []
Toggle Status Area [Hide, Lock]
Go to Layout ["Splash Screen"]
Pause/Resume Script ["0:00:03"]
Go to Layout ["Data Entry"]
```

Toggle Text Ruler   Windows

What it does: Hides or shows the text ruler.

Options: [1] Show/Hide/Toggle
              Refresh window

When to use: When text editing requires the ruler.

Considerations: When the text ruler is showing, the Toggle Zoom Window script step does not zoom to a larger window to accommodate.

Application: This script step is not widely used. It could be useful when entering content for a form letter.

Script Examples (Toggle Text Ruler)

1. Adjust for text ruler in layout
One of the disadvantages of showing the text ruler is that it occupies space in the current layout. Zooming the window does not adjust for the ruler. To fix this, a separate layout must be created and zoomed.

```
Toggle Text Ruler [Show]
Comment ["Zoom to a layout that accounts for the text ruler."]
Go to Layout ["Ruler Zoom Layout"]
Toggle Window [Zoom]
Go to Layout [original layout]
```

Toggle Window   Windows

What it does: Manipulates the window with Hide, Maximize, Zoom and Unzoom options.

Options: [1] Zoom/Unzoom/Maximize/Hide (Mac)
Zoom/Restore/Maximize/Minimize (Win)

When to use: When window control needs to be used on database windows.

Application: This script is widely used because of its ability to resize the window to the size of the layout. The layout is defined by the last part and the farthest object to the right. The Zoom feature is used when moving from one layout to another to make the window resize to the dimensions of that layout.

CLOSE.FP3

Technique File:
Resize Window on
Close

Other options aren't used as frequently, but can be useful. For instance, there is a technique called Resize Window on Close (CLOSE.FP3) on the CD that shows how to make sure the window is always in the upper left hand corner at startup. This technique uses the Maximize option of the Toggle Window script step.

Script Examples (Toggle Window)

1. Show splash screen

A common use of the Toggle Window script step using its Zoom option is to commercialize a FileMaker Pro solution with a splash screen. A splash screen often has a different window size than the data entry layout, so the Window is zoomed before and after the splash screen displays

```
Comment ["Typical startup script."]
Go to Layout ["Splash Screen"]
Toggle Window [Zoom]
Pause/Resume Script ["0:00:03"]
Go to Layout ["Data Entry"]
Toggle Window [Zoom]
```

Undo   Editing

What it does: Undoes the last action performed, if possible.

Options: [1] None

When to use: When the last action performed needs to be undone.

Considerations: As soon as you exit a record, the Undo item under the Edit menu becomes Can't Undo. This limits the usefulness of the feature.

Application: The best example of this rarely used script step is to offer users a button that corrects typing errors. However, most users are familiar with this feature as a menu item, so a button is redundant.

Unsort Sort/Find/Print

What it does: Unsort places your records in creation order. Creation order is the sequence in which the records were originally created. It is tracked by an internal date mechanism which cannot be changed.

Options: [1] None

When to use: When it is desired to have the found set of records in their creation order.

SORTPORT.FP3
Technique File:
Sorting Portals

Key information: When you create a new record in a sorted found set, the new record created (or duplicated) will be placed right after the currently selected record. If the records are unsorted, the new or duplicated record will be created at the end of the found set. Therefore, Unsort is a common step used in record looping scripts.

SORTPRT2.FP3
Technique File:
Sorting Portals 2

Application: This script step is useful when you are sorting portals. There is an example of how to sort portals on the CD called Sorting Portals (SORTPORT.FP3) and Sorting Portals 2 (SORTPRT2.FP3).

Windows only

What it does: Updates the OLE link for a container field. If you don't specify a field, the currently selected field will be updated.

Options: [1] Specify field

When to use: When it's needed to link an image or data stored in a container field to another application via an OLE link.

Application: Pictures of your products, created in Photoshop or other graphics program, can be linked to a FileMaker Pro invoicing system. Any modifications to the original art can be updated using the Update Link script step.

View As | Windows

What it does: Allows you to toggle a layout between viewing as list or form.

Options: [1] View as List (pop-up)
[2] View as Form (pop-up)
[3] Toggle (pop-up)

When to use: When a layout should be switched from one view to another.

START.FP3

Root Directory of CD

Application: There is a technique for using the View As List and View as Form options to make a single layout serve the dual purpose of both list view and form view. This script step is used in the START.FP3 file when viewing Other Products and Services.

Script Examples (View As)

1. Dual purpose layout

It's possible to make one layout serve as both the list view and form view. The trick is to use a body part to hold list related information and a sub-summary part. When the view is list, the sub-summary part is hidden, but appears in form view. A global field added to the sub-summary part completes the technique. A script attempts to paste into the field, but can only do so when the view is form view. You can check for this value and determine which mode to toggle to.

```
Comment ["READ ME: The freeze window prevents the user from seeing
         the paste that occurs."]
Freeze Window
Comment ["READ ME: The paste literal attempts to paste to the
         global field. If the view is list, nothing will be pasted
         because only the body will accept modifications. If the
         view is form, the value will be pasted."]
Paste Literal [Select, "Global", "1"]
Comment ["READ ME: You must make sure that the global field is on
         the part of the layout that is visible in form view.
         Otherwise this script won't work."]
If ["Global = 1"]
    View As [View as List]
    Set Field ["Global", "0"]
Else
    View As [View as Form]
    Set Field ["Global", "1"]
End If
```

Chapter 5

Intermediate/Advanced

ScriptMaker Fundamentals

7.0 ScriptMaker & Multi-file scripting

Understanding how ScriptMaker interacts with multiple FileMaker Pro files is an integral part of creating powerful systems. Without the ability to communicate between files using scripts, the power of automation would be limited to a single file.

Try comparing a complex database system to a company. Think of each department within the company as a different file in the database system. As each department has a specialty, so does each file in the system. For instance, accounting handles the monetary operations while human resources focuses on employee issues. The same is true for your database system. A typical invoicing system has a file for invoices and one for customers.

By treating each FileMaker Pro file like a department that only deals with certain tasks, you create an environment for specialization. This increases efficiency and productivity. In the case of the invoicing solution, the file that handles the actual invoices only knows how to create, reconcile and print invoices. The invoices file does not know about the information contained within the contacts file, just as the employees in accounting know nothing about human resources (or at least not enough to run the department). The way these departments work together to accomplish a common goal, like payroll, is through communication. Your database solutions should communicate equally as well. When the job gets too complex for a single file, you can benefit by sharing information using multi-file scripting.

7.1 Database files that "talk" to each other

Open this file and follow along

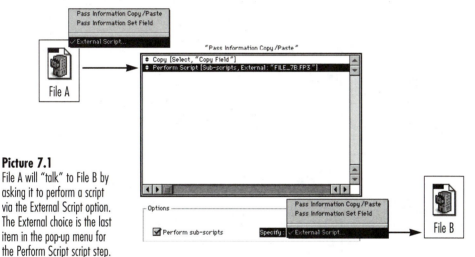

07_A.FP3

Chapter File:
Moving Data
Between Files

Files communicate with each other using the Perform Script script step. The External option in the Perform Script step is what makes the scripts in other files available (see Picture 7.1). If you understand how sub-scripts work, External scripts are essentially the same (see Chapter 3 for a discussion of sub-scripts). The only difference, is the sub-script is located in another file.

Picture 7.1
File A will "talk" to File B by asking it to perform a script via the External Script option. The External choice is the last item in the pop-up menu for the Perform Script script step.

There are many reasons to run a script from another FileMaker Pro file. The reasons are as diverse as the solutions that can be created with FileMaker Pro. Researching the CD ROM Technique Files for examples of how to use the Perform Script step will aid the learning process.

Ending up in the right file

When using the External Script option of Perform Script, it is important to be aware of the location where ScriptMaker completes the processing of a

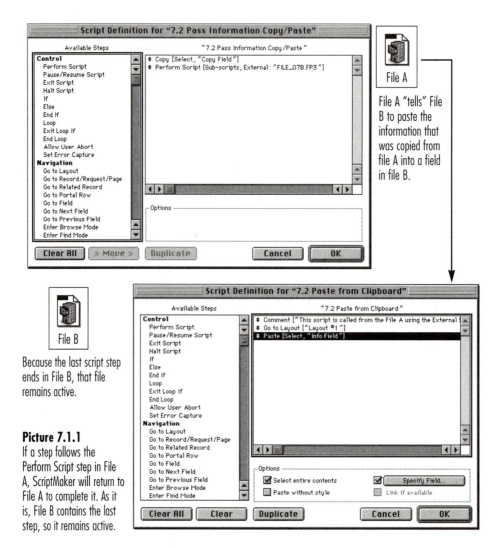

File A

File A "tells" File B to paste the information that was copied from file A into a field in file B.

File B

Because the last script step ends in File B, that file remains active.

Picture 7.1.1
If a step follows the Perform Script step in File A, ScriptMaker will return to File A to complete it. As it is, File B contains the last step, so it remains active.

script. If calling an External script is the last step, the
file containing that sub-script will remain active. If
you want the calling file to remain active at the end of
a script process, at least one additional step is
required – even if that script step has no real function.

07_A.FP3

Chapter File:
Moving Data
Between Files

Take the example of File A and File B. File A tells
File B to paste a piece of information (see Picture
7.1.1). As it's written, File B will be active at the end
of the process. What's required for us to end up back

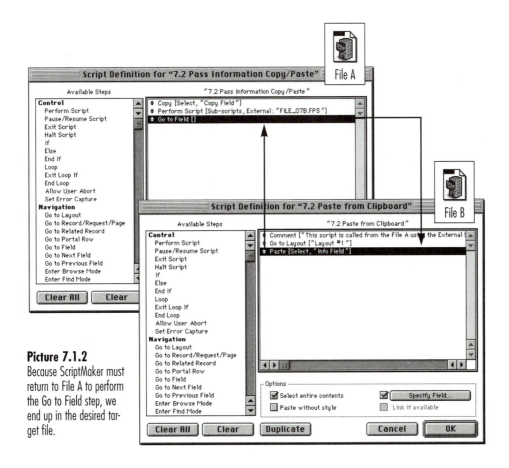

Picture 7.1.2
Because ScriptMaker must
return to File A to perform
the Go to Field step, we
end up in the desired target file.

in File A, is the addition of at least one more step to the script in File A. By doing this, ScriptMaker will return to File A to perform the last steps of the script. The additional step that you add can be as simple as a Go to Field that has no specified field (see Picture 7.1.2). The objective is to cause ScriptMaker to end its script in the proper file. Another way to control the active file is to add a Halt step at the end of the script in File A, or use the Open Script step in File B to make the desired target file come to the front. There are many ways to end up in the right file. Depending on your needs, use one of these techniques or experiment with your own.

7.2 Passing information with Set Field

Open this file and follow along

◎ **07_A.FP3**

Chapter File:
Moving Data
Between Files

Passing information from one file to another via a script should almost always happen through a relationship. Using a relationship and Set Field is much more efficient than Copy and Paste. Consider these points:

• Set Field does not erase the contents of the clipboard.
• Neither the originating nor the target field need be present on the current layout.
• The target file does not need to be activated.

Leaving the contents of the clipboard undisturbed prevents losing information placed there by the user. Using Set Field allows you to omit fields from a layout, thus conveniently hiding the data being manipulated. Copy and paste are inefficient because they require the fields to be present on the current layout.

With previous versions of FileMaker Pro, the only option for passing data from one file to another was using copy and paste. Version 3.0 introduced relationships and Set Field, making the copy and paste method obsolete. However, there are a few instances when you would want to Copy and Paste information. Moving data from Browse to Find mode is a good example.

Picture 7.2
The most basic of all relationships is based on an auto-enter serial number.

Setting up a relationship from one file to another creates a **data path** that allows files to communicate. The Chapter file on the CD ROM (07_A.FP3) covers how a basic relationship based on a serial number allows data to be moved from one file to another. Moving data can be even more powerful when using a relationship with Set Field and a constant. The next section will cover how to design this type of relationship.

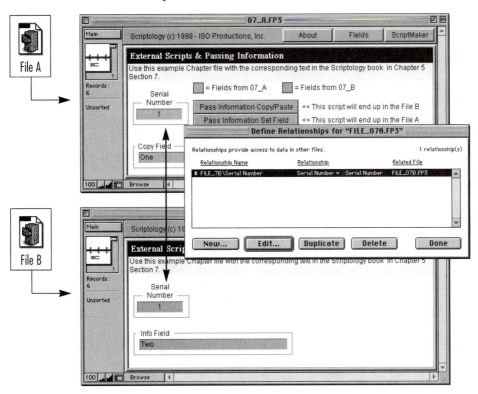

Passing Information Sample: Copy Paste ("OK" Method)

ScriptMaker script: 07_A.FP3 "7.2 Pass Information Copy/Paste"

This script copies the information from "Copy Field" in file 07_A.FP3 and then tells file 07_B.FP3 to paste the information into "Info Field".

```
Copy [Select, "Copy Field"] (This will replace what the user has in their clipboard)
Perform Script [Sub-scripts, External: "07_B.FP3"]
```

ScriptMaker script: 07_B.FP3 "7.2 Paste from Clipboard"

This script will paste the text copied to the field into the field "Info Field".

```
Go to Layout ["Layout #1"]
Comment ["Whenever using Copy or Paste you MUST be on a layout that
         has the referenced field"]
Paste [Select, "Info Field"]
```

Passing Information Sample: Set Field ("BEST" Method)

Relationship: 07_A.FP3 "FILE_07B\Serial Number"

This relationship associates File A to File B using the Serial Number field.

Relationship Name	Relationship	Related File
FILE_7B\Serial Number	Serial Number = ::Serial Number	07_B.FP3

ScriptMaker script: 07_A.FP3 "7.2 Pass Information Set Field"

The script in file 07_A.FP3 uses the Set Field step to "push" the information over to the field specified in file 07_B.FP3.

```
Set Field ["FILE_7B\Serial Number::Info Field", "Case(
Serial Number = 1, "One",
Serial Number = 2, "Two",
Serial Number = 3, "Three",
Serial Number = 4, "Four",
Serial Number = 5, "Five",
Serial Number = 6, "Six",
"I can't count that high"
)"]
```

7.3 The constant game

A constant is anything that is unchanging. In this example a calculation field, containing a value of one (1), serves as the constant (see Picture 7.3). The purpose of using a constant for a relationship is to create a **data channel.** A data channel is a relationship that's always open and links all records in one file to all records in another file. There are two types of constant relationships – one based on stored values and the other unstored.

Before discussing the differences between the two, you'll want to know the reason you would want all records in one file to relate to all records in another file. The answer is, to pass global data between the two files. No matter what record is being browsed, with a constant relationship you can push global data from one file over to the related file using a script. Because global field values are the same on every

Picture 7.3
Creating a calculation which results in "1" will always result in one for all records in a database.

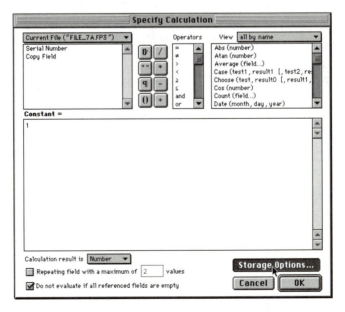

PREF.FP3

Technique File:
Preferences

MEMORY.FP3

Technique File:
Remember Record

record, these are the only values you will want to change using a constant relationship. This method of transferring data between global fields can be used in the example of a preferences file which stores user specific settings (see Chapter 17 for more information on preferences files). For instance, you might want to allow the user to choose whether the results of a find are shown in list view or form view. Another use of global field manipulation is remembering the last record used (found in MEMORY.FP3).

Stored constant relationships

Open this file and follow along

07_C.FP3

Chapter File:
Constant
Self-relationship

A stored constant relationship means the calculation field set to one (1), is indexed (see Chapter 8 Section 14.4 for more about the index). Relationships typically rely on the match field in the related file to be indexed (stored). When you match a constant field in one file to a constant field in another file you create a data channel (see Picture 7.3.1). With the constant relationship in place you can use a Set Field script step to set any data in any global field in the related file. This avoids any methods of transferring global

Picture 7.3.1
A relationship based on a constant creates an open data channel.

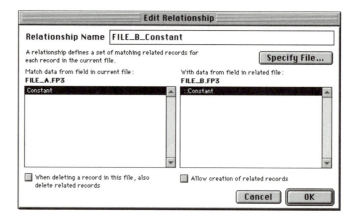

data between files using copy and paste. Because a constant is always the same, you know the relationship will work at any time without having to worry about a specific match. File 07_C.FP3 showcases a same-file relationship that is based on a stored constant. This allows any record to see all other records in the database.

Unstored constant relationships

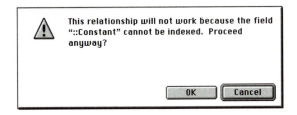

GLOB_REL.FP3

Technique File:
Global Relationships

While a relationship expects that the match field in a related file is indexed, it is not always necessary. If the storage settings of a constant calculation are set to unstored, the calculation field will not contribute to the size of the file by adding to the index. What isn't known by many FileMaker Pro users is that an unstored constant relationship, or even a relationship between two globals, will still function for transferring global data between files. When two unstored constants are used as match fields you will be presented with a dialog box that says the relationship will not work (see Picture 7.3.2). With the knowledge that global data can still be transferred between global fields this dialog can be ignored and the OK button clicked.

Picture 7.3.2
The bad relationship dialog box can be ignored if global values are being passed using a constant relationship.

> ⚠ This relationship will not work because the field
> "::Constant" cannot be indexed. Proceed
> anyway?
>
> [OK] [Cancel]

8.0 Looping Operations

To help understand the concept of looping, think of the process of opening your mail. You open the first letter and decide what to do based on the contents. After you finish, you open the next letter, and the next, until there are no more. This is a repetitive process, as is a loop within a script. The Loop and End Loop steps surround the steps you want to repeat.

Understanding a common loop

The definition of a loop

A loop is a sequence of steps that cycle forever. A loop would continue endlessly without some sort of control or condition to tell it when to exit the loop.

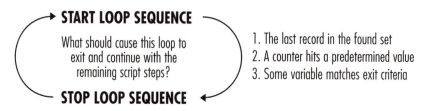

START LOOP SEQUENCE

What should cause this loop to exit and continue with the remaining script steps?

STOP LOOP SEQUENCE

1. The last record in the found set
2. A counter hits a predetermined value
3. Some variable matches exit criteria

The iterations of a loop are controlled by conditional steps such as:

- Go to Record/Request/Page [Exit after last, Next]
- Exit Loop If
- Halt (when used in combination with the If step)
- Exit (when used in combination with the If step)

All of the above steps allow you to exit a loop, but are used under different conditions. Knowing what works best for the given situation is a matter of practice. The easiest exit method is the Go to Record/Request/Page [Exit after last, Next] script step, because it stops the loop once it hits the last record. The last three loop exit options require more planning.

8.1 The almighty counter

COUNTER.FP3

Technique File:
Better Counter

Controlling a loop is as simple as stopping the mail process after you open the last letter. If you start with six letters and open them until zero letters remain, you have just simulated a **descending counter**. The counter is the **control value** necessary in many looping situations. A counter is most often a global number field, because it takes up less space in the file and the same value can be accessed from every record. Because counting is a linear process, it doesn't matter whether you count up (**ascending counter**) or down (**descending counter**) since the number of repetitions will be the same.

If you're counting down from 100 to zero, you'll initialize your global to 100 and decrement the global by some value, usually by one, each time you complete one cycle of the loop. The typical method of exiting a loop is to use the Exit Loop If step and set the condition based on whether you are counting up or down – zero if descending and 100 if ascending.

The diagram on the following page depicts the process of using a counter to know when to stop processing mail.

Descending counter

The primary question to ask when using a counter is "When do I exit the loop? On what value?"

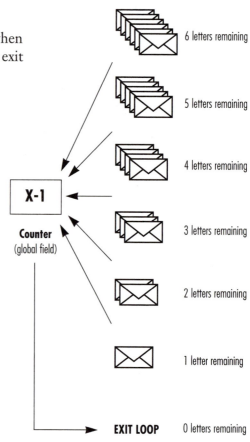

6 letters remaining

5 letters remaining

4 letters remaining

X-1

Counter
(global field)

3 letters remaining

2 letters remaining

Exit condition

After each letter is opened and read, a cycle has been completed and the counter is reduced by one (1). Leave the loop when the unopened letter count equals zero.

1 letter remaining

EXIT LOOP   0 letters remaining

8.2 Record Looping

Looping through records is the most basic use of the looping function (see Picture 8.2). It is the easiest to implement and also the most common. Start by finding a set of data you want to work with. Whether you choose a **subset** of records or the whole database

Open this file and follow along

08_A.FP3

Chapter File:
Basic Record Loop

depends on your needs. Go to the first record in this set of data and start the loop. Perform the steps within the loop and then go to the next record. What makes record looping so easy is the check box included as part of the Go to Record/Request/Page script step. Checking the Exit after last option, causes the loop to exit once the last record is processed.

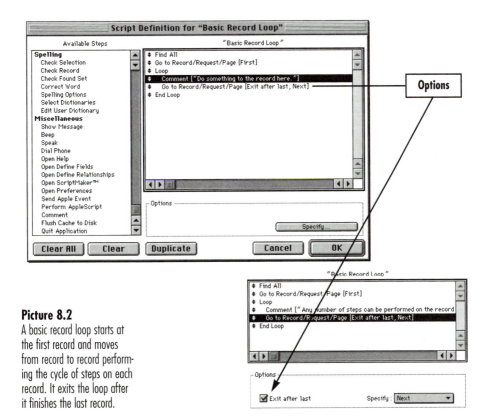

Picture 8.2
A basic record loop starts at the first record and moves from record to record performing the cycle of steps on each record. It exits the loop after it finishes the last record.

MARK.FP3

Technique File:
Marking Records by
Category

Understanding a record loop

A record loop is the simplest of all loops because there's a built in condition where ScriptMaker will exit the loop when it hits the last record in the found set.

```
Find All
Go to Record/Request/Page [First]
Loop
   Comment ["Any number of steps can be performed on the record here."]
   Go to Record/Request/Page [Exit after last, Next]
End Loop
```

8.3 Data Looping

Open this file and follow along

08_B.FP3

Chapter File:
Data Looping

LISTSORT.FP3

Technique File:
Sorting Lists

Where record looping moves through the records in a found set, data looping is based on the data within a single record. Data loops are most commonly used with lists. When storing data in a field, you can delimit the values. The best delimiter is the return character as it clearly separates each value. A typical data loop will cycle through an entire list, comparing the number of returns to the counter, exiting when they are equal. Instead of exiting the list at a predefined counter limit, the data loop can also test each item against a condition. Once the criteria is met, the number of returns counted to that point will be returned, representing the position in the list.

The object of the Chapter file provided on the CD ROM (08_B.FP3) is to take a return separated list, stored in a global field, and create a new record with each item. A calculation uses the Middle, Position and PatternCount functions to parse the text based on the

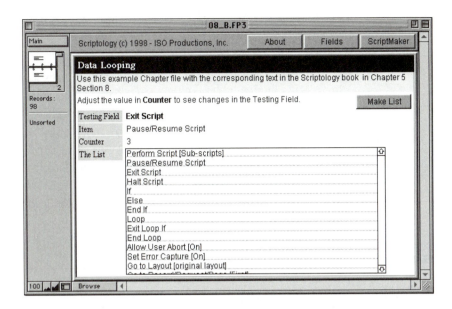

Picture 8.3
In the 08_B.FP3 Chapter file, the list of script steps is delimited by a return character.

Open this file and follow along

08_C.FP3
Chapter File:
Steps for Data Looping

Counter field. PatternCount determines how many times the loop should repeat by counting the number of returns.

The Position function accepts 4 parameters; text, search string, start and occurrence. The Counter field provides the value for the occurrence parameter, which allows the Position function to locate the start of the next line item. The Middle function uses embedded functions to parse out the line item between the two return values.

In Picture 8.3, "Exit Script" is the third item of The List field. If you change the value in the Counter field, the corresponding list item will be returned in the Testing Field. The Testing Field is a calculation that simulates what the script does but without creating new records. Examine this calculation in file 08_C.FP3 to understand how the calculation portion of the script works. Skip to Chapter 7, Calculation

Fundamentals, for a more detailed discussion of this complex calculation.

The example of parsing out list values uses a conditional Exit Loop If statement in order to stop the loop from running. The condition for exiting the loop is based on a counter value matching the PatternCount value of the number of returns. If you're unaccustomed to complex calculations the following example may seem very daunting. Make sure to open 08_C.FP3 and examine the calculations used.

Exiting a data loop based on a condition

ScriptMaker script: Conditional Exit

```
Comment ["READ ME... This script is designed to move the data from the
          global field The List into the field named Item."]
Go to Record/Request/Page [First]
Set Field ["Counter", "1"]
Set Field ["Item", "Case(Length(The List) <> Position(The List, "¶", 1,
    PatternCount(The List, "¶")) and Counter = PatternCount(The List,
    "¶") + 1, Right(The List, Length(The List) - Position(The List,
    "¶", 1, PatternCount(The List, "¶"))), Middle(The List,
    Position(The List, "¶", 1, Counter - 1) + 1, Position(The List,
    "¶", 1, Counter)  Position(The List, "¶", 1, Counter - 1) - 1))"]
Loop
  Go to Record/Request/Page [Next]
  Set Field ["Counter", "Counter + 1"]
  Set Field ["Item", "Case(Length(The List) <> Position(The List, "¶",
      1, PatternCount(The List, "¶")) and Counter = PatternCount(The
      List, "¶") + 1, Right(The List, Length(The List) - Position(The
      List, "¶", 1, PatternCount(The List, "¶"))), Middle(The List,
      Position(The List, "¶", 1, Counter - 1) + 1, Position(The List,
      "¶", 1, Counter) - Position(The List, "¶", 1, Counter - 1) -
      1))"]
▶ Exit Loop If ["Counter = Case(Length(The List) <> Position(The List,
      "¶", 1, PatternCount(The List, "¶")), PatternCount(The List, "¶")
      + 1, PatternCount(The List, "¶"))"]
End Loop
```

8.4 Portal Looping

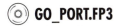

GO_PORT.FP3

Technique File:
Go to Portal

Looping through a portal is as easy as looping through records. With a record loop, the Go to Record/Request/Page [Next] step is used. To loop through rows in a portal, use the Go to Portal Row [Next] step. When looping in portals, it's important to note two things; the number of portals on the layout and their layer position. Working with multiple portals requires knowing how to direct your script to the correct portal. Use the Go To Field script step in your script to choose the related field within the target portal. Otherwise, the portal placed on the layout first will be selected. You can change the position of the portal within the layout layer scheme by using the menu items in the Arrange menu (i.e. Bring to Front, Bring Forward, Send to Back, and Send Backward). Once the correct portal is selected you can cycle through the rows with a loop.

Picture 8.4
Because of how objects are layered in the layout it is best to use a Go to Field script step to target the proper portal when more than one is used.

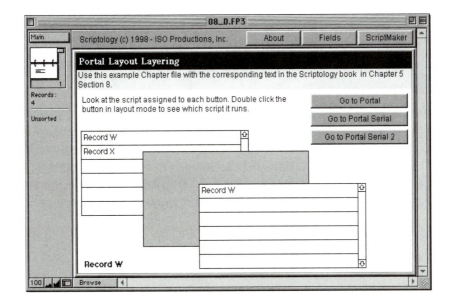

If you have only one portal on a layout you won't need the Go To Field step. It's good practice, however, to include the Go to Field script step in case a second portal is added later.

When working with a portal loop there are a few important issues to remember. The first is if/when your script exits the portal to perform some other operation, such as a copy and paste, the script will lose the position and row number of the portal it was looping through. To remedy this you can include a Set Field script step that will set the Status(CurrentPortalRow) to a global field. It's then possible to return to the portal row that you left off at by using a Go to Portal Row by field value.

The second item you need to remember is whether or not the relationship for the portal has the option of Allow record creation checked. If the relationship is set to allow record creation then the method used for exiting the portal loop needs to be adjusted. The standard check box option, Exit after last, for a Go to Portal Row [Next] script step will not work if you're using a Set Field or another script step that adds data to the portal. The reason for this is that FileMaker will make a new record in the related file if the Allow record creation is turned on. What ends up happening is an infinite number of newly created related records. The simple solution to this problem involves using an Exit Loop If based on a counter value. A Count(Related::Field) function is used to get the total number of related records in the portal.

Looping from portal row to portal row: record creation disallowed

The basics of a portal loop, when record creation is disallowed, are very similar to a record loop. The Go To Field step targets the correct portal if there is more than one on the layout.

☐ Allow creation of related records

```
Go to Field [Select/perform, "Relationship::Text Field"]
Set Field ["Relationship::Text Field", ""New Data""]
Loop
     Go to Portal Row [Select, Exit after last, Next]
         Set Field ["Relationship::Text Field", ""New Data""]
End Loop
```

Looping from portal row to portal row: record creation allowed

The difference when a relationship is set to allow record creation, is the exit mechanism. If you are modifying the data in the portal, new records will be created indefinitely. A new control for the loop is required.

☑ Allow creation of related records

```
Set Field ["Counter", "Count(Relationship::Text Field)"]
Go to Field [Select/perform, "Relationship::Text Field"]
Set Field ["Relationship::Text Field", ""New Data""]
Loop
     Set Field ["Counter", "Counter - 1"]
     Exit Loop If ["Counter = 0"]
     Go to Portal Row [Select, Next]
     Set Field ["Relationship::Text Field", ""New Data""]
End Loop
```

8.5 Loop Troubleshooting

The easiest way to prevent trouble when using loops is to make sure the loop cycles through the whole set of data and performs a complete cycle on each record

Bookmark this page
You should use this list when
having problems with loops.

or field it is processing. Here is a checklist you can use to determine if something is going wrong with your loops.

Loop Troubleshooting

Things to check
- ❑ Is the criteria for exiting being met?
- ❑ Did you initialize the counter (if used)?
- ❑ Did you preset the first record's data if necessary?
- ❑ Are you performing the loop's cycle on the last record or field?
- ❑ When does the Exit Loop happen? Before or after all data has been processed?
- ❑ Does the Go To Next Record step have the Exit after last check box checked – if needed?

A real world example of loop troubleshooting occurs when looping through records and deleting or omitting records that meet certain criteria. When a record is deleted or omitted, FileMaker Pro moves to the next record rather than the previous. This eliminates the need for the script to navigate to the next record. If you don't stop the script from going to the next record, some records will be skipped.

A common looping sequence

Loop steps
1.) Initialize your counter – if used.
2.) Preset any data on the first record – depends on how the loop is exited.
3.) Start the loop cycle – the individual steps of the loop.
4.) If a record loop, check the exit on last record option.
5.) If a data loop, watch for a correct evaluation of an Exit Loop script step.
6.) Decrement your counter – if used.
7.) Repeat loop until End.

The technique file SORTPORT.FP3 on the CD ROM shows how to loop while considering that Omit leaves off at the next record instead of the previous.

9.0 Conditionals

Imagine a restaurant with only one entree, a golf game with a single club or television with only the news; decisions would be unnecessary. Life, like manipulating a database, however, is about making choices. Scripting a database without being able to make choices would require a different script for every single action. Conditional decisions within scripts give you those choices in FileMaker Pro.

When a computer makes a logical decision, it is based on a binary digit – a 1 or 0. These two numbers can be represented by any pair of opposites; on or off, black or white, true or false, etc. If we understand this, logical decisions become much easier. To return a boolean value, a calculation or script step that uses the calculation dialog box can test a situation and return a boolean value. The example of sorting through your mail will clarify how logical decisions operate.

IF the letter looks like junk mail THEN throw it into the trash otherwise, (ELSE) put it into the keep pile. Written in FileMaker Pro, the statement looks like this.

If (mail = "junk mail", trash, keep pile)

As each observation is made, a decision follows. Only one of two outcomes is possible. Since there are only two choices, a computer can calculate the outcome of many conditions very quickly. The outcome of a conditional statement can be another conditional statement. This technique is called **conditional branching**.

The following sections not only cover the If script step, but calculation functions as well. Combining script steps with calculation functions makes a static script into a dynamic script. Once you know how to coordinate these tools, you will be able to ask your database any question.

9.1 Single If statements

If statements are used as either a step in ScriptMaker scripts or a function in a calculation. An If statement, will return one of two possible results. The result, when used in a script, allows you to run a choice of script steps while the result of a calculation returns one of two values. Even though there are structural differences between scripts and calculations, the processing of an If statement is the same for both.

Example logical statements

Where, Field A = Your First Name
Where, Field B = Your Last Name

ScriptMaker script: "My Script"

An example that uses a basic If script step

```
If ["Field A = "My Name""]
  Perform Script [Sub-scripts, "My Script"]
End If
```

Calculation: "My Calculation"

When Field A is my name then result in the value "It's me.".

```
If (Field A = "My Name", "It's me.", "It's not me.")
```

Comparing calculations and scripts using If

Calculation:

If (test, result if true – value 1, result if false – value 2)

Script Step:

If [test]
   result if true – script 1
Else
   result if false – script 2
End If

Comparison:

Test – numeric value or logical expression
Result If True – script step 1 or return value 1
Result If False – script step 2 or return value 2

Note:

The If statement has a counterpart, called Case, which is only available in calculations. The Case and If function have a few minor cosmetic differences, but accomplish the same task. Upcoming sections will discuss the differences and why it is better to use the Case function. For now, it is sufficient to say that the Case statement is easier to manage.

In section 9.2, examples of single If statements used with logical operators (AND, OR, NOT, XOR) are shown. Logical operators expand the possibilities of If statements by allowing more than one test to be evaluated. Combining If calculations and logical operators within an If script step, extends the capabilities even further. Understanding how to implement multiple conditions is the key to creating advanced scripts.

The Case statement

Case statements function exactly like If statements. They evaluate test clauses in order of occurrence. The structure of the basic Case statement looks like this:

Case(Test A, Result 1, Test B, Result 2, Test ..., Result ..., Default Result)

Important info ▶

Using this format, a Case statement could test an unlimited number of conditions. Each condition you check for, is simply followed by a comma and the result you want returned when that test is true. You can supply a default result at the very end if you wish, but none is required. This is one of the important differences between the Case and If statements. An If statement requires two possible results; one for a true test and one for false. With the Case statement, a false test does not require a result value to be returned – a null value will automatically be returned if none is specified.

As soon as one of the tests evaluates to true, the value following that test will be returned. If none of the tests evaluate to true, the final default value will be used.

If(
Field A = "My Name", "It's me",
"It's not me."
)

is exactly the same as

```
Case(
Field A = "My Name", "It's me",
"It's not me."
)
```

Its good practice to start getting into the habit of using the Case statement in your calculations. In upcoming sections, you'll find out more reasons why the Case statement is superior to the If statement.

9.2 Logical Operators

Open this file and follow along

09_A.FP3

Chapter File:
Understanding Logicals

Logical decisions are made in FileMaker Pro scripting using conditional statements. Conditional statements often include more than one logical decision. A good example is the thought process you go through when looking through your mail. If you notice that the envelope is addressed to current resident and the stamp says bulk rate, based on these two conditions, you can classify the mail as junk mail. In order to combine logical decisions, you need to use logical operators. In the junk mail example, the logical operator AND is used. The mail needs to have bulk rate postage AND current resident as the recipient for it to be classified as junk mail. Here are the logical operators available in FileMaker Pro:

AND
OR
XOR
NOT

The operators NOT and XOR are used less frequently than AND and OR. In most situations, using the AND and OR operators will suffice to make your logical decisions work. Here are some examples of logical operators in action.

Understanding the AND operator

With the AND operator, all conditions must be met.

ScriptMaker script: "My Script AND"

When Field A is my first name and Field B is my last name, perform "My Script AND"

```
If ["Field A = "My First Name" and Field B = "My Last Name"]
    Perform Script [Sub-scripts, "My Script AND"]
End If
```

When, Field A = My First Name

Result = Script "My Script AND" will run

Calculation: "My Calculation AND"

When Field A is my first name and Field B is my last name, result in the value "It's me".

```
If (Field A = "My First Name" and Field B = "My Last Name", "It's me",
"It's not me.")
```

When, Field A = Your First Name
When, Field B = Your Last Name

Result = "It's me"

When, Field A = Your First Name
When, Field B = A Friend's Last Name

Result = "It's not me"

Understanding the OR operator

With the OR operator, either one or the other must be true.

ScriptMaker script: "My Script OR"

When Field A is my first name or Field B is my last name, do Script "My Script OR"

```
If ["Field A = "My First Name" or Field B = "My Last Name"]
    Perform Script [Sub-scripts, "My Script OR"]
End If
```

When, Field A = Your Last Name

Result = Script "My Script OR" will run

Calculation: "My Calculation OR"

When Field A is my first name or Field B is my last name, result in the value "It's me".

```
If (Field A = "My First Name" or Field B = "My Last Name", "It's me",
"It's not me.")
```

When, Field A = Your First Name
When, Field B = Your Last Name

Result = "It's me"

When, Field A = Your First Name
When, Field B = A Friend's Last Name

Result = "It's me"

When, Field A = A Friend's First Name
When, Field B = Your Last Name

Result = "It's me"

When, Field A = A Friend's First Name
When, Field B = A Friend's Last Name

Result = "It's not me"

NOTE: Obviously you wouldn't use the "OR" operator to test these conditions, but the above script and calculation return the proper results.

Understanding the XOR operator

With the XOR operator, either one or the other can be true but not both.

ScriptMaker script: "My Script XOR"

If Field A is my first name xor Field B is my last name, show a message stating that your full name has not been entered.

```
If ["Field A = "My First Name" xor Field B = "My Last Name"]
    Show Message ["You haven't entered your full name"]
End If
```

When, Field A = Your First Name
When, Field B = Your Last Name

Result = Script "My Script XOR" will run

Calculation: "My Calculation XOR"

When Field A is my first name xor Field B is my last name, result in the value "Full name entered".

```
If (Field A = "My First Name" xor Field B = "My Last Name", "Partial
name entered", "Full name entered")
```

When, Field A = Your First Name
When, Field B = Your Last Name

Result = "Full name entered"

When, Field A = Your First Name
When, Field B = A Friend's Last Name

Result = "Partial name entered"

When, Field A = A Friend's First Name
When, Field B = Your Last Name

Result = "Partial name entered"

Understanding the NOT operator

NOT operators precede the statement being evaluated.

ScriptMaker script: "My Script NOT"

When Field A is not your first name, the "My Script NOT" is performed. This means it would perform on any name other than your own.

```
If ["Not Field A = "My First Name""]
    Perform Script [Sub-scripts, "My Script NOT"]
End If
```

When, Field A = Your First Name

Result = No script will run

Calculation: "My Calculation NOT"

When Field A is not my first name, result in value "It's not me".

```
If (Not Field A = "My First Name", "It's not me", "It's me.")
```

When, Field A = Your First Name

Result = "It's me"

When, Field A = A Friend's Last Name

Result = "It's not me"

The NOT is different from the other logical operators. Instead of comparing statements, it returns the opposite of the statement it precedes. Think of it as working the same as it would in a common english statement. "I am NOT hungry" is the opposite of "I am hungry".

If you didn't have logical operators, your conditional scripts wouldn't be very efficient. Without logical operators, you would have to embed multiple if statements to accomplish the same task. This would increase the length of your scripts significantly.

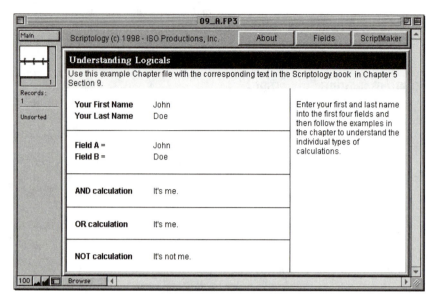

Picture 9.2
Use the file named 09_A.FP3
to work with the logical
operators.

Similar Results

Key knowledge

There's no one best way to arrive at the same result with logical statements in
FileMaker Pro. All of the following statements are exactly the same!

```
If (not Field A = "My First Name", "It's not me", "It's me.")
If (Field A ≠ "My First Name", "It's not me", "It's me.")
If (Field A <> "My First Name", "It's not me", "It's me.")
If (Field A = "My Friend's First Name", "It's not me", "It's me.")
```

When, Field A = Your First Name

Result = "It's not me"

Making Scripts and Calculations Shorter with Logical Operators

Logical Operators can reduce a nine step script to just five steps, or reduce the number of nested If statements a calculation uses. Fewer steps or functions means faster processing.

If Script without Logical Operators

If you don't use Logical Operators in conditional scripts, they become unnecessarily complicated.

```
1. If ["Cholesterol > 300"]
2.     Show Message ["Unhealthy"]
3. Else
4.     If ["Fat Grams > 50"]
5.         Show Message ["Unhealthy"]
6.     Else
7.         Show Message ["Healthy"]
8.     End If
9. End If
```

If Script with Logical Operators

Logical Operators make conditional scripts shorter.

```
1. If ["Cholesterol > 300 or Fat Grams > 50"]
2.     Show Message ["Unhealthy"]
3. Else
4.     Show Message ["Healthy"]
5. End If
```

If Calculation without Logical Operators

Notice that a calculation without logical operators has two If statements making it more difficult to follow.

```
If (Cholesterol > 300, "Unhealthy", If (Fat Grams > 50, "Unhealthy",
  "Healthy"))
```

If Calculation with Logical Operators

Logical Operators create a more readable formula.

```
If (Cholesterol > 300 or Fat Grams > 50, "Unhealthy", "Healthy")
```

If Statements are faster with Else

Using the Else script step increases the efficiency of conditional scripts. The indentation with Else steps also makes the script easier to read.

If Script without the Else step

This script requires the processing of all the If statements.

```
If ["Fat Grams > 300"]
  Show Message ["Unhealthy"]
End If
If ["Fat Grams < 300 and Fat Grams > 50"]
  Show Message ["Moderate"]
End If
If ["Fat Grams < 50"]
  Show Message ["Healthy"]
End If
```

If Script using the Else step

Using Else allows the script to Exit as soon as any condition is found to be true.

```
If ["Fat Grams  > 300"]
  Show Message ["Unhealthy"]
Else
  If ["Fat Grams < 300 and Fat Grams > 50"]
     Show Message ["Moderate"]
  Else
     Show Message ["Healthy"]
  End If
End If
```

9.3 Multiple If statements

Using more than one If statement allows you to test for multiple criteria. While the single If statement is useful, complex operations require testing more than one condition. In any solution, the ideal is to check all input for every possible variance. In the case where you want to filter out all of the junk mail, it is helpful to process each item as thoroughly as possible. The multiple If structure makes this possible.

With the mail example, there are three different tests to determine whether to keep or discard a piece of mail. This solution, may help filter out the junk mail, but it is by no means foolproof. By checking more conditions, however, it would provide a more thorough solution.

In the days before FileMaker Pro 3.0, multiple conditions where handled by embedding another If statement within one of the results (true or false) of an enclosing If statement. Here is an example in common english.

If(
Your age is less than 19, You're a teenager,
If(Your age is between 19 and 65, You're an adult,
If(Your age is over 65, You're a senior citizen,
You must be dead
)))

Notice that the last result provided reads "You must be dead". This is the default result and would be returned if there was no age provided. As you can see the multiple If statements can become very lengthy and difficult to decipher.

Why Case is better

When considering a conditional that has multiple requirements you are almost always better off using the Case statement rather than the If. The reason is that this function is much more efficient and works in the same manner as the If statement. Here is the above common english calculation using Case.

```
Case(
Your age is less than 19, You're a teenager,
Your age is between 19 and 65, You're an adult,
Your age is over 65, You're a senior citizen,
You must be dead
)
```

The simplicity of the Case statement makes it the best choice for multiple conditions.

Simple CASE statement

Example calculation
This calculation looks for three characteristics on your mail.

```
Case (envelope = "bulk rate stamp", trash, envelope = "hand written",
keep pile, addressee = "current resident", trash, maybe keep pile)
```

Simple CASE statement (easier to read)

Example calculation
This is the same calculation as the previous in an easy-to-read format. This hypothetical calculation looks for multiple mail characteristics.

```
Case (
envelope = "bulk rate stamp", trash,
envelope = "hand written", keep pile,
addressee = "current resident", trash,
maybe keep pile
)
```

Making your calculations easier to read is key to becoming more proficient in FileMaker Pro. Since FileMaker does not care if you have returns in your calculations, you can write calculations which are more readable and can be revisited later without a high relearning curve.

Embedded IF statement vs. Case

Evaluating mail with Scripts and Calculations can be accomplished with embedded If statements. There is no script counterpart for the Case statement.

Example Calculation (If)

This calculation tests your mail for three different criteria.

```
If( envelope = "bulk rate stamp", "trash",
If( envelope = "hand written", "keep pile",
If( addressee = "current resident", "trash", "maybe keep pile")))
```

Example Calculation (Case)

This calculation accomplishes the same thing as the If statement above. Notice that the word Case is not repeated and there aren't as many closing parentheses.

```
Case (
envelope = "bulk rate stamp", trash,
envelope = "hand written", keep pile,
addressee = "current resident", trash,
maybe keep pile
)
```

Example Script

This script tests your mail for three different criteria.

```
If [envelope = "bulk rate stamp"]
    Perform Script [Sub-scripts, "Trash"]
Else
    If [envelope = "hand written"]
        Perform Script [Sub-scripts, "Keep Pile"]
    Else
        If [addressee = "current resident"]
            Perform Script [Sub-scripts, "Trash"]
        Else
            Perform Script [Sub-scripts, "Maybe Keep Pile"]
        End If
    End If
End If
```

In the calculation and script in the above examples, you can see that you are watching for three criteria. If it has a bulk rate stamp you trash it, if it's hand written you keep it and if addressed to current resident you trash it. Otherwise, all other mail goes into the maybe keep pile.

While much can be accomplished with the multiple embedded IF statements, they are not quite as efficient as the Case statement. The Case allows you to expand the number of conditions while reducing the overhead. Overhead is the extra Ifs and parentheses that are necessary when using multiple embedded If statements.

Once you understand that the functionality of the Case statement is exactly the same as an If statement, you may never need to use If in your calculations. Since there is no Case available within ScriptMaker, the If step must still be used.

10.0 ScriptMaker Optimization

Few users of FileMaker Pro know how to optimize their scripts. Optimization involves the concepts covered in Chapter 3.0, such as organization and modular script design, as well as understanding the subtleties of ScriptMaker to achieve maximum speed.

Freeze Window will speed up any script that requires FileMaker Pro to redraw the window. Some good examples include:

• Looping scripts that switch between records.
• Complex scripts that pass data between files using Perform Script.
• Scripts that navigate to many different layouts.

- Any scripts that change modes a lot.
  e.g. switching between Find/Browse/Preview

This single script step can increase the speed of some scripts by many times. FileMaker Pro uses CPU cycles to tell the display circuitry on the computer what to draw when the appearance of the window changes. By adding a Freeze Window, you are telling FileMaker Pro not to redraw the screen until all the steps in the script are complete.

The best way to speed up any operation, is to know what options you have available. In some cases, it may be better to use a calculated replace (covered in Chapter 11 Section 17.2) rather than a looping script that sets a value in each record. The looping script has to use multiple script steps to cycle through the records, setting a calculated value in each one. A calculated replace is much more efficient because it takes a single script step that uses your calculation to act on the column of data in the database table. Whenever a calculation is applied to a set of records, the calculated replace will work much faster.

11.0 ScriptMaker & Portal/Relationships

◎ DBINDB.FP3

Technique File:
Database in a
Database

There are many tricks of the trade when it comes to using ScriptMaker and portals. One of these tricks is knowing that looping through a portal doesn't require it to be visible on a layout when in Browse mode. There are four steps to making a portal invisible:

1) Set it to have a scroll bar.
2) Set it to have only one row.
3) Hide the portal by changing the pen
   and fill color to the same as the background.

4) Shrink the portal to less than 25 x 25 pixels.

In most instances you don't even need to have related fields in the portal.

Open this file and
follow along

11_A.FP3

Chapter File:
Go to Related Record

Another nuance of working with portals and scripting is revealed when including a button in the top portal row. This button will repeat on all the rows in the portal. If the Go to Related record step is part of the script attached to the button, FileMaker Pro will go directly to the related record displayed in that portal row.

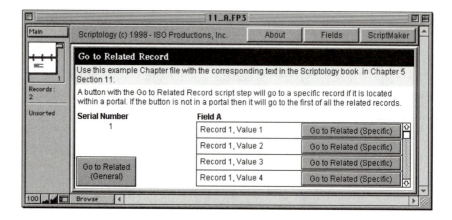

Picture 11.0

A button running the Go to Related Record step will take you to the first record of the related set of records. Placing that same button in the portal allows you to open the record related to the portal row the button was clicked in.

You can read more about the specifics of portals in Chapter 13.

Test yourself to see what you've learned.

1. **Files communicate with each other using?**
   - ○ Set Field
   - ○ Perform Script: Pass Data...
   - ○ Perform Script: External Script...
   - ○ All of the above

2. **When performing a script from one file to another, which file is left active?**
   - ○ The file containing the last script step
   - ○ The file with the End Active File step
   - ○ The first file opened
   - ○ All of the above

3. **Which method is best for moving data between files?**
   - ○ Copy and paste
   - ○ Set Field through a relationship
   - ○ A lookup field
   - ○ All of the above

4. **The advantages of Set Field are? Check all that apply.**
   - ❏ Fields don't need to be on the layout
   - ❏ A target file containing the field being set can remain inactive
   - ❏ Data manipulation can happen behind the scenes
   - ❏ Set Field works only with Booleans

5. **A constant relationship involves what criteria?**
   - ○ The match field in both files must be the same for all records
   - ○ The constant should adjust from record to record
   - ○ The relationship must be indexed
   - ○ All of the above

6. **What causes a loop to exit in ScriptMaker?**
   - ○ The last record in a found set is reached with Exit after last turned on
   - ○ A condition is met by the calculation criteria of an Exit Loop If
   - ○ An Exit or Halt script step is activated
   - ○ All of the above

7. **A counter controls what?**
   - ○ A descending data loop
   - ○ An ascending record loop
   - ○ Any loop that doesn't use a condition or the Exit after last option of Go to Record
   - ○ All of the above

8. **The Loop script step is limited to?**
   - ○ Working with the found set
   - ○ One field on the record
   - ○ Go to Portal Row [Next]
   - ○ All of the above
   - ○ None of these options

9. **A portal loop may loop indefinitely if?**
   - ○ The Exit Loop if is not used
   - ○ Set Field is used and Allow record creation is turned on
   - ○ The last related record is related to another database
   - ○ All of the above

10. **The functionality of the IF and CASE statement differ by?**
    - ○ Their order of result placement
    - ○ The ability to have more conditions using CASE
    - ○ The requirement of a default value
    - ○ All of the above

11. What do the commas represent in the following; If(test,true,false)?
- ○ Else, Then
- ○ Then, Else
- ○ Otherwise, While
- ○ While, Else

12. The XOR function will return the false value if?
- ○ All conditions in the test are met
- ○ Only one condition is met
- ○ No conditions are met
- ○ All of the above

13. When using multiple If script steps the Else will?
- ○ Allow additional conditions
- ○ Make the script quicker
- ○ Speed up conditional evaluation
- ○ All of the above

14. Optimizing ScriptMaker includes which of the following? Check all that apply.
- ❏ Using Freeze Window to prevent the window from refreshing
- ❏ Using Exit to stop a script early
- ❏ Using Perform Script to modularize
- ❏ Breaking down larger scripts

15. Adding a button into the first portal row will...
- ○ Appear in all portal rows with data
- ○ Link directly to that related record when attaching a Go to Related Record
- ○ Show only related records with the show option of Go to Related Record checked
- ○ All of the above

Answers:

Answers: 1. Perform Script : External Script"... 2. The file containing the last script step 3. The match field in both files must be the same for all records 6. All of the above 7. All of the above 8. None of these options 9. Set field is used and Allow record creation is turned on 10. The requirement of a default value, CASE does not require a default value 11. Then, Else 12. All conditions in the test are met 13. All of the above 14. Options 1, 3 & 4 should be checked. 15. All of the above

What you should have learned
- How to make FileMaker Pro files communicate
- The importance of file specialization and communication
- The one script step that is the link between files: Perform Script
- How script steps can affect which file is left active
- That a relationship, used with Set Field, is more effective than copy and paste
- How to use a constant relationship to create a data channel
- How to perform repetitive tasks using loops
- How to test conditions using If, Case, and Multiple If
- The usage of the logical operators AND, OR, XOR and NOT
- Techniques to optimize scripts
- Tricks for working with Portals

More technique files for this chapter...

SUB_NUM.FP3
Numbering Sub-Summaries

How to number the records with each break of a sub-summary.

CLAIRVOY.FP3
Clairvoyance

Demonstrates the technique for simulating type ahead using looping scripts.

EMAILS.FP3
Extracting Email Addresses

Uses a looping script to grab email addresses.

FREEZE.FP3
Freeze Window

How to speed up a loop with the Freeze Window script step.

EMAIL.FP3
Parsing Email

Uses a data loop to parse the contents of a single field into many fields.

RETURNF.FP3
Return to the Same Field

Demonstrates how to use a looping script to return to the previously selected field.

MISSING.FP3
Missing Numbers

Find the gaps in a sequence of serial numbers using a looping script.

DUP_PORT.FP3
Duplicating Portals

Return to the original field after completing a process that requires leaving the field.

Chapter 6

ScriptMaker Debugging

12.0 Debugging your scripts

There's a saying that coding, or in our case scripting, is 20% inspiration and 80% debugging. For some reason the law of trial and error seems to be a fundamental part of scripting. There's usually no getting around it, even for the seasoned FileMaker Pro user. When you're creating a complex script that involves more than a simple new record or delete record step, you can expect to come across problems with your script. Some scripts are easy, while complex operations will take you hours to debug.

In this chapter, you'll find many techniques for debugging your scripts. You'll learn to expect your script to work incorrectly the first time on all but very basic scripts. This is true, regardless of your level of expertise. The difference between a good scripter and a bad one is that the good one knows how to troubleshoot scripts more effectively through the use of sound techniques.

As with organizing scripts, discussed in chapter three, there are no built-in features for debugging. You have to devise your own. Debugging styles in FileMaker Pro vary from developer to developer. Use this chapter as a starting point for developing your own process.

12.1 Using the Pause script step

Pausing your script is a great trick when troubleshooting. In conventional programming, you have a tool called a debugger. It performs operations such as a trace or a step through. This allows the developer to step through each line of code, while seeing the

Picture 12.1

Using a Pause/Resume step within a loop is very useful for debugging a script.

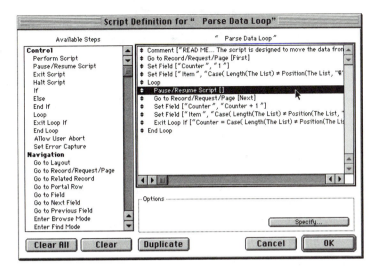

results one line at a time. In much the same way, Pause script steps make FileMaker Pro step through the script. By placing a pause at crucial points, you can verify that the correct values are being calculated, data is being modified or scripts are performing the right operations.

Another technique for stepping through scripts is using the Show Message step. This step allows you to return a message at points in the script where you want to be notified. This is especially helpful when trying to track the current position in a script that has multiple sub-scripts.

The best way to debug a longer, more complex script is to duplicate the script before you start. This way, you leave the original intact. You may only need to reorganize the script or add a single step. If you put multiple pauses in the original script, you have to remember where you put them and then take them out when the script is functional.

12.2 Breaking your script into smaller parts

As you add functions and features to your script, it can become frighteningly complex. In Chapter 3, we covered how you can take a modular design approach when using ScriptMaker. The benefits of a modular design become very obvious when needing to debug a script. As with any problem, solving a smaller part of the whole will always be easier than trying to solve the whole thing at once. In the example below there are two distinct database functions. The first is determining the results of a find. The second is using the final results to determine which view the user should be taken to. By going into the scripts and sub-scripts

Picture 12.2

The core part of the script only has one function; it enters Find, when the results are returned, other scripts run.

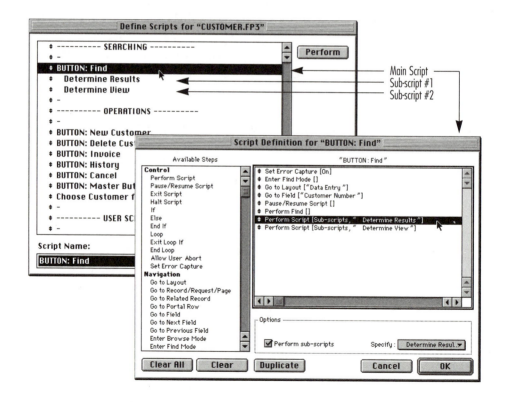

we can break down what would be one large script into three parts. Doing this allows us to troubleshoot the smaller sub-scripts much more easily. The following list of steps will help you break out your scripts.

Breaking down your ScriptMaker scripts

Steps to follow
- Duplicate your main script
- Look for logical breaks where the script begins a different process
- Clear all other steps that do not belong to that process
- Make sure the new sub-script does what it is supposed to do
- Open your main script and add a Perform Script step calling the new sub-script
- Clear the steps that are now being handled by the sub-script

Practicing these steps will shed light on the scripting process by helping you think clearly about how scripts should work. The more you practice, the less troubleshooting you will need to do.

12.3 Using temporary calculation fields for testing

The calculation dialog box is the same whether you are writing a formula in a script, designing a calculated replace or defining a calculation field. This continuity can be used to debug your scripted calculations more efficiently.

Imagine you are working on a complex Set Field calculation that's part of a script with hundreds of steps throughout many sub-scripts. Every time you want to test the Set Field step, you need to run the entire script. This could take more time than is necessary for testing purposes. A better method for debugging the Set Field calculation is to create a temporary calculation field via Define Fields. Create a new calculation with an arbitrary name, like "temp" or "test". Once the formula is working as intended, copy and paste it into your Set Field step. Here are the script steps that use calculations:

Paste Result
Replace
Set Field

Debugging your scripts with this technique is most efficient when working with a small number of records. Including records not required to test the features of the calculation will diminish the benefits of this technique by wasting time. The more records you add, the longer new or modified calculation fields take to process when exiting Define Fields.

Picture 12.3
A "temp" calculation lets you test for field results before using the calculation in a script.

12.4 Field required on layout

One of the most common scripting problems is a script that doesn't work because the referenced field is not present on the layout. FileMaker Pro will not give warning if the field you are trying to paste into is not on the current layout. The following steps require the referenced field to be present:

Go to Field
Go to Next Field
Go to Previous Field
Cut
Copy
Paste
Clear
Paste Literal
Paste Result
Paste from Index
Paste from Last Record
Paste Current Date
Paste Current Time
Paste Current User Name
Replace

When using any of the above script steps, you can avoid the requirement of having the field on every layout by creating a script that goes to a layout containing all fields in the database. The script would then return to the layout from which it was initiated. This script should be independent and called as a sub-script when needed.

12.5 Field and script highlighting

! Power Tip

Use the Overview section of Access Privileges to determine the layouts where a particular field is used. Just click on the field and black bullets will appear next to the layouts where the field is present.

One of the more frustrating aspects of a larger database project is keeping track of where a particular field or script is referenced in other scripts. There may be cases where you think of a new process which allows you to eliminate a field or script. Since FileMaker Pro doesn't provide any conventions for finding out which scripts call a particular sub-script, we must highlight the script with some sort of recognizable indicator. This is done so scripts and fields can be scanned to make sure a script or field that may still be needed is not accidentally deleted or changed.

To find a script, field or layout, you can temporarily put noticeable characters within its name. By using bullets or some other character in a long sequence you can quickly scan for the existence of that script or field in another script or calculation.

Picture 12.5
You can see that, by prefacing a script with a number of characters, you can scan for the usage of that script in other scripts.

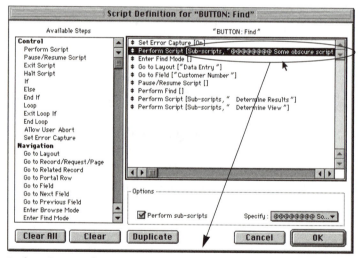

Perform Script [Sub-scripts, "@@@@@@@@ Some obscure script"]

Scanning for script or field names, when you've made them stick out, becomes much easier.

Test yourself to see what you've learned.

1. **Stepping through a script to debug it incorporates which tools?**
   - ○ The trace tool and stop points
   - ○ Pause and Show Message
   - ○ The debugger and step through function
   - ○ All of the above

2. **When a Set Field is not functioning it is best to...**
   - ○ Run a script each time to test
   - ○ Use a sub-script with Set Field
   - ○ Create temporary calculations
   - ○ All of the above

3. **The best method for preventing lost work with a broken script is to...**
   - ○ Save a copy of the database
   - ○ Create multiple sub-scripts
   - ○ Duplicate the script
   - ○ All of the above

4. **Tracking down where a script or field is used can be done using?**
   - ○ A name change
   - ○ Noticeable prefix characters
   - ○ The Show Message script step
   - ○ All of the above

Answers:

Answers: 1. Pause and Show Message 2. Create temporary calculations 3. Duplicate the script 4. Noticeable prefix characters

What you should have learned
- A foundation for troubleshooting scripts
- Use of Pause and Show Message steps to debug scripts
- Why smaller scripts save time
- How to use calculation fields to perfect script calculations
- How to locate where scripts, layouts and fields are used

Calculation Fundamentals

13.0 Beyond single function calculations

Many FileMaker Pro users find it pretty easy to use a single FileMaker Pro function. Using a simple Left(Last Name, 1) to get the first letter of a person's last name is quite easy. When you go beyond this single function and start combining functions, you begin to access the power in FileMaker Pro calculations.

Building a database is like building a house. You could build a house with only lumber, a hammer, and nails. But, if you want the house to be attractive, comfortable, functional, etc., there is a lot more required. The same is true with FileMaker Pro calculations. Making the transition from single-function to multi-function calculations will enable you to make your databases more functional and easier.

Here are some examples requiring complex calculations:

- Parsing a first and last name from a single combined name field
- Pulling a list item from a return delimited list
- Converting decimal numbers to fractions
- Formatting phone numbers and currency fields
- Determining fiscal months and quarters
- And many more...

13.1 Functional Foundation

FileMaker Pro can do just about anything you can think of when it comes to organizing, processing, and transferring data within a file structure. But, the integrity of any structure, including that of a

FileMaker Pro database, depends entirely on the strength of the foundation. The foundation in this case is your ability to understand the operation of each and every function. Let's repeat that for clarity. Your ability to understand each and every FileMaker Pro function will determine how much you can do with your database. Before you move onto complex calculations that integrate multiple functions, it is important to understand the individual functions themselves.

While writing this book, it was decided that explaining the great techniques, describing the benefits of automating processes, and even providing examples of working solutions would be useless until we put the power of knowledge into your hands. It was decided that for you to feel in control, you have to be responsible for learning, practicing, and understanding the tools available to you. The level of understanding you want to achieve with FileMaker Pro rests entirely on this one concept – understanding functions.

This may seem a little drastic at first, however, if you understand functions you will be light years ahead of the learning curve whenever you see someone else's solution, or when you have something explained to you – like Scriptology is attempting to do. So, what do we recommend? Here it is. This is what Scriptology is all about in one sentence. Learn every function in a way that allows you to understand it, then practice it at least three different ways. If you do this, and write them out on paper, you will always know how to take small bites from a big problem. Working from the basics in this way will provide you the confidence that allows you to feel like you can do anything.

FileMaker Pro Functions
Appendix B in this book and the FUNCTNS.FP3 reference file on the CD ROM are a good place to go when you have questions about a calculation function.

There are roughly 125 different functions. Some you may use all the time, some never, but all are important if you want to know FileMaker Pro inside and out. You will find a Functions Reference file on the CD ROM that accompanies Scriptology. This file contains all the functions in one place and includes an explanation of the operation that each performs. This is a nice reference and will save you a lot of time, but the key is to learn these functions. There is no way around it. If you pick 5 or 10 a day, depending on the difficulty of the function, you can learn all of them in about 20 days. If you're willing to do that, you may be able to ask for a raise at work, start developing your own shareware as a hobby, or quit your day job all together and start creating FileMaker Pro solutions for a living. The knowledge learned here will overlap with many other areas of computers as well. Take the time, and do the grunt work. Whoever made up the term no pain, no gain must have been talking about learning the basics in any area. People are used to instant gratification, but learning the functions one by one, is more like an investment in your future. It will pave the way to creating calculations containing multiple functions.

13.2 Going in reverse - building your calculation

The best way to begin working on a complex calculation is to start with the main function and then create the parts that contribute to the main calculation. Let's say you want to extract a section of text from within a long list of values. Using the Middle function, you can extract a static piece of text from a list. In other words, you can grab the same section of text from the same field if you provide static parameters. However, if you use the Position function, within the Middle function, to return a value for one of the Middle function's parameters, the calculation becomes dynamic.

Going in reverse requires that you complete the subparts first. In order to do this, you need to know what tools you have. Learn the use of each function by practicing each one on very simple, one-step examples. Once you understand the individual functions, using them is just like digging into a tool box for the tool that fits the job. In the following example, it's important that you completely understand the parameters that can be supplied to the Middle and Position functions. Refer to Appendix B or the FUNCTNS.FP3 Reference file on the CD ROM.

FUNCTNS.FP3

Reference File:
Calculation Functions

Parsing out a list item

Open this file and follow along

The following list is contained in one field in the Chapter files (13_A.FP3, 13_B.FP3 and 13_C.FP3) on the CD ROM . Each file builds on the other, making it easier to understand the final product. Each of the files grab a line based on a number in a field. Here is the list that each contains:

13_A.FP3

Chapter File:
Parsing out of a list 1

Cat
Dog
Bird
Horse
Elephant

13_B.FP3

Chapter File:
Parsing out of a list 2

The objective is to dynamically extract one of the values from the list. You need a calculation field which returns the value from a specified line item in the list above. To vary the item you isolate in the list, you will need a value that **controls** what line is specified. This field is called "Control". If Control contains a one (1),

13_C.FP3

Chapter File:
Parsing out of a list 3

the calculation should return "Cat", line two (2) will be "Dog" and so on. See the dissection below to get a complete understanding of the process.

Parsing a list: Calculation dissection

Field Name	Field Type	Field Value
The List	Text	A return-delimited list of items
Counter	Global number	A variable number
Result	Calculation Text	The value from the list

Calculation: 13_A.FP3 "Result"

The complete calculation looks into the middle of the The List field and uses the Counter field to determine which line item it returns. Start with the middle function when breaking it down.

```
Middle (text, start, size)
```

We now know we want something from the middle of The List

```
Middle (The List, start, size)
```

We need to start at the beginning of each line. Because we know each item is separated with a return character "¶", that's a good place to start.

```
Middle (The List, Start at the return character, size)
```

We want to grab the size of the entire line item. This includes all spaces and punctuation.

```
Middle (The List, Start at the return character, for the length of the line)
```

We can now define our starting position and size. Beginning with the start parameter, use the Position function since it will tell us the position of the "¶" character. Use the Counter field to control which occurrence of the "¶" character to locate. By subtracting 1 we go backwards one occurrence to the previous "¶" character that's in front of the line the Counter is looking for. Because the Position function finds the exact position of the "¶" character we need to go forward exactly one character (+ 1) to start grabbing text at the first letter or number of the line.

```
Position(The List, "¶", 1, Counter - 1) + 1
```

This function now results in a number we can plug into the start parameter.

```
Middle(The List, Position(The List, "¶", 1, Counter - 1) + 1, size)
```

Now we need to determine how much text to grab. The size is controlled by the distance between the two returns. This can be figured by finding the ending "¶" character and the starting "¶" character. We found the starting character above with the Position(The List, "¶", 1, Counter - 1) function. All we need to do is go to the "¶" character at the end of the list item and subtract from the starting character found with the start portion of the calculation. In order to grab the very first character of the line we have to back up one character by subtracting 1 to end up at the first "¶" character.

```
Position(The List, "¶", 1, Counter) - Position(The List, "¶", 1, Counter - 1)
- 1
```

When we plug this last part into the main calculation we get a result that extracts individual line items from a list, based on the value found in the Counter field.

```
Middle(The List, Position(The List, "¶", 1, Counter - 1) + 1, Position(The
List, "¶", 1, Counter) - Position(The List, "¶", 1, Counter - 1) - 1)
```

The complex part is that our calculation doesn't account for the last value. Since we are using the return character "¶" to control where we start, and length of text we grab, we need to test for a "¶" at the end of the list. This adds complexity, making the calculation look like the following. Take the calculation apart to better understand it. Being able to read and understand the following means you're close to mastering FileMaker Pro.

```
Length(The List) <> Position(The List, "¶", 1, PatternCount(The List, "¶"))
and Counter = PatternCount(The List, "¶") + 1,

Right(The List, Length(The List) - Position(The List, "¶", 1,
PatternCount(The List, "¶"))),

Middle(The List, Position(The List, "¶", 1, Counter - 1) + 1, Position(The
List, "¶", 1, Counter) - Position(The List, "¶", 1, Counter - 1) - 1)
)
```

13.3 Determining the end result

Bookmark this page
You should use this list any time you are about to attempt a complex calculation.

This may seem basic, but it is very important. If you clearly understand what you want your calculation to do before you start writing it, the process will be much smoother. Ask yourself the questions in the list below to limit the time you spend racking your brain trying to figure out where to start.

Key questions

Things to ask about your calculation
- Where is the data coming from?
- How many fields are involved?
- Are there any unique features about the data?
- What is the result going to be? Number? Text?
- Do I need to convert the data formats? (TextToNum, etc.)
- What is the mathematical outcome?
- What functions will I need to use?
- Should the calculation be stored or unstored?

Once you've considered your calculation, it'll be much easier to design. If you start writing your calculation immediately after inspiration, it's likely you'll run into trouble. Plan your calculation carefully by considering all the possibilities. You might even want to work through the process on paper before writing the calculation.

13.4 A better view

Reading complex calculations can be difficult. You can add a level of professionalism and quality to your calculations by making a few modifications to their structure. This is done by using the entire available area of the calculation entry box. Add spaces and returns where needed to make the calculation read better. Using an example Case statement (see the example on the next page), open the statement by including a return after the first parenthesis and close the statement with a return before the last parenthesis.

Separating long calculations at the comma dividing the parameters also adds readability. If you have multiple results, such as with true/false (Boolean) resulting calculations, allow for some space by adding a return between them. If the calculation becomes so large that simply adding spaces and extra lines won't do the trick, you can add extra spaces in the form of lines. Adding six or more spaces before the start of a calculation within a calculation more clearly defines what starts where.

A unique trick that can be used for internal documentation of a calculation is to use the following function.

COMMENT.FP3

Technique File:
Commenting Files

```
Left("Whatever kind of documentation you want to
include.", 0) &
```

Add your functioning calculation to the end of this formula. The Left function will return nothing, leav-

ing the result of your formula. Remember, the best
way to understand your own work is to be able to
read it quickly and clearly.

Examples of calculation readability

Bad example

This calculation is barely readable compared to the one that follows.

Huh? ➤

```
Case(Length(The List) <> Position(The List, "¶", 1, PatternCount(The
List, "¶")) and Counter = PatternCount(The List, "¶") + 1, Right(The
List, Length(The List) - Position(The List, "¶", 1, PatternCount(The
List, "¶"))), Middle(The List, Position(The List, "¶", 1, Counter - 1)
+ 1, Position(The List, "¶", 1, Counter) - Position(The List, "¶", 1,
Counter - 1) - 1))
```

Good example

This calculation is written so the first part is the test, the second
part is the true result and the third part is the false result. Within
each part there is a calculation that determines a value.

Open ➤
```
Case(
```

Test ➤
```
Length(The List) <> Position(The List, "¶", 1, PatternCount(The List,
"¶")) and
Counter = PatternCount(The List, "¶") + 1,
```

True ➤
```
Right(The List, Length(The List) - Position(The List, "¶", 1,
PatternCount(The List, "¶"))),
```

False
(Default) ➤
```
Middle(The List, Position(The List, "¶", 1, Counter - 1) + 1,
Position(The List, "¶", 1, Counter) - Position(The List, "¶", 1,
Counter - 1) - 1)
```

Close ➤
```
)
```

Test yourself to see what you've learned.

1. **Building a complex calculation is easier using what process?**
    - ❍ Breaking out sub-calculations
    - ❍ Building in reverse
    - ❍ Starting with the result in mind
    - ❍ All of the above

2. **The foundation needed to be a proficient FileMaker Pro user is?**
    - ❍ Knowing calculation functions
    - ❍ Understanding how layouts work
    - ❍ Understanding how to make multiple query requests
    - ❍ All of the above

3. **Making calculations more readable is done by...**
    - ❍ Labeling them well in the layout
    - ❍ Using comments in a developer layout
    - ❍ Adding returns and spaces
    - ❍ All of the above

4. **Which function can be used to document inside a calculation?**
    - ❍ TextToNum
    - ❍ Left
    - ❍ Position
    - ❍ All of the above

5. **A counter field used in a parsing calculation makes the calculation?**
    - ❍ Faster
    - ❍ Static
    - ❍ Dynamic
    - ❍ All of the above

6. **Making a literal quote character (") part of a calculation result uses?**
    - ❍ & """" &
    - ❍ & "" &
    - ❍ & """""" &
    - ❍ All of the above

Answers:

Answers: 1. All of the above 2. Knowing calculation functions 3. Adding returns and spaces 4. Left 5. Dynamic 6. & """" & (double quotes withing a set of quotes returns a literal quote)

Chapter 7 Highlights

What you should have learned
- How to start with simple calculations to build a foundation
- How to approach a complex calculation
- Making your calculations readable for understandability
- How starting with the end in mind makes the calculation clear

More technique files about calculations...

DECIMAL.FP3
Decimals to Fractions

How to convert decimal numbers into fractions.

DOLLAR.FP3
Dollars to Text

Converting numbers to words. Can be used for a check writing program.

CSZ.FP3
Extracting City, State & Zip

Extracts city, state and zip into separate fields if they have been entered together into a single field.

FISCAL.FP3
Fiscal Month and Quarter

Calculating the fiscal month and quarter since FileMaker has no functions for these features.

PHONE.FP3
Phone Number Formatting

Formats a phone number field no matter what entry method is used.

Intermediate/Advanced

Calculation Debugging

14.0 Debugging your calculations

The natural tendency when debugging calculations is to try and solve the problem in your head. You might rethink what it is you want the calculation to do and why it's not working, or you might start breaking down the calculation to make sure you wrote it correctly. Everybody's thought process is a little different. It definitely helps to think about what is happening, but it can be confusing to try and calculate all but the simplest of formulas in your head.

When you know what the calculation needs to return, but the result is not meeting your expectations, it helps to work it out by hand – with pencil and paper. This will give you a complete understanding of how each function is supposed to work and what is happening at each step. Going through the process of manually figuring your work a few times will enable you to think about it more clearly. This sounds obvious but few people try working through their calculations in this manner. Doing so can save many frustrated hours in front of your computer. Most experts work through their problem calculations on paper.

Even better than learning the power of working your problem out on paper is being able to avoid them in the first place. By breaking down the calculation into its component parts, you can build the calculation one function at a time. This will allow you to understand each part well enough to construct a solid complex formula. See Chapter 7 Section 13.2 – Building your calculations in reverse – for more information.

Even with the best planning, your calculation development is bound to fail in many instances. This chapter covers techniques for debugging calculations when you aren't able to avoid them.

14.1 Plugging in values

One of the most fundamental techniques for troubleshooting a calculation is to use sample data. When a formula is not calculating as expected, it is helpful to create an example using known results, substituting the values for the field references and working it out on paper.

Try working on a calculation that extracts the first and last name from a field containing the full name. For this example, assume that the LeftWords and RightWords functions do not exist. To prevent this particular calculation from becoming more complicated than necessary, all first and last names are assumed to be single words and no middle names are present. The formula for extracting the first name field looks like the following and functions correctly:

```
Left(
Full Name, Position(Full Name " ", 1, 1) - 1
)
```

However, the formula for the Last Name field is not working:

```
Right(
Full Name, Position(Full Name, " ", 1, 1) -
Length(Full Name)
)
```

This second formula keeps returning an empty (null) value. The logic behind this second calculation is to find the location of the space between the first name and last name and subtract from the length of the entire name to determine how many characters from the right constitute the last name.

A debugging technique that can help in this type of situation is writing the formula down on paper and working it out by hand. Keep in mind that most functions return a number value. So, a complex calculation with field and function names can be reduced to a simple formula with just text and numbers. Substituting sample data will give you insight into why the function is returning a null value. Let's take the example of "Bob Jones". Write each letter of the name down on paper including the space between the first and last name. Number each character from one to nine (see Picture 14.1).

Picture 14.1
Every character in a text field is counted. This includes spaces and punctuation.

Name ⟶ Bob Jones
Character Position ⟶ 123456789

Now plug-in the values from the specific example:

```
Right("Bob Jones", Position("Bob Jones", " ", 1,
1) - Length("Bob Jones"))
```

Locate the position of the space in the sample data and use the character number as the result for the Position function:

```
Right("Bob Jones", 4 - Length("Bob Jones"))
```

Count the number of characters in the sample data and use the value as the result of the Length function:

```
Right("Bob Jones", 4 - 9)
```

Now it is much easier to see why the formula is not working. It is trying to grab a negative number of characters:

```
Right("Bob Jones", -5)
```

To fix this formula, switch the order of the Position and Length functions so positive numbers are returned. Here is the correct formula:

```
Right(Full Name, Length(Full Name) - Position(Full
Name, " ", 1, 1))
```

This debugging technique can be used on most calculations, not just text functions. Think of this technique as an algebraic equation. The unknowns in this example are the Full Name field and the result from the Position and Length functions. As you go through the stages of inputting data, you'll be able to see why FileMaker Pro is returning the incorrect result even though your logic may seem to be correct.

14.2 Separating the functions

When a calculation isn't working, a good idea is to separate the formula into pieces. This procedure is similar to building your calculations in reverse (see Chapter 7 Section 13.2), but can also be used to debug your calculations. The best way to describe this technique is to start with an example of a calculation that is not working properly.

Let's say you're trying to extract items from a return separated list based on a number in another field. The formula requires the combination of several functions and is quite complicated. Even experts run into problems when writing this type of calculation from scratch. The following formula (which does not work properly) references a return separated list in a field named List and a number in a global field named List Choice.

Open	`Middle(`
Test	`"¶" & List & "¶",`
True	`Position("¶" & List & "¶", "¶", Position("¶" &` `List & "¶", "¶", 1, List Choice), 1),`

False (default)	`Position("¶" & List & "¶", "¶", Position("¶" &`
	`List & "¶", "¶", 1, List Choice), 2) -`
	`Position("¶" & List & "¶", "¶", Position("¶" &`
	`List & "¶", "¶", 1, List Choice), 1)`

Close	`)`

This formula is supposed to grab the correct line item depending on the number in the global List Choice field.

The Problem

Open this file and follow along

14_A.FP3

Chapter File: Debugging Complex Calculations

The problem with this formula, is that the result of the item retrieved includes a paragraph return character at its beginning. Since the formula relies on line items being between the return character from the previous line and the return character of the current line (see Picture 14.2), it is necessary that extra return characters be added to the beginning and ending of the List field. In order to demonstrate how to solve this problem, let's separate the individual functions and test them.

Item 1¶
Item 2¶
Item 3

Picture 14.2
Item 2 is between the return from line one and the return of line two.

Since this formula is so complicated, you're better off troubleshooting the pieces to find out why an extra character is being grabbed. The `Middle (text, start, size)` function has other functions embedded within it. The best way to break down this formula is to isolate the start and size parameters, each of which contain the following formulas:

Start parameter portion of the formula:

Start parameter	`Position("¶" & List & "¶", "¶", Position("¶" & List & "¶", "¶", 1, List Choice), 1)`

Size parameter portion of the formula:

Size parameter	`Position("¶" & List & "¶", "¶", Position("¶" & List & "¶", "¶", 1, List Choice), 2) - Position("¶" & List & "¶", "¶", Position("¶" & List & "¶", "¶", 1, List Choice), 1)`

When these portions of the whole are analyzed as separate calculations, the reason the extra return character is "grabbed" becomes more evident. For instance, let's say you had a list of names in the List field:

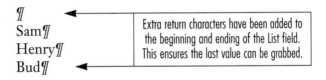

¶
Sam¶
Henry¶
Bud¶

Extra return characters have been added to the beginning and ending of the List field. This ensures the last value can be grabbed.

NOTE: The "¶" symbols above would not normally be seen in the text. They are the FileMaker Pro representation of return characters.

SCROLL.FP3

Technique File:
Scroll Through

When a two is placed in the List Choice field (attempting to extract Henry), the Start calculation returns a five and the Size calculation returns a six. Counting five characters from the beginning of the list, without forgetting the return characters, leaves you at the return character just after "Sam". This is the extra return character being grabbed.

GRAB.FP3

Technique File:
Grab a Value from a List

Even the size parameter of six is wrong since the item "Henry" is only five characters long. Plugging different numbers into the List Choice field reveals that the starting point is always one character too early and size is one character too long. With the problem in hand, the solution is easy. Add one to the start calculation and subtract one from the size calculation. Here are the working formulas:

Start formula:

```
Position("¶" & List & "¶", "¶", Position("¶" &
List & "¶", "¶", 1, List Choice), 1) + 1
```

Size formula:

```
Position("¶" & List & "¶", "¶", Position("¶" &
List & "¶", "¶", 1, List Choice), 2) -
Position("¶" & List & "¶", "¶", Position("¶" &
List & "¶", "¶", 1, List Choice), 1) - 1
```

Plugging them back into the main function completes the formula:

Open	`Middle(`
Test	`"¶" & List & "¶",`
True	`Position("¶" & List & "¶", "¶", Position("¶" & List & "¶", "¶", 1, List Choice), 1) + 1,`
False (default)	`Position("¶" & List & "¶", "¶", Position("¶" & List & "¶", "¶", 1, List Choice), 2) - Position("¶" & List & "¶", "¶", Position("¶" & List & "¶", "¶", 1, List Choice), 1) - 1`
Close	`)`

If you started off looking at this calculation, you would no doubt think it was impossible to fix. Being aware of each part, however, enables you to think clearly by tackling a small portion of the problem at a time.

14.3 Common mistakes with calculations

This section answers the question "Why won't my calculations work?". The most common reason calculations return an incorrect value is because the result type is set incorrectly. For instance, if a function returns a date value and the result type is set to number, the date will be converted to a number (e.g. 2/2/98 converts to 729422). A similar problem occurs when the value type expected by a FileMaker Pro function is not the same as the value provided by a referenced field (e.g. The Left function requires a text field but a number field is provided by mistake).

Picture 14.3
Make sure the calculation formula returns the same type as the result type pop-up menu.

This result

should match

This setting

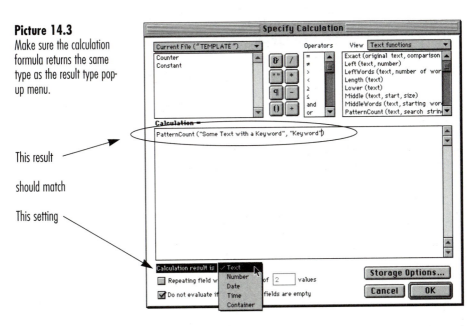

The final result type of a calculation should always be uppermost in your mind. A simple mistake can cause a calculation to return an incorrect result for no apparent reason.

Embedded expectations

Embedded functions (functions within other functions) need to return the result type required by the parameter it replaces. For instance, the Left function has two parameters; a text and a number parameter. If you use a function in place of the number parameter, it needs to return a value of type number. If it returns a text value, the calculation may not work properly. In many cases, the problem can be solved by using one of the following conversion functions:

TextToNum( )
NumToText( )
TextToDate( )
DateToText( )
TextToTime( )
TimeToText( )

Picture 14.3.1
Watch for the result types of embedded functions. If necessary, use a conversion function like TexToNum.

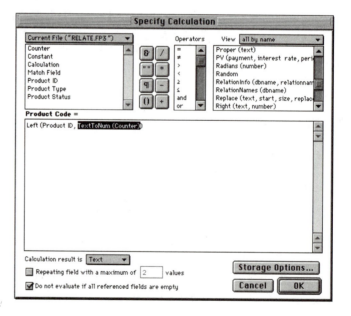

FUNCTNS.FP3

Resource File:
FileMaker Pro Functions

Use the Appendix B in this book or the Functions Reference on the CD to determine the result type for each function.

14.4 Storage settings

It's important to understand the FileMaker Pro index because there are many situations where the outcome of a calculation is dependent upon the index of a field. The index for a calculation field is controlled by the storage settings dialog (see Picture 14.4).

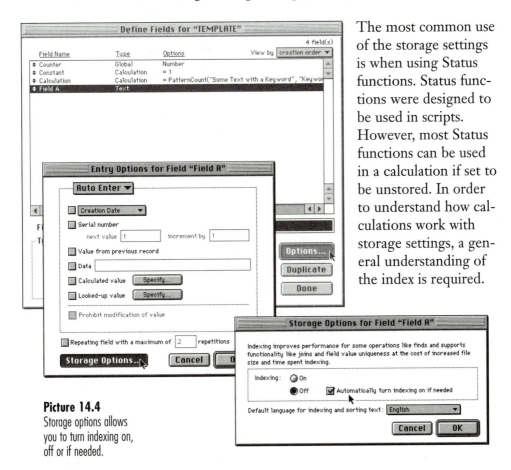

The most common use of the storage settings is when using Status functions. Status functions were designed to be used in scripts. However, most Status functions can be used in a calculation if set to be unstored. In order to understand how calculations work with storage settings, a general understanding of the index is required.

Picture 14.4
Storage options allows you to turn indexing on, off or if needed.

The index – What is it?

When the index is turned on, each FileMaker Pro field stores a list of the unique values in that field (see Picture 14.4.1). The index of a single field is comprised from all values for that field in the database. Duplicate values are stored only once and only the first 20 characters of each word are indexed. For example, if you have the word "cat" in the same field on three different records, the index displays the word "cat" once with references to each of those records. This keeps the size of the index small so searches are quick.

Picture 14.4.1
In order to view the index values of a field, it must be selected. After the field is selected, choose From Index under the Paste Special sub-menu under the Edit menu. This can be invoked with a power key of Command-I on Macintosh or Control-I on Windows.

The index and calculations

The index for a field provides for much more than speedy searches. One function of the index is to store the results of calculations. Without the index, calculations would simply display a value rather than store the result. Since unstored calculations do not get indexed, they are recalculated each time the screen is refreshed.

STATUS.FP3
Technique File:
Updating Status
Functions

The index is not always under your control, but knowing how a FileMaker Pro database will react is the key to designing a sophisticated system. For instance, you don't need to store the index for a calculation or a field that is never searched. Or, if a calculation field is never displayed on a layout, there's no reason to have it store the calculation results. Each indexed field in the database contributes to the overall size of the file. Suffice it to say, understanding when and where calculations are, or can be, unstored will help you design and troubleshoot a database more effectively.

Examples of calculation storage

Calculations that reference global fields are automatically unstored because global fields cannot be indexed. Global fields contain a single value so there's no reason to index it. However, this creates problems for calculations based on global fields, in that they are always unstored. If the unstored calculation needs to display in list view, the redraw will likely be slow since the formula needs to recalculate for each record. Scrolling will also slow the display redraw since each record that scrolls into view will recalculate.

Calculations that reference related fields are also unstored because the file that contains the calculation does not have access to the index for the related field. Rather than store the index of every field in every file for a solution, calculations based on related fields become unstored. One workaround to this problem is to use a lookup instead of a related field. Lookups aren't automatically updated and increase the size of the database, but used sparingly they can help create speedier calculations.

When using Status and Design functions in a calculation formula, it's necessary to check the storage setting option "Do not store calculation results" (see picture 14.4.3). If this option is not checked, the calculated result will never refresh. For instance, placing the Status(CurrentFoundCount) function in a calculation will give the same number of records as were present when it was initially formulated, even if the new found set of records changes. If the calculation is set to unstored, the calculated value will reformulate every time the screen refreshes (e.g. a new record is shown).

Picture 14.4.3
Set calculation storage to "Do not store calculation results" when using Status or Design functions.

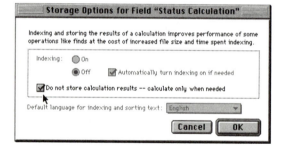

The GetSummary function is an interesting function. It stores values when the database is sorted by the break field parameter. Once the database is unsorted, the values disappear. For example, let's say you wanted to sort a calculation field based on the values from a GetSummary function. This is impossible since the instant you performed the find, the database would be unsorted and the former values for the GetSummary function would be lost. All calculations based on the GetSummary function are unstored.

More than basic indexing

It is sometimes advantageous to reset the language type for the index of a text field. With normal indexing, FileMaker Pro indexes characters from the alphabet and numbers of the current language. By setting a text field to index using ASCII, you can have an index that uses values not normally indexed, thereby allowing for more specific searches. Setting the index language to ASCII (see picture 14.2.3) is done via the Storage Options dialog and it increases the number of characters that are indexed. Values not normally indexed include the following characters: !, ", #, $, %, (,), *, +, ;, <, =, >, ?, @, [, \,], ^, _, `, {, |, }, ~, †, °, ¢, £, §, •, ¶, ®, ©, ™, ´, ¨, ≠, ∞, ±, ≤, ≥, ¥, µ, ∂, Σ, ∏, π, ∫, Ω, ¿, ¡, ¬, √, ƒ, ≈, ∆, «, », …, –, —, ", ", ÷, ◊, ¤, ‹, ›, ‡, ·, „, ‟, ‰, 1, ˆ, ˜, ¯, ˘, ˙, ˚, ¸, ˝, ˛, ˇ.

Picture 14.2.3
You can increase the range of the FileMaker Pro index by changing the language to ASCII.

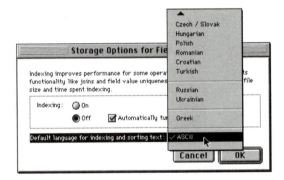

Dangerous keys

Without knowing some of the specifics of how the index is used by relationships, it's possible to create complex relational keys that break and do not provide stable relationships. There are two key pieces of information that you need to determine if a complex key will break. The first is the language setting.

⚠ Power Tip

The following characters are sometimes used in relationship keys and are not indexed by default:

    &   (ampersand)
    ,   (comma)
    -    (hyphen)
    .   (period)
    /   (forward slash)
    :   (colon)
    '   (apostrophe)

When creating long calculated keys based on them; watch out.

If it's not ASCII then certain characters will not be indexed. For example, with the language setting of English the two following keys are seen by the relationship as the exact same thing.

123456789-101112131415
123456789101112131415

The dash character in the first string of numbers is not indexed so you can imagine that it is not really there if the language is English. Therefore the two strings become the exact same. Only when the field's index language is changed to ASCII will the dash character be recognized as a division in the first key, making it different than the second key.

The second factor to consider is the 20 character limit on the index. Since only the first 20 characters of each word are indexed a complex key cannot exceed this amount before some division in the key is used. For example, the two keys below are seen as the same no matter what.

12345678901234567890**1**
12345678901234567890**2**

While the language setting of the index has no direct bearing when debugging a calculation, it's good to be aware of this when designing your database.

Rules of the FileMaker Pro index

How indexing affects your files
- Indexed fields increase the overall size of your files.
- Indexing decreases search times.
- Indexing is turned on automatically when a field is searched unless the option for automatically turning on the index has been unchecked.
- Non-indexed fields, when searched, are temporarily indexed.
- List views draw more slowly on screen when fields are not indexed.
- Relationships require indexed fields to work. (Except global relationships)
- Global fields are not indexable.
- Calculations can be set to unstored and become unindexed.

Chapter 8 Overview & Quiz

Test yourself to see what you've learned.

1. **The most common problem with non functioning calculations is?**
   - ○ Too many embedded functions
   - ○ Global fields are referenced
   - ○ The result type doesn't match the result of the calculation
   - ○ All of the above

2. **Which field reference makes a calculation unstored?**
   - ○ Global fields
   - ○ Text fields
   - ○ Container fields
   - ○ All of the above

3. **The database index is?**
   - ○ Specific fields as arranged in Define Fields
   - ○ All the unique values of each stored field
   - ○ The field specific data from calculation fields
   - ○ All of the above

4. **The best method for testing a calculation subpart is to?**
   - ○ Add extra lines between functions
   - ○ Create an independent calculation
   - ○ Reference another calculation's result
   - ○ All of the above

5. **The screen refreshes faster in list view using?**
   - ○ Stored calculations
   - ○ Unstored calculations
   - ○ Stored global fields
   - ○ All of the above

6. **Changing a field's index language to ASCII causes? Check all that apply.**
   - ❑ The period to be recognized
   - ❑ The space to be recognized
   - ❑ The dash to be recognized
   - ❑ The colon to be recognized

Answers:

Answers: 1. The result type doesn't match the result of the calculation 2. Global fields 3. All the unique values of each stored field 4. Create an independent calculation 5. Stored calculations 6. Options 1,3 and 4 should be checked.

What you should have learned
- How to work out your calculation problems on paper
- How to break down your calculations into separate pieces
- How to use sample data to discover calculation problems
- Why a calculation result type is important when debugging
- Why the field type is important when working with embedded functions

Technique files that relate to this chapter

SCROLLER.FP3
Stay Scrolled

An alternative to scrolling fields which allows the field to save the scroll position even when the field is exited.

TEXT_TO.FP3
Blank Calculation Results

How to use the type conversion functions (e.g. TextToNum) to prevent question marks from displaying for blank results.

STRIP.FP3
Remove Extra Returns

If a data entry person accidentally enters extra returns at the end of an entry, this formula can remove them.

NAMES.FP3
Extracting Names

Extracts first, last and middle names from a single into separate fields.

Validations

Advice

This chapter discusses a few highly advanced techniques that depend on a solid understanding of relationships and the way lookups function. If you don't already have a solid foundation in these areas then skip to Chapter 12 and return later.

15.0 Making FileMaker Pro use the right information

One of the more powerful features added to a database is validation. Validations provide the ability to limit the values accepted by a field. This allows you to direct user input and reduce entry errors by presenting error messages.

There are many types of validations. Basic validations are covered by the validation options for text, number, date and time fields. The standard validation options include ❶ watching to see if the value in a field is of a certain type (number, date or time) , ❷ determining whether a field is not empty , ❸ if a value is unique to the field , ❹ whether data already exists in the file , ❺ if it's a member of a value list , ❻ in a certain range , ❼ or the best option of all, that of meeting a certain condition as defined by a calculation .

Picture 15.0
The validation options of any text, number, date or time field and in special cases, a global field.

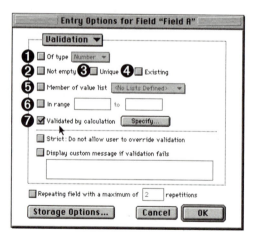

This chapter covers validation by calculation, validating global fields and other uses of FileMaker Pro validations. Let's start with validation by calculation since it's the most powerful of all the validation techniques in this chapter.

15.1 Understanding validation requirements

! Power Tip

1 = True

Yes, be *true* to the *one* you love.

0 = False

No, it's *false* that I have *zero* belongings.

The phrases above should help you remember what the Boolean values should equal. Italicized words represent the various ways to specify a Boolean.

When validating by calculation there are only two possible outcomes; true or false. If it's true, the predefined criteria has been satisfied, and if false, FileMaker Pro will consider the input incorrect.

Any question that allows only two answers is considered a Boolean operation. A value of one (1) to a computer using boolean logic will always represent the following; On, True, or Yes. A zero (0), on the other hand, always returns the opposite; Off, False, or No. The only thing to remember when writing a validation calculation is whether you want the result to be a 1 or a 0.

If a field meets the validation requirements, the result is a one. Anything that results in a false or zero will show a message that the field does not meet the expected criteria. It's important to note that FileMaker Pro will also consider any non zero value to be a true value. In many cases the easiest method for writing a calculated validation is to use a Case statement with result values of (0) zero and (1) one.

Picture 15.1
Number fields can be for-
matted as Boolean values.

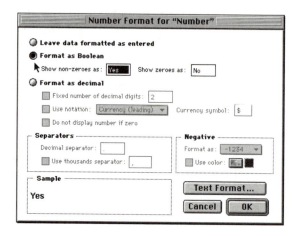

Using numbers as Boolean

If fields being used in your calculated validation happen to be numbers, it's possible to format their display as Boolean values. The Field Format options
available for number fields can format output as
Boolean (see Picture 15.1).

Checking for multiple criteria

**Open this file and
follow along**

15_A.FP3

Chapter File:
Validating Phone
Numbers

Most calculated validations require that you validate
for more than one criteria. For example, a field may
require an input of twelve characters – ten numbers
(character counts differ from number counts) and two
dashes. The following example validates a U.S. phone
number in the format XXX-XXX-XXXX. The AND
operator enables you to check that all requirements
are met.

Calculated Validation Exercise

Validation Calculation: Field name "Phone Number"

The following is a calculation that would appear in a calculated validation for a U.S. formatted phone number stored in a text field.

```
Middle(Phone Number, 4, 1) = "-" and
Middle(Phone Number, 8, 1) = "-" and
Length(Phone Number) = 12 and
Length(TextToNum(Phone Number)) = 10
```

If all tests are met then the result is (1) one.

(1) The field must have a dash at the fourth position:

```
Middle(Phone Number, 4, 1) = "-"
```

AND

(2) The field must have a dash at the eighth position:

```
Middle(Phone Number, 8, 1) = "-"
```

AND

(3) The field must be twelve characters long:

```
Length(Phone Number) = 12
```

AND

(4) The field must contain only numbers and the length of those numbers must equal ten:

```
Length(TextToNum(Phone Number)) = 10
```

If all of the criteria are met, the result for the validation equals one (1) or true. If just one part of the validation does not evaluate to true, an error message will be displayed.

Validations using Case statements

Open this file and follow along

15_B.FP3

Chapter File:
Validating Email
Addresses

A Case statement allows you to add substantially more power to a validation. The power comes with the ability to test multiple conditions. If the first condition is met, a result will be returned. If the first condition is false, another test will be performed until at least one condition is satisfied. As long as the final result of a calculated validation is a one (1) or a zero (0), it doesn't matter the type or number of tests performed. The calculation below validates an email address by verifying that no spaces have been included and there's one at sign (@). If any one of the evaluations in the Case statement are met then the result is zero or false. If all evaluations pass, the result is one.

As long as you remember that a calculated validation result must be either a one (1) or a zero (0), you're free to design any calculated validation you want.

Calculated Validation Exercise

Validation Calculation: Field name "Email"

The following calculation would appear in a calculated validation for a standard email address field named "Email".

```
Case(
PatternCount(Email, " ") <> 0, 0,
PatternCount(Email, "@") > 1, 0,
PatternCount(Email, "@") < 1, 0,
1
)
```

NOTE: Notice that the validation calculation references the field it is validating.

15.2 Using validations creatively

Users of FileMaker Pro continuously ask for new features. Many requests are made for features that can be developed using a little creativity. By doing so, you can accomplish tasks previously considered impossible. The following examples will give you insight on how to use the validation feature to its full potential, often in ways never intended.

Validating Global Fields

◎)) **GLOBAL.FP3**

Technique File:
Validating a Global
Field

Currently, FileMaker Pro provides no options for global fields other than setting the field type and whether it's repeating. However, globals can be validated using the following technique.

In order to validate a global field all you need is to create a regular numeric or text field and set all of your validation criteria. After you have set the validation criteria, simply change the field to a global field of the same type. This is done by highlighting the field in Define Fields, choosing Global as the field type and clicking the Save button. The validation information will be retained by the field.

Let's say you have a global field with a pop-up menu attached. The problem is that users keep entering custom values that cause problems. Adding a validation to this global field could be used to prevent the problem.

This quirk has been around since FileMaker Pro 3.0 was released. It is an excellent FileMaker Pro trick that will not cause problems when converting databases from 3.0 to later versions.

Setting validations for globals

This is a chart of the validations that can be applied to global fields.

<u>Yes</u>	<u>No</u>
In Range	Not Empty
Of Type	Unique
Member of Value List	Existing
Calculated Validation	

Single entry fields

Open this file and follow along

◎ **15_C.FP3**

Chapter File:
Single Entry Fields

The Access Privileges feature in FileMaker Pro is the most common method for preventing modification to data. You can lock users out of layouts, records and fields as well prevent modifications to a record once the data has been entered. What isn't possible is preventing modifications at the field level.

There is a validation technique for locking a field so that data may be entered only once. Once the field has been exited, an error message will appear on any subsequent attempts to modify the field. Additional features include allowing password access via a control field.

The inside secret to this technique lies in the auto-enter options of a field. By adding an auto-enter (by calculation) field, whatever is entered into the field being validated will automatically be copied into the auto-enter field. The auto-enter will only occur the first time a value is entered into the validation field. A simple calculated validation comparing the two fields is all that's needed to prevent future modifications to the validation field. If the two fields don't

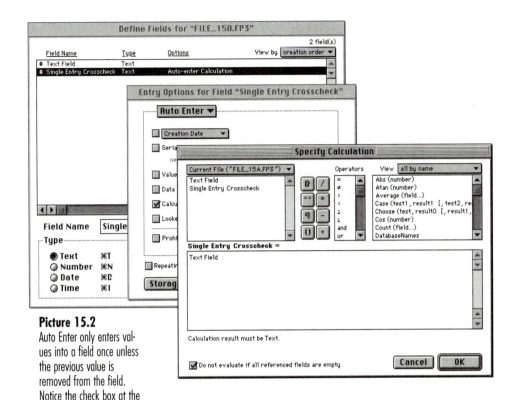

Picture 15.2

Auto Enter only enters values into a field once unless the previous value is removed from the field. Notice the check box at the bottom that reads Do not evaluate if all referenced fields are empty.

PREVENT.FP3

Technique File:
Prevent Modification

match, an error message will appear warning the user that the field is not modifiable. You'll find this technique on the CD ROM in both 15_C.FP3 and PREVENT.FP3.

This technique could be used in an invoicing system. All users need to be able to enter invoices, but once a value is accepted, only the person who created the record should be able to modify certain fields. Add a field that auto-enters the user name when a record is created and an additional test to the validation that checks to see if the person modifying the record is also the current user. This will provide a level of security not possible with access privileges.

Cross-field validations

Open this file and follow along

We highly recommend you use the file on the CD ROM along with the book explanation since this technique is quite complicated.

15_D.FP3

Chapter File:
Cross Field Validations

In a database that tracks Internet IP addresses, you want to prevent duplicate addresses. Tracking a single IP address is simple using the Unique validation option. However, in some cases it's possible for a single machine to have two IP addresses. You could use a single record for each IP address, but if you wanted to store the IP addresses according to machine it would require two fields on one record. The dilemma is that it's necessary to verify that the IP address is unique across both fields and for the entire database. This can be accomplished with a technique called cross-field validations.

The first concept you need to be familiar with is the order FileMaker Pro uses when evaluating data entry.

FileMaker Pro's Order of Evaluation

The steps FileMaker Pro goes through when evaluating new data
1. Lookups are triggered and data is copied into the lookup field
2. Validations occur on any fields in the record
3. Relationships are resolved and data on the screen is refreshed

Most attempts to validate across multiple fields involve using a relationship. Since validation occurs before the resolution of a relationship, the validation will occur before the relationship is updated (see FileMaker Pro's Order of Evaluation above). The workaround is to use a lookup since it evaluates before a validation. A calculation that concatenates the IP address fields, two **self relationships** and a lookup field for each IP address are all that's needed.

The calculation named "Relationship calc" is written as follows:

```
IP address 1 & "¶" & IP address 2
```

The result of the calculation on a record might look like this:

192.128.256.256
192.128.256.251

The carriage return between the two IP addresses enables the two values to be seen as separate match values for a relationship.

Picture 15.2.1
Using a lookup to cross check other fields in the database allows for cross-field validations.

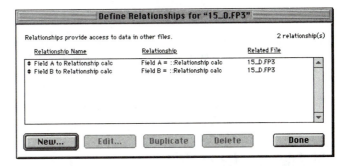

The **self relationships** use the IP address fields on the left side and the calculation field on the right side (see Picture 15.2.1). There's a relationship for each field to be validated. Two lookup fields are added and are based on the two self relationships. To cross check the fields, the value from the calculation is copied during the lookup. It really doesn't matter which field is copied as long as the field does not contain only a

Picture 15.2.2
The trick to resolving cross-field validation is to use a value you know will be used if there are NO matches. Any other match will trigger the validation.

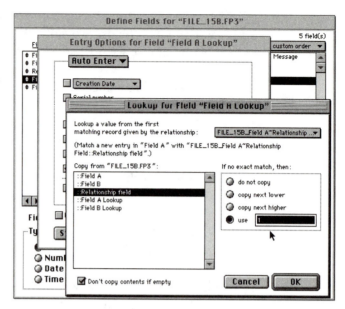

one (1). What matters is, the value copied when there are no matching records. When no match occurs, a one (1) is copied as specified in the lookup options (see Picture 15.2.2). The (1) one is used by the validation to signal that the values are okay to use.

Now that the groundwork has been laid, you can create the calculated validation on the IP Address fields. The calculations are simple:

Field Validation for IP Field 1

1. How Field 1 checks Field 2 for occurrences of a value
Because FileMaker Pro lookups are triggered before validations occur, it is possible to lookup a value and then perform a validation based on the value.

```
Case(
IP Address 1 = IP Address 2,  0,  - Error because the same IP is in both fields
IP Address 1 Lookup = 1,  1,  - There are no matches in the rest of the database so validate to true
0
)
```

Field Validation for IP Field 2

1. How Field 2 checks Field 1 for occurrences of a value

Because FileMaker Pro lookups are triggered before validations occur, it is possible to lookup a value and then perform a validation based on the value.

```
Case(
IP Address 2 = IP Address 1, 0, - Error because the same IP is in both fields
IP Address 2 Lookup = 1, 1, - There are no matches in the rest of the database so validate to true
0
)
```

The validations check to see whether or not the IP Address Lookup fields contain the numeric value one (1), as well as to make sure the same IP Address is not used in both entry fields. If they contain a one then the entry is valid, otherwise a duplicate is present. The chapter example file 15_D.FP3 breaks this technique down.

Validating for duplicates

Open this file and follow along

One of the more common practices for a database is removing duplicates. Instead of searching for duplicates after they have been entered, a better solution is to be alerted about a duplicate as soon as it is entered.

15_E.FP3

Chapter File:
Duplicate Validations

The first step in validating for duplicates is creating a calculation that uniquely identifies a record. The example file on the CD that accompanies this section simply concatenates a first and last name field. It's likely that using just a person's full name will return more than one person in your database with the same name (e.g. John Smith).

DUP.FP3

Technique File:
Duplicate Warning

The following are a couple of example calculations that will help you design your own unique record identifier.

Unique identifiers for records

1. Concatenating values to make a unique identifier

Identifying a record requires that there be some sort of unique attribute. If there isn't a value like a social security number, email address or IP number, it may be necessary to create one out of the data available.

```
First Name & " " & Last Name & " " & LeftWords(Address, 1)
```

or this...

```
First Name & " " & Last Name & " " & Right(Phone, 4)
```

There is no master calculation that will work for everyone. Think about what combination of information allows you to uniquely identify that record before designing a custom calculation.

UNIQ_VAL.FP3

Technique File:
Validating Calc Fields

Notice the spaces between the quotes in the calculations above. FileMaker Pro only indexes the first twenty characters of each word and the index is used when a lookup is performed. The spaces are concatenated between each field to ensure that each word never gets longer than twenty characters. For instance, the following two strings would be considered the same by the index:

JohnTimothySmith1234568
versus
JohnTimothySmith1234567

as opposed to

John Timothy Smith 1234568
versus
John Timothy Smith 1234567

which are seen as two different strings.

! Power Tip

When using concatenated keys for relationships, make sure the key does not exceed 20 characters per word (see Chapter 14 about the FileMaker index and storage settings). The first 60 characters of the field is the maximum length of a relationship key.

After creating your unique identifier calculation, you can concentrate on how to show a validation error message for the duplicate. All you need is a **self relationship** using the the field that checks for duplicates as the match field and a validation calculation.

Lookups are evaluated before validations. A lookup, named "Validator", based on the duplicate checking calculation, as the trigger field, can determine if a matching record exists. In the Chapter file provided for this section, the Validator field copies the Last Name field into itself. If there is no exact match, a one (1) is entered (see Picture 15.2.3).

Picture 15.2.3
Using a default value when there is no match allows you to check fields with a validated calculation.

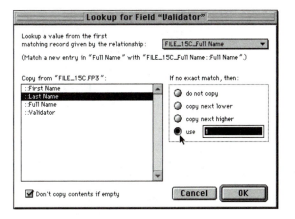

A one is entered when there is no match because the Validator field is used in the validation calculation. A one is evaluated as true and zero is evaluated as false. If a last name is copied in the lookup, the text will be evaluated as zero. Actually, the characters "y" and "t" will be evaluated as ones so these need to be removed before the validation occurs. The formula that appears in the chapter file is on the following page.

Validation calculation for duplicate checking

1. Example of what to do

Even though a lookup is based on a relationship, it is resolved before a validation occurs. This makes it possible for validation calculations to check for duplicates. (see Chapter file 15_E.FP3)

```
TextToNum(
Substitute(
Substitute(

Validator,

 "y", ""),
 "t", "")
)
```

The nested Substitute function removes any letters that could be incorrectly evaluated as the Boolean value of one (1). For instance, if the last name "Smith" is pulled into the Validator field, the nested Substitute functions will return "Smih" instead. With the name Smith the "t" would be used by FileMaker Pro to evaluate as true. Any text other than "y" and "t" will be evaluated as zero and thus return the error message from the field validation.

There are many techniques available for removing duplicates from a database. This validation technique can be employed to prevent duplicates from being entered in the first place.

Test yourself to see what you've learned.

1. **Validations resulting in a Boolean false, a zero (0), will?**
   - ○ Do nothing
   - ○ Show the validation message
   - ○ Trigger a lookup
   - ○ All of the above

2. **Validating for multiple criteria can involve the use of...**
   - ○ A Case statement
   - ○ The AND operator
   - ○ The OR operator
   - ○ All of the above

3. **A global field can only be validated if?**
   - ○ A calculation is linked to it
   - ○ It contains a value before setting the options
   - ○ Validation options are set before it's converted into a global
   - ○ All of the above

4. **A field set to use an auto-enter calculation referencing another field will?**
   - ○ Copy the value into the field the first time data is entered and the referenced field is exited
   - ○ Copy the value each time the field is changed
   - ○ Enter the value when a record is created
   - ○ All of the above

5. **The order of evaluation for FileMaker Pro is?**
   - ○ Relationships, lookups and validations
   - ○ Validations, lookups and relationships
   - ○ Lookups, relationship and validations
   - ○ None of the above

6. **When validating for duplicates, what feature is most important?**
   - ○ Lookup
   - ○ Replace
   - ○ Find
   - ○ All of the above

7. **How many characters are indexed per word?**
   - ○ 60
   - ○ 40
   - ○ 20
   - ○ 10

8. **How many characters are indexed for a relationship?**
   - ○ 60
   - ○ 40
   - ○ 20
   - ○ 10

Answers:

Answers: 1. Show the validation message 2. All of the above 3. Validation options are set before it's converted into a global 4. Copy the value into the field the first time data is entered and the referenced field is exited 5. None of the above 6. Lookup 7. 20 8. 60

What you should have learned
- How to use basic validations
- How to implement powerful calculated validations
- Validating global fields
- Unique ways of using validations for checking data including; cross-field validations, duplicate validations and single entry fields

More technique files about validations

RECORD.FP3
Preventing Record Modification

Three methods for preventing record modification using validation and passwords.

VALID.FP3
Layout Validation

Limiting a field validation to a particular layout.

FALSE.FP3
Always Validate False

Shows how to prevent a field from being modified without a password scheme or additional calculation fields.

CREDIT.FP3
Credit Card Checker

Validate credit cards with a script. Validation calculation to make sure the card has not expired.

Value Lists

16.0 Defining Value Lists

One of the new features in FileMaker Pro 4.0 is the Define Value Lists menu item. It can be found in the File menu under the Define sub-menu. This is great for accessing and defining value lists quickly. The other method for adding, deleting and adjusting value lists is to enter Layout Mode and choose the Field Format menu item from the Format menu while a field is selected. Once presented with the dialog box, the rest is a matter of selecting the type of list (pop-up list, pop-up menu [pull-down], check box or radio button). With FileMaker Pro 4.0 the new method for defining value lists is a real time saver since you don't have to enter layout mode.

Picture 16.0
Define a value list first by selecting the field and then selecting the type of value list.

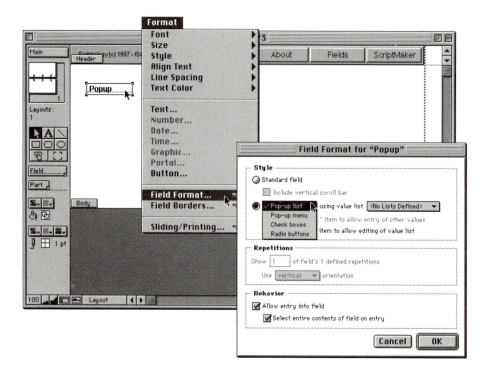

The different format styles

Picture 16.0.1
The Other option for Pop-up menus allows for custom input. The Edit option gives user access to the values in the value list.

Most users know radio buttons allow one selection and check boxes allow as many choices as checked. The difference between pop-up menus and pop-up lists, however, is more subtle. Pop-up menus are restricted to the defined value list, but can include an option for "Other" which allows custom input. The pop-up list, on the other hand, allows custom input from the user by clicking twice in the field. The first click shows the value list while the second enters the field allowing input. Both enable the designer to include the Edit option, allowing the user to make changes to the attached value list.

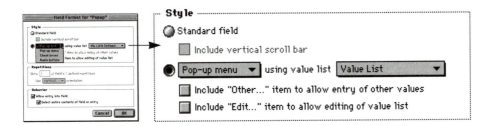

Dynamic Value Lists

One of the most useful value list options is the "Use values from a field:" found in the Define Value Lists dialog box (see Picture 16.0.2). Selecting this option will change your lists from static to dynamic by incorporating the index values from another field. Typically, these are used in pop-up menus and pop-up lists, but what few people know is that they can also be used with radio buttons and check boxes. Making the field large enough to accommodate all the possible choices is an important point to remember when using this technique.

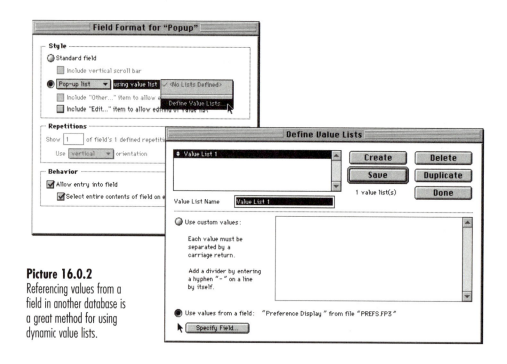

Picture 16.0.2
Referencing values from a field in another database is a great method for using dynamic value lists.

Multiple selections

Whenever selecting multiple items from a pop-up menu or radio buttons (selecting with the shift key depressed) the values are stored in the field as a return-delimited list. If multiple items are ever incorrectly selected in a radio button field, hitting the delete key twice after selecting the field will clear all the contents of the field.

One of the more intriguing aspects about radio buttons and check boxes is that any value in the field not part of the value list will be hidden. For instance, let's say you have a radio button with an associated value list of Apple, Orange and Grape. After a lot of data

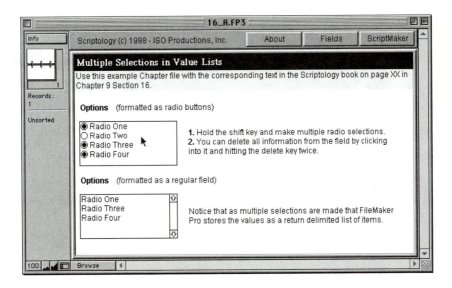

Info | Scriptology (c) 1998 - ISO Productions, Inc. | About | Fields | ScriptMaker

Multiple Selections in Value Lists

Use this example Chapter file with the corresponding text in the Scriptology book on page XX in Chapter 9 Section 16.

Records:
1

Unsorted

Options (formatted as radio buttons)

⦿ Radio One
○ Radio Two
⦿ Radio Three
⦿ Radio Four

1. Hold the shift key and make multiple radio selections.
2. You can delete all information from the field by clicking into it and hitting the delete key twice.

Options (formatted as a regular field)

Radio One
Radio Three
Radio Four

Notice that as multiple selections are made that FileMaker Pro stores the values as a return delimited list of items.

100 | Browse

Picture 16.0.3

Because FileMaker Pro must store all selected values in a field, it does so by actually storing the selections as a return delimited list of items.

Open this file and follow along

⊚ **16_B.FP3**

Chapter File:
Check box values

has been entered into the database, you may decide to change the Grape value list choice to Banana.

The previously selected Grape option will cause "Grape" to remain in the fields on the records where it was selected. It will be hidden from view, however, because only items in the value list are displayed in fields formatted as check boxes or radio buttons.

So the change from

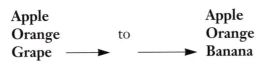

Apple		**Apple**
Orange	to	Orange
Grape ⟶		⟶ Banana

means records with the previous selection of Grape will still contain that value. In most cases this won't cause problems, but there's no reason to have it remain in the field. The best way to get rid of this extraneous data is to use a calculated Replace (see

---

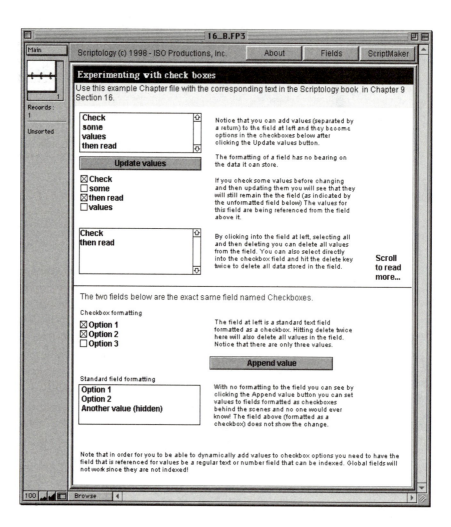

Picture 16.0.4
16_B.FP3 demonstrates how check boxes store their values.

Chapter 11 Section 17) with the Substitute function. It may be possible to use this knowledge about radio buttons and check boxes for something productive but think of it more as a troubleshooting technique.

Facts about fields formatted as value lists (check boxes, radio buttons, pop-ups)

- Multiple values selected are stored in fields as individual values separated by a return character.
- Radio buttons and check boxes can be dynamic - they can adjust their selectable values based on the contents of another field.
- Clicking in a field formatted as check boxes or radio buttons and hitting the delete key twice will delete all the data from the field.
- Fields formatted as radio buttons or check boxes can store more values than are available in their associated value lists.

16.1 Hierarchical decisions

You've seen how values in a pop-up menu can come from a statically defined list or from another field (dynamic). A popular request for a FileMaker Pro feature is hierarchical value lists (also known as conditional value lists). Conditional value lists are two or more linked pop-up menus. A choice from one pop-up menu determines what is shown in another pop-up menu. For instance, a choice of chocolate from the ice cream pop-up menu might show you Rocky Road, Chocolate Chip and Double Chocolate from the flavor pop-up menu. For now, all conditional pop-up menu techniques require a script in order to work.

Power Tip

FileMaker, Inc. may add a feature for conditional pop-up menus in a future release of FileMaker Pro.

Knowing that values can be referenced from any field, in any FileMaker Pro file, provides you with the opportunity to create conditional lists. If you haven't played with the option for referencing values in another field, the rest of this chapter will make little sense (see Picture 16.1). There are many conditional menu techniques, and all of them require using a script to change the contents of the second list. The scripts that enable this capability are covered in the next section.

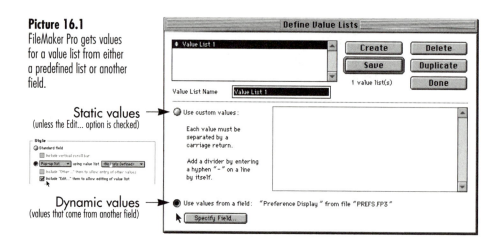

Picture 16.1
FileMaker Pro gets values for a value list from either a predefined list or another field.

Static values
(unless the Edit... option is checked)

Dynamic values
(values that come from another field)

The basics

By combining FileMaker Pro's features, you can create the effect of hierarchical or conditional menus. There are many different methods – each with advantages and disadvantages. Learn all of them in order to make the best choice for your solution:

• Portal method
• Multiple files method
• Calculation method
• Relationship method

The trick to understanding conditional menus is understanding that the FileMaker Pro index stores all the values for each field as separate words. The values in field x on record 1, if different than those in field x on record 2, will merge together to create a larger value list possibly including undesirable values as options. The objective is to isolate those values that correspond to a selection made from the first menu. Because a script must be invoked, conditional menu techniques require the use of a pop-up list rather than a pull-down menu. The characteristics of a pull-down menu do not allow it to be activated by a script. It can only be activated using the mouse. A pop-up list, however, can be displayed by entering the field via keyboard or mouse and continues to display the list until a selection is made. This enables you to attach a script to the pop-up list field that sets the correct choices for the conditional menu. Once the choices are set, the menu can be shown via the Go to Field script step.

It is important to use the files on the CD ROM along with this section since the techniques here are described in theory. Once you understand the general concept, pick apart the files on the CD ROM for a full appreciation of the specifics.

Hierarchical menus

HIERMENU.FP3

Technique File:
Hierarchical Menus

The portal method is the easiest of all conditional menu techniques. The first pop-up list serves as the **primary key** for a relationship. When a choice is made from the first pop-up list, a portal displays records from a related file corresponding to that choice. The portal doesn't store the choice, but transfers the data to a second field using a script once the selection is made. By incorporating a second layout, you can create a visual simulation that makes the portal seem like a pop-up list. Use the example on the CD ROM (HIERMENU.FP3) to see how well a second layout can trick the user into believing a pop-up list, rather than a portal is being shown. A second layout isn't necessary for this method to function, but is a nice visual effect for the user interface.

The biggest advantage of this method is the ease of implementation. It has a straightforward design with very few script steps. This technique can also be used, without modification, in a multi-user scenario. However, the use of multiple layouts and a portal make this solution less professional looking.

Multiple file conditional menus

COND.FP3

Technique File:
Conditional Menus

The second method for conditional menus incorporates two additional files to accomplish the task. Each possible choice corresponds to a record in one file, while the choices for the second pop-up list are stored in another file. For instance, foods are stored in one database according to type (e.g. Apples, Oranges, and Grapes as Fruits, Chicken, Beef and Pork as Meats) while the choices for the current pop-up menu are stored in another database (e.g. Apple, Oranges, Grapes). For this example, let's refer to your file as "File 1" and the additional files as "File 2" and "File 3".

A script attached to the second pop-up list initiates the Go to Related Record step. This important step locates all the related records in File 2. There is an option on the Go to Related Record step, titled "Show", which locates only the records related to the current master file record. Since the first pop-up list is the match field in the relationship, the found records correspond to the choice made from the first pop-up list.

The next script step uses the Copy All Records step to capture a return separated list of values. This list is a subset of the records in File 2 because of the Go to Related script step in the previous script. A Perform Script step calls a script in File 3 which pastes into a field. File 3 contains one record and a single field called "Choices". This is where the list of values is pasted.

At the completion of the sub-script in the third file, the original file regains control and finishes the remaining script steps. These steps activate the second pop-up list that's based on the values copied from the second file into the "Choices" field in the third file. This list is now visible thanks to the Field Format option that allows you to use the values from the "Choices" field in File 3.

This technique is also fairly easy to implement. The scripts are not that complicated and it functions fairly quickly. There are two disadvantages; disruption of the clipboard and multi-user implementation. If a user manually copies a graphic or text clipping into the clipboard, the Copy All Records step in the script will erase the contents of the clipboard. Another drawback is the use of this solution in a multi-user setting. Since adding a record to track each user's pop-up choices would create a value list incorporating many pop-up choices from each user, the value list for the second menu would be as large as the number of selections made by users.

Calculated conditional menus

COND2.FP3

Technique File:
Conditional Menus 2

The third conditional menus method uses a second file to store each set of choices on a record. If you have ten choices in the first pop-up list, there will be ten records in the second file. Each of those ten records will store the corresponding choices for the second pop-up list. When the second pop-up list is triggered, a script marks the record in the second file corresponding to the selection made in the first pop-up list. This causes a calculation to return the results for the second pop-up list. The only record in the second file that returns values from the calculation is the one marked. Hence, it is necessary for the script to unmark the record used for the previous pop-up.

The advantage to this method is the ability to add another level of conditional menus, without increasing the number of files. As with most of the other methods, the biggest disadvantage with this technique is that it cannot be used in a multi-user scenario.

Single file conditional menus

POPUP_1.FP3

Technique File:
Conditional Menus 3

The fourth method is one of the best methods since it relies on a single FileMaker Pro file and uses succinct scripts. All that's needed is a self relationship, a few fields and some short scripts to track the record last used for a pop-up list. When the second pop-up list is triggered, the script locates the previous record, removes the contents of the field storing the pop-up choices and places the new choices in the current record.

The records are tracked using a **self relationship**. The match fields in the relationship are a global field on the left side and a serial number on the right side. Each record is assigned a unique serial number when it is created. The global field stores the previously selected record's serial number. This allows the relationship to uniquely identify a record at any time. It enables the script to use the Set Field step to erase the pop-up choices from the previous record and place the new choices on the current record. Therefore, the index for the second value list options only contain those relevant to the selection made in the first value list.

The biggest advantages with this technique are the use of a single file and short scripts that run very quickly. Again, the disadvantage is the inability to implement this solution in a multi-user scenario. Of the four hierarchical menu solutions, only the portal technique is viable in a multi-user environment.

16.2 Click into pop-ups

Open this file and follow along

FileMaker Pro doesn't always deal with pop-up lists in a desirable way. On some occasions, it is preferable for the user to click directly into a field to enter custom options, at other times they will want to pop-up a menu with predefined choices. This can be accom-

16_B.FP3

Chapter File:
Check box values

Picture 16.2
By dechecking the Behavior setting of Allow entry into field you can place one field on top of another. Clicking into the field will "click through" the field on top and enter the field underneath it.

Clicking into the field does not produce a value list.

Clicking the pop-up arrow provides the value list.

By placing a copy of the field on top of the original you can achieve layout object layering. The field on bottom is a non-entry field and has a value list. The field on top is a standard field that allows entry into the field.

plished with the pop-up list feature built-in to FileMaker Pro, but the user must click twice to enable custom data entry. A pop-up menu can also accomplish the task, but requires the user to choose the "other" option from the pop-up menu, type the entry into a dialog and click a button to accept the data. The solution offered in this section allows the user to use a single click on the field for custom data entry, and click on an arrow button beside the field to display a value list.

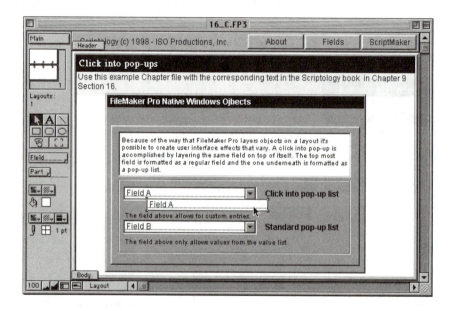

POPUP.FP3

Technique File:
Pop-up menus

To make this happen, it is necessary to understand how FileMaker Pro treats layered objects. If a field is placed on the same layout twice, a script using the Go to Field step will activate the field placed on the layout first, regardless of whether the field is set to allow entry or is in the current tab order or not. The trick to this technique is to place a copy of the field without formatting on top of the field formatted as a pop-up list. The bottom field formatted as a pop-up list should also be taken out of the tab order.

To complete the interface for this solution, add a button to the right of the fields. This button, with an attached Go to Field step, is the only way to access the pop-up list. When tabbing or clicking through the fields, the pop-up list will not appear because it has been removed from the tab order and set to non-entry.

Chapter 10 Overview & Quiz

Test yourself to see what you've learned.

1. **Fields formatted as a pop-up, check box or radio button store multiple values in the field by?**
   - ○ Adding them with the Edit... options
   - ○ Adding them to a hidden field
   - ○ Separating them with a return
   - ○ All of the above

2. **Value lists that are dynamic come from?**
   - ○ Related fields
   - ○ Fields in the same database
   - ○ The field's index
   - ○ All of the above

3. **It's possible to have more than one occurrence of a field on a layout.**
   - ○ With the same formatting
   - ○ With different formatting
   - ○ With a scroll bar
   - ○ All of the above

4. **Pop-up menus don't work well for hierarchical value lists because?**
   - ○ A script must be activated
   - ○ They are too slow
   - ○ The Other... option breaks the link
   - ○ All of the above

5. **Check boxes, radio buttons, pop-up lists and pop-up menus are all?**
   - ○ Field formats
   - ○ Different field types
   - ○ The same field type
   - ○ All of the above

6. **What is the best conditional pop-up menu technique for a multi-user environment?**
   - ○ Hierarchical Menus
   - ○ Multiple file conditional menus
   - ○ Calculated conditional menus
   - ○ All of the above

7. **Multiple selections in a radio button field can be done using?**
   - ○ Control key
   - ○ Shift key
   - ○ Shift and Control keys
   - ○ It's not possible

Answers:

Answers: 1. Separating them with a return 2. All of the above 3. All of the above 4. A script must be activated 5. Field formats 6. Hierarchical Menus 7. Shift key

What you should have learned
- How FileMaker Pro stores multiple choices from value list selections
- How to create dynamic value lists
- How to implement conditional menu techniques
- How to optimize data entry and interface functionality with pop-ups

More technique files about value lists

LISTS.FP3
Field Based Value Lists

Value lists generated from two fields show all possible values for both fields.

SCROLL.FP3
Scroll Through

An alternative to pop-up menus. This file cycles through values found in a regular text field.

RADIO.FP3
Radio Buttons

A file that instructs how to make radio buttons look attractive in the Windows OS.

Data Operations

17.0 Powerful FileMaker Pro techniques

Until recently, FileMaker Pro has been considered merely an end-user database system. Other database platforms, with roots in the relational market, have long had a strong hold on the high-end market. However, FileMaker Pro can handle most of the same data tasks as these rivals. In fact, most database systems are more appropriate for FileMaker Pro since the development process requires a fraction of the time.

In this chapter you'll learn about some of the more powerful techniques for manipulating data. As you are reading, remember that FileMaker Pro can accomplish almost any task, if you give it the chance. You just need to consider the range of features and how they can be combined to accomplish a task.

17.1 The Replace function and using it for power

Picture 17.1
The Replace option is one of the most useful tools for data manipulation.

Replace is one of the scariest commands in FileMaker Pro. If used incorrectly, data in a field across the entire database can be wiped out. Think of it the same as you would the Find/Replace feature in your favorite word processor. It replaces all the data in the current found set for the selected field. The power of Replace can cause havoc, but it can also save time. When the time comes to change all values in a field, it's much quicker to use Replace than any other method (e.g. such as a record looping script). After invoking the Replace dialog, you are given the option to replace the field contents of all found records with the value that is currently in the field, with serial

Picture 17.1.1

The value in the field at the point you start the replace will be the value used for all records in the found set.

```
═══════════════ Replace ═══════════════

Permanently replace the contents of the field
"Name" in the 60 records of the current found set?

● Replace with: "Some other value"
                                    ▶

○ Replace with serial numbers:

    Initial value: [1              ]

    Increment by:  [1              ]

    ☐ Update serial number in Entry Options?

○ Replace with calculated result:  [ Specify... ]

                          [ Replace ] [ Cancel ]
```

numbers, or with a calculated result (see Picture 17.1.1). The current value of the field and the serial numbers are pretty straightforward; it's the calculated replace that is the most powerful and will be covered in the following sections.

17.2 Calculated Replace statements

Open this file and follow along

◎ **17_A.FP3**

Chapter File:
Using Replace Options

Think of a conference where there are 25 people wearing red shirts, 36 people wearing orange shirts and 14 people wearing blue shirts. With a magical power, you could make all people wearing red shirts turn to purple, those wearing orange change to green and those in blue change to pink. This magical power in FileMaker Pro is called a calculated Replace. Instead of replacing the same thing on every record in the found set, a calculated Replace can make decisions based on the contents of each record. The result is the placement of custom values on each record.

Performing a calculated replace accomplishes the same result as a looping script which cycles through all the records in a found set. The looping script can

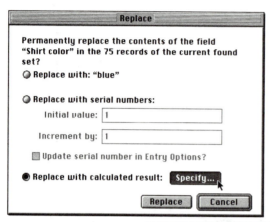

SUB_NUM.FP3

Technique File:
Numbering
Sub-Summaries

perform conditional script steps to determine how to manipulate each record. The calculated Replace works nearly the same as a looping script, but is much faster. Using the shirt example, the Case statement in the calculated Replace can change the shirt colors (see Picture 17.2).

Picture 17.2
By using a Case statement within a calculated Replace, you can control the shirt color conversion.

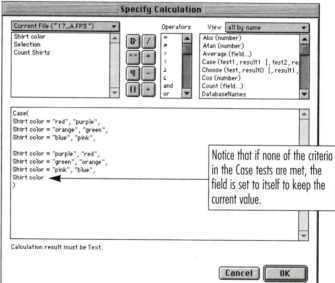

Avoiding problems with Replace

It's not advisable to give users access to perform a manual Replace. In order to prevent accidental Replaces, use Access Privileges to remove it from the Mode menu. This is done by creating a limited password with the Editing Only option selected (see Picture 17.2.1). If a Replace is accidentally performed, it is almost impossible to undo the damage unless a backup of the database has been made.

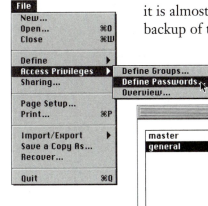

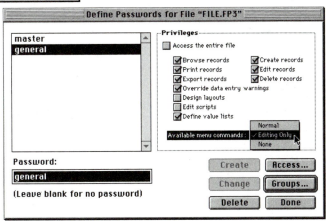

Picture 17.2.1
Using Access Privileges to define a limited password with Editing Only capabilities, limits a user's ability to use the Replace function.

⚠ Power Tip

FileMaker Pro saves on idle (i.e. records are not being edited and scripts are not running). FileMaker Pro will save no more than every five seconds.

There are ways to correct errant Replaces, but they are quite drastic. Do not rely on these techniques, but use them as a last resort. The first method will work if FileMaker Pro is set to save at specified times. The default setting is to save during idle times, but can be changed via Preferences in the Memory settings area. It is possible to set FileMaker Pro to save the database to disk at specified intervals of 10, 15, 30 or 60 minutes. If an errant Replace has occurred, you must

---

force quit the program (Command-Option-Esc on Macintosh or Control-Alt-Del on Windows) before the next save occurs. There is a possibility that this could damage your database beyond repair, so make sure you have a backup. Most likely, the database will open after performing a consistency check and work fine. The data in the database should be the same as it was before the replace was performed.

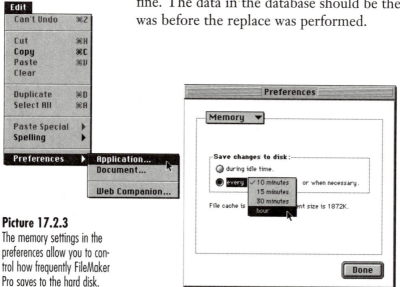

Picture 17.2.3
The memory settings in the preferences allow you to control how frequently FileMaker Pro saves to the hard disk.

Another way to catch an unintentional Replace is to interrupt the Replace. The advantage of this technique is that you don't have to set your database to save at intervals. In order for this method to work, the Replace cannot have finished yet. If it finishes, the replaced data will be saved immediately. To interrupt the computer, turn the computer off or try force quitting FileMaker Pro and restart your computer (Command-Option-Esc on Macintosh or Control-Alt-Del on Windows). Most likely, your database will open after performing a consistency check. If it does not, you will need to use the Recover command to fix the file. If Recover does not work, you'll need to revert to a backup.

WARNING ▶ These solutions should be used as a last resort only. If you are the one who performed the errant Replace rather than a user, these solutions may work well. To prevent yourself from performing an errant Replace, read the entire Replace dialog before continuing. Simply reading the dialog and confirming the action really will prevent most Replace problems.

17.3 Data piggybacking

Open this file and follow along

◎ **17_B.FP3**

Chapter File:
Set Field
Appending & Striping

Data piggybacking is useful for optimizing the data structure in your FileMaker Pro files. It allows you to place multiple pieces of data in a single field instead of creating a field to store every single piece of information. This technique is familiar to anyone who has done any type of programming, though in most cases, the terminology is different. The term "piggybacking" is used here because it is easy to remember.

Most complex database solutions will contain fields that are not visible to the user. These fields usually store data specific to the operations, or any data that the user simply does not need to see. Data piggybacking optimizes these operations by storing more than one piece of information per field. This reduces the number of fields in Define Fields which increases the efficiency of your solution.

For example, suppose you are storing IP address related information in a field. IP addresses can be stored in a field along with port data, but be accessed separately. Simply append the port number to the existing IP address, adding a distinguishing separator between the two pieces of data. A dash could be used as the delimiter between the IP address and the port number. Any time you need to reference the port number, use a calculation that grabs the end of the

Regular IP address	192.255.138.45
IP address with port number	192.255.138.45-80

TCP/IP address. This can be accomplished by using the Position function in the following calculation:

```
Right(IP Address, Length(IP Address) - Position(IP
Address, "-", 1, 1))
```

[!] Power Tip

Common delimiters are the return character (symbolized in FileMaker Pro by ¶), a colon, dash, comma (comma delimited) and the tab (tab delimited) character.

This calculation simply extracts the value that was appended to the end of the IP address and sets it to another field for further manipulation. The Position function looks for the location of the dash within the field. Subtracting the position of the dash from the total length of the field returns the number of characters occupied by the port number. The number of characters is used as the parameter for the Right function in order to grab the port number.

The most common implementation of this calculation is in a Set Field script step. Set Field allows you to add, move or remove the port number from the end of the IP address. The example above moves the port number to another field. The following calculation deletes the port number from the IP address storage field:

```
Left(IP Address, Position(IP Address, "-", 1, 1) -
1)
```

The purpose of this information is not specific to IP addresses but helps highlight a method for compiling multiple pieces of data into one field. As long as you the developer, know the specifics about how the data is being stored in a field, you can use calculations and scripts to work with, compare and manipulate data. The general term for this technique is "piggybacking".

Any character can be used as a delimiter between data in a field. The key is to select a character that will not be part of the data placed in the field. For instance, if you are placing phone numbers in a data piggybacking field, the dash will not work. In this case, an asterisk might work better. Other common delimiters include the carriage return, comma, pound sign, exclamation point and carat. Pick the character that works for you and your data.

17.4 Set Field power – appending extracting & subtracting

Open this file and follow along

◎ **17_C.FP3**

Chapter File:
Set Field Operations

⚠ Power Tip

Set Field is capable of referencing the same field it's set to perform on. For example, Using Set Field on a field named Text Field can reference Text Field within its calculation settings.

The previous section briefly discussed the Set Field script step. Set Field is one of the most powerful script steps because it works whether or not the field is present on the current layout, through relationships and on any type of field (unlike copy and paste which require fields to be on the layout). In addition, Set Field utilizes calculation formulas which make it able to manipulate data better than any other script step. With the Set Field command, you can control almost any aspect of your database. Using it allows you to perform mathematical, text, graphic and any operation you can imagine. Think of Set Field as a calculation that can be invoked on the fly at any time. With this capability, you can control any piece of data, anywhere in your group of files.

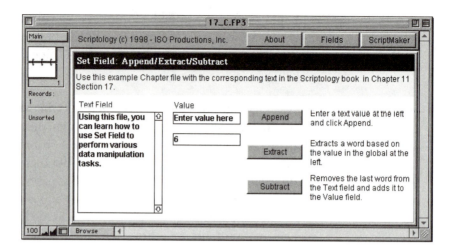

Picture 17.4
17_C.FP3 contains a few examples of scripts that use Set Field to append, extract and subtract data from a field.

 **FUNCTNS.FP3**

Reference File:
Calculation Functions

The following sections cover how to use Set Field to append, subtract and extract data. These techniques use the Position(), Left(), Right(), Middle(), Length() and other text functions. Make sure you are familiar with the basic operation of these functions before continuing. Look to Appendix B or the Reference file on the CD ROM called FUNCTNS.FP3. In addition, use the Chapter file on the CD ROM titled 17_C.FP3 to assist in the following sections.

Appending data

> **! Power Tip**
>
> A direct import from one FileMaker Pro database to another is, in some cases, the quickest way to get information from file to file. Another way is to use a script with multiple Set Fields to move the data in a batch.

Appending data to a field is the simplest technique. All you have to do is concatenate two fields. Here is the example from 17_C.FP3:

```
Text Field & " " & Value
```

The above calculation is used in a Set Field script step. The specified field is the Text Field which is the same as the field referenced in the calculation. This is what allows the calculation to append to itself. You set a field to itself plus the contents of another field.

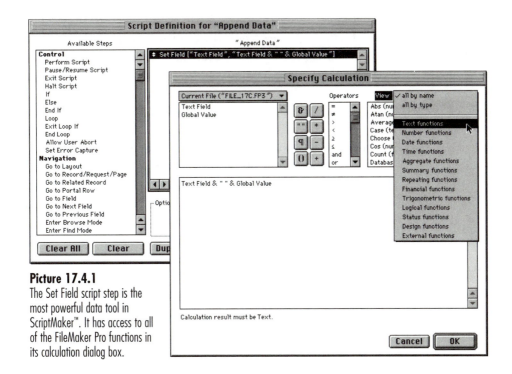

Picture 17.4.1
The Set Field script step is the most powerful data tool in ScriptMaker™. It has access to all of the FileMaker Pro functions in its calculation dialog box.

Extracting data

Extracting data involves two Set Field steps. The first Set Field step places the value in another field and the second step removes the value from the origin field. Here is the calculation that moves the data:

```
MiddleWords(Text Field, Number, 1)
```

This calculation uses the MiddleWords() function to grab one word starting from a value provided by the Number field. When you look at 17_C.FP3, you'll see that the Number field is a global field. If the value in the Number field is a two, the Set Field calculation will grab the second word in the Text Field. For more extraction where characters are counted, the Middle() function may work better than MiddleWords().

Once the specified word has been moved to the Value field, it can be removed from the Text Field with a second Set Field step. Here is a calculation that works well for most scenarios:

```
Substitute(Text Field, Value & " ", "")
```

This calculation uses the Substitute function to locate data from the Value field in the Text Field. Since the value you extracted from the Text Field is now in the Value field, the Substitute function will search for that word in the Text Field. It will be replaced with a null value ("") per the replace string parameter. A space character is added to the Value field so only whole words are removed. For instance, say you moved the word "the" to the Value field. The Substitute function would remove the beginning of the word "theory" or the middle of the word "other" because they contain the characters "the". By adding a space to the end of the value, you can search for just the word "the". Unfortunately, this trick does not account for the word "the" followed by punctuation. It will also remove multiple occurrences of "the " if the field contains more than one. The best solution is to use a more complex calculation that removes the word in much the same way it was moved to the Value field. Here is a calculation that works well:

```
LeftWords(Text, Number - 1) & " " &
RightWords(Text, WordCount(text) - number)
```

This calculation works by grabbing all the words before and after the word specified by the Number field and concatenating them together. Since the calculation is set to the same field where the information resides, the word is removed.

Subtracting data

Subtracting data is a lot like extracting data. The difference is that the formula in 17_C.FP3 removes the last word from the Text Field. What makes this example interesting is the avoidance of the RightWords, LeftWords and MiddleWords functions. Without these functions, the formula becomes far more difficult, but teaches much more. Compare the following formulas with the previous section to see how to implement these calculations succinctly. Here is the formula used in the first Set Field step to move the last word in the Text Field to the Value field:

```
Right(

Text Field,

Length(Text Field) - Position(Text Field, " ", 1,
PatternCount(Text Field, " "))

)
```

This formula shows how to use the PatternCount function to determine where the last space in the Text Field is located. This enables the calculation to locate the last word since it follows the last space.

The calculation that removes the last word from the Text Field works in reverse to the previous calculation. It grabs all the characters before the last space and sets them to the Text Field. It also looks for words ending in a period. If the last character in the Text Field is a period, it is not grabbed along with the last word.

```
Left(

Text Field,

Length(Text Field) -
Length(RightWords(Text Field, 1)) - 1 -
(Case(Right(Text Field, 1) = ".", 1, 0))

)
```

Once you understand how the subtraction technique works, try using the LeftWords, RightWords and MiddleWords functions to make the calculation shorter.

17.5 Record isolation

Open this file and follow along

There may be times when you need to isolate a particular record in FileMaker Pro. For example, you could present the user with a preview of a single record or export just the current record. There are many applications for this technique so learn it well.

17_D.FP3

Chapter File:
Isolating Records

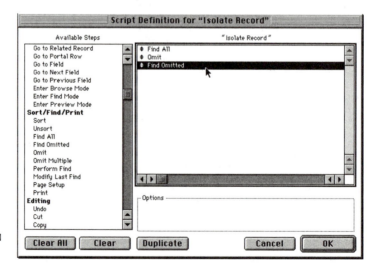

Picture 17.5
Isolating a FileMaker Pro record can be done using a simple three step script.

◎ ISOLATE.FP3

Technique File:
Isolating a Record

◎ PREVIEW.FP3

Technique File:
Previewing the
Current Record

Isolating a record is actually very simple. To explain it well, it's best to start with a discussion of how found sets work in FileMaker Pro. If FileMaker Pro is showing five records out of a database of ten, you have a found set of five. If you are currently on record number three of those five, performing a Find All from the Select menu will leave you on record three with a found set of all ten records. With this knowledge, the script for isolating the current record will make more sense:

```
Find All
Omit
Find Omitted
```

Find All keeps the current record selected, so omitting the current record removes the record you want to isolate from the found set. The Find Omitted script step reverses the found set. Since the found set contained all the records in the database minus the record you were trying to isolate, reversing that found set leaves you with a found set of one record, the record you wanted to isolate. Any script steps that follow will function on the single record rather than the entire found set.

17.6 Global fields and network considerations

If you are planning on creating a FileMaker Pro database that will be shared over a network, there are some considerations you need to make with regards to data and how it is stored. One of the primary considerations is how global fields operate.

Global fields on a **client** (guest) are stored in memory on each users local machine. Changes to a global field do not affect anyone else on the network. This can be confusing at first, but is very necessary and powerful. Imagine what would happen if every user updated the same global field value. The value would change for everyone each time the value was modified. In the case of regular fields, only one person at a time can change the values on a record. This is called record locking. Since global fields transcend records, they need to be tracked locally. This enables a designer to keep universal data for each user so it is available on every record. Once you get used to how global fields work in a multi-user scenario, they become very powerful.

Another point to remember about global fields is how they are initialized. When a user opens a multi-user database, the initial values come from the host machine. Therefore, it is important to initialize global fields with a startup script, or else they may contain an undesirable value. To initialize a global field on startup, add a Set Field to a script that is run on startup. This allows you to override what is set on the host.

17.7 Flagging Data

Open this file and follow along

◎ **17_E.FP3**
Chapter File:
Flagging Data

Flagging data means using a calculation to mark a record according to its condition or status. A flag serves as an indicator or warning as to the status or type of data. A good example of marking a record occurs with a credit card example. A calculation field called Message watches the credit card number field to make sure it has the correct number of digits based on the credit card type. If the credit card does not have the correct number of digits, the record is flagged with a warning notification in a calculation field.

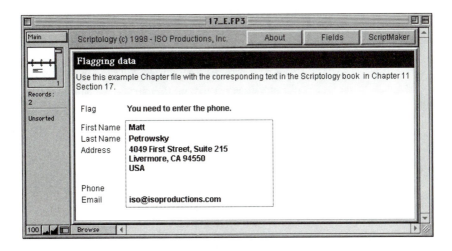

Picture 17.7
The 17_E.FP3 file will show you how a standard message flag is used.

Another good example involves a looping script. The script loops from record to record, flagging records that meet a particular criteria. For instance, you might want to mark all the duplicate records in a database, find them and delete the found set.

(◎) **CREDIT.FP3**

Technique File:
Credit Card Checker

(◎) **MARK.FP3**

Technique File:
Marking Record by Category

Flagging data is a very important concept in FileMaker Pro. You can give users visual cues on screen in the user interface, control a script to make a logical decision, search for data and much more. The uses are as varied as can be imagined. Even so, flags, when used inefficiently, can cause database slow downs. One of the more common uses of a flag is to mark past due invoices. A flag can be used to mark any record that is older than the invoice creation date. Here is a calculation that will flag invoices if they are older than 30 days and haven't been paid:

```
Case(
Creation Date + 30 < Today and Status = "Unpaid",
"Past Due",
""

)
```

The problem with the above calculation is that it recalculates every time you launch the database on a new day. If you have thousands of records, this can take a long time to process. Most likely, you don't check overdue invoices every day, so you don't need to waste your time recalculating the Today function every day. A better solution is to use a script that locates past due invoices when they are needed:

```
Enter Find Mode []
Paste Result [Select, "Invoice Date", ""<" &
DateToText(Status(CurrentDate) - 30)"]
Set Field ["Status", ""Pending""]
Perform Find []
```

The Paste Result script step is used because Set Field can only place date values into a date field. Any values other than a date will attempt to be coerced into a date format by the Set Field step. However, Paste Result does not convert the data, but places it as is.

Finding past due invoices is a great example for considering all the possible outcomes when developing a feature for a solution. Always design three different methods for implementing a feature and analyze the advantages and disadvantages. The most obvious solution is not always the best.

When an on screen visual indicator is desired, the first formula can be used with the Status(CurrentDate) replacing the Today function. Setting the storage option to unstored will provide the user of the database with the visual indication of the status of the invoice.

```
Case(
Creation Date + 30 < Status(CurrentDate) and
Status = "Unpaid", "Past Due",
""
)
```

Chapter 11 Overview & Quiz

Test yourself to see what you've learned.

1. **A calculated replace performed on a field is limited to?**
   - ○ Using fields other than the one being replaced
   - ○ Using the field being replaced
   - ○ Using Global fields
   - ○ None of the above

2. **The term "data piggybacking" refers to?**
   - ○ Grouping data into one field separated by delimiters
   - ○ Using a dash to delimit two values
   - ○ Using one field to reference another field
   - ○ All of the above

3. **The most powerful data manipulation script step is?**
   - ○ Copy
   - ○ Perform Script
   - ○ Set Field
   - ○ If/Then/Else

4. **The three steps for isolating a records are?**
   - ○ Find All, Find Omitted, Omit All
   - ○ Find All, Omit Multiple, Find Omitted
   - ○ Find All, Omit, Find Omitted
   - ○ All of the above

5. **In a multi-user environment, global fields are stored on a client machine in?**
   - ○ The global field itself
   - ○ The computer's memory
   - ○ The hard disk
   - ○ All of the above

6. **Uses for flagging data are?**
   - ○ User interface feedback
   - ○ Conditional decisions
   - ○ Database environment controls
   - ○ All of the above

7. **Which formula will append the value of "1" to the field named Text?**
   - ○ "Text" + 1
   - ○ Text & "1"
   - ○ & "1"
   - ○ None of the above

Answers:

Answers: 1. None of the above 2. Grouping data into one field separated by delimiters 3. Set Field 4. Find All, Omit, Find Omitted 5. The computer's memory 6. All of the above 7. Text & "1"

What you should have learned
- Why the Replace function is so powerful and how to use it
- How to piggyback data
- Why Set Field is so useful and how to use it
- How to isolate a record
- How global fields interact with a networked environment
- When to flag records

More technique files about data operations...

FINDOMIT.FP3
Scripting the Omit Box

Making a script that checks the omit box in the status area while in Find mode.

PREVIEW.FP3
Previewing the Current Record

Directions on isolating the current record so that it can be viewed in Preview mode.

REPLACE.FP3
Simulating Find & Replace

A technique that utilizes the Replace feature and the Substitute function to duplicate the Find/Replace feature.

LABEL.FP3
Printing Multiple Labels

This trick shows a fairly easy method for printing multiple copies of a single label. It uses a record isolation script.

SUB_NUM.FP3
Numbering Sub-summaries

Uses the Replace feature and a relationship to restart the numbers at each sub-summary break.

BACK.FP3
Back and Forward

Simulates the back and forward buttons from a web browser using Set Field and other script steps.

LISTSORT.FP3
Sorting Lists

Demonstrates how to sort a list of values in a field using the Set Field script step.

Understandable Relationships

18.0 Lookups vs. Relationships

In flat-file database systems, (which FileMaker Pro was prior to version 3.0), there are few ways to make correlations between data. FileMaker Pro actually introduced a type of relationship between files called a lookup. Version 3.0 kept this feature and now offers the ability to use a lookup as well as related files. Both methods of data exchange are useful for a variety of database actions.

You should be familiar with a Macintosh Alias, or Windows Shortcut. These two features give you a pointer to an actual file or application on your computer. The advantage is being able to have multiple pointers to one file without duplicating the file or application. This saves a tremendous amount of hard drive space. For example, Microsoft Word may be located in your Programs folder, but you also want to be able to launch it directly from an icon on your desktop. The same is true for data in a FileMaker Pro file. You may need to access information from several different databases, but want to store it in a single file. In this case, a relationship would work exactly like a Shortcut or Alias; it let's you see data stored in external files. In contrast, a lookup does not point, but rather duplicates your data. This would be like putting a full copy of Microsoft Word in multiple places on your hard drive.

Because you can avoid duplicating data, it would seem that a relationship is always better than a lookup. The truth is, it depends on the situation. If you just want to display the most current data in different places, you would use a relationship. A relationship allows you to make one modification and have it reflected wherever that information appears. On the other hand, a lookup makes a copy that reflects the state of that information at the time it's being used. If you need to track a price that may fluctuate at some point in time, you will want to use a lookup. For example, lookups would be better used between a product and invoice database because you would want to maintain, on the original invoice, the price at which a product was ordered. In contrast, a common use of a relationship is between a customer information and an invoice file. You will always want to keep the most current phone number for the customer, so you would use a relationship to ensure that changes in one place are reflected in every other.

Compared to a flat-file database, relational databases are more efficient since they don't have to store multiple copies of the same information. With this efficiency comes complex sounding terms like **data normalization** (the optimization of a database by limiting the amount of data duplication). These classic concepts in database theory have all kinds of rules about how to store data in a relational system. The good part about FileMaker Pro is that you don't have to know these concepts in detail to design a perfectly functional database environment.

18.1 What's a lookup?

As discussed in the previous section, a **lookup** copies data from a field in one database to a corresponding field in another database. As in the case of an orders database, this is exactly what you want to happen. With most products, the price changes over time, but you'll want to keep a record of the original price on the invoice. A lookup will maintain the price over time unless the lookup is triggered again.

When using a lookup, there's a field referred to as the match field (sometimes called a trigger field). This field matches data from one FileMaker Pro file to data in another. When a value in one file matches a value in another file, it triggers the lookup. Unless a Relookup is performed or the trigger field is modified, the copied data will never change.

Picture 18.1
A lookup actually duplicates data from the product file into the line items file.

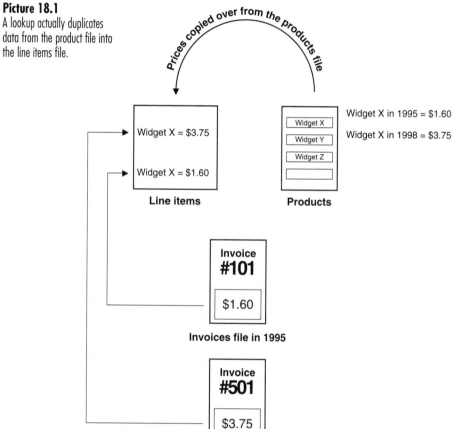

INVOICE.FP3

Technique File:
Invoice

A good example of when to use a lookup is in an invoicing system. It records purchases in a file called Invoices. A purchase could include one or many items. Each item from the Invoices file is stored on a separate record in the Line Items file and is displayed in the Invoices file using a portal. All the products the company sells are stored in a file named Products. Price modifications are entered in the Products file. When a new invoice is created, you want the current price from the Products file to be copied into the Line Items file. A lookup is used so that data is copied and not referenced. Otherwise, a price change in the Products file would change all the referenced prices in the Line Items file and, in turn, update all the prices in the Invoices file. This adjustment would change all the invoice totals, upsetting the accounting end of your operations. The product price on the invoice should never change, even if there is a price increase. It's not desirable to look at an invoice from two years ago and have the price of Widget X at the same price it is today (see Picture 18.1).

When the Invoice file creates a new line item, that line item needs to find the current price. With each product, you'll more than likely have a Product ID. This is a unique value associated to the product. When a new invoice is created and a new line item is added, you enter the Product ID and this triggers FileMaker Pro to copy the associated price. When the Product ID number entered into a line item matches one in the products file, FileMaker Pro will actually duplicate the price associated with that product and store it in the price field of the Line Items file. This data value is now stored in the Line Items file and is not referenced, as it would be with a relationship. It is important to note that the data exists in both the Line Items file and the Products file. Over time, the price in the Products file may change without affecting the price stored in the Line Items file.

18.2 What's a relationship?

While lookups copy data from one file to another, a relationship only references the data. Think of it as a window into another database. FileMaker Pro knows what data to show through the use of a match field. A **match field** enables a record from one file to display information from a record in another file. In the case of a customer file, you may have more than one customer with the same name. A unique match field, such as a Customer ID field, will allow you to link the two files together while avoiding duplicates. Adding a Customer ID to the Invoice file will allow you to link to the related record in the Customer file. With each new invoice, a Customer ID will be entered and display that customers data on the invoice.

Picture 18.2

A relationship uses one field to make a match based on a common field. This allows one file to see all the data in another file's record when there is matching data between the records.

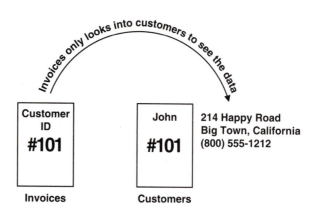

Techno babble

When speaking of relationships, database developers use terms like primary file, master file, parent file, main file and possibly a few others. They all represent the file from which the relationship is established. The other side of the relationship is commonly referred to as the child file, secondary file or some other term denoting it as the referenced file in the relationship. When it comes to a relationship key, what FileMaker, Inc. refers to as a match field is commonly called master key or primary key and these will be matched with a foreign key or a secondary key. Look to the Glossary for definitions of these terms.

Setting up a relationship

Creating a working relationship basically requires two criteria. Follow these steps before creating a relationship and you can't go wrong.

Step 1: First, the two match fields in a relationship must be the same type; Text, Number, etc. If the relationship option for creating new records will be used, the match field on the right side of the relationship (the related file) cannot be a calculation field.

Step 2: On the right side of the relationship the field must be indexed. There are exceptions to this rule as demonstrated in the Technique file titled Global Relationships (GLOB_REL.FP3).

Once both of these criteria are met, you can add fields to your layout displaying data from the related file. It is possible that a record will match a single record or many records in the related file.

! Power Tip

If you use a global field on the right side of a relationship, FileMaker Pro will warn you that the relationship will not work. If, however, you have a global field on both sides of the relationship and display only related global fields, that message can be ignored.

GLOB_REL.FP3

Technique File:
Global Relationships

Types of relationships

[!] Power Tip

When it comes to many-to-many relationships, FileMaker Pro match fields are "or-based" relationships. When a match field has multiple values separated by returns, FileMaker Pro will show the records related to each match value.

When working with FileMaker Pro, or any relational database, you're bound to hear terms like one-to-many, many-to-one, and many-to-many. For example, a single customer may order many times from you. In this situation you have a one-customer to many-invoices relationship. On the other hand, you have many items on one invoice creating a many-items to one-invoice relationship. When you have many invoices, each of which has many items, a many-to-many relationship is needed.

(○) **MANYMANY.FP3**

Technique File:
Many-to-Many

The best way to become familiar with the different relationship types is to work through examples. There are three basic examples on the accompanying CD ROM. These Technique files are:

(○) **MANYMAN2.FP3**

Technique File:
Many-to-Many (Join)

Many-to-Many
Many-to-Many (Join)
Invoice

(○) **INVOICE.FP3**

Technique File:
Invoice

The objective of this book is to discuss advanced techniques not covered in other FileMaker Pro books. While we have provided a few examples of the basics, you should either already have a good understanding of the different relationship types or refer to the manual that came with FileMaker Pro for more examples.

Same-file relationships

There's no standard term for this aspect of relationships. You'll hear the terms self-relationship, self-join and same-file relationship. It merely means that a relationship is used to relate the file to itself. When creating a relationship, FileMaker Pro asks you to choose a related file. All you have to do to create a same-file relationship is choose the file you are creating the relationship from. An example is a database about animals. There are many types of animals with many different classifications. One of the categories is Birds. By creating a relationship where the field Category is used on both sides, the database will show the other records in the same database that have the same category. You would display these via a portal. For instance, while on a record for the Yellow-billed Magpie, the portal would show records for Common Scrub Jay, Red Tail Hawk, and any other birds in the database.

A common technique for same-file relationships is to use a global field on the left side of the relationship. Since a global field shows the same value on all records, the portal based on a global relationship will display the same related information on every record. A working example of this technique can be seen in the INDEX.FP3 file on the CD ROM.

Picture 18.2.1
A common technique for showing related records from the same file is through a same-file relationship with a global field as the match field. This is used in the INDEX.FP3 file on the CD ROM.

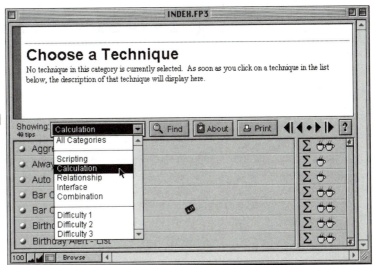

This file displays the Technique files in a portal based on the Category pop-up menu. For instance, you can select the calculations option from the pop-up list which displays all the techniques relating to calculations (see Picture 18.2.1).

When using same-file relationships, it is important to understand how to use the check box options in the Edit Relationship dialog (see Picture 18.2.2). The check box on the left allows you to delete related records. A common use for this is in an invoicing scenario. When an invoice is deleted, you also want the related line items to be deleted as well. Never check this box when using a same-file relationship. It will create the effect of cascading deletes. Think back to the animals database. Deleting the Yellow-billed Magpie would delete all birds because of the same-file relationship by Category.

Picture 18.2.2
By relating a file to itself you create a same-file relationship. With this type of relationship it is dangerous to check the option of deleting records on the bottom left.

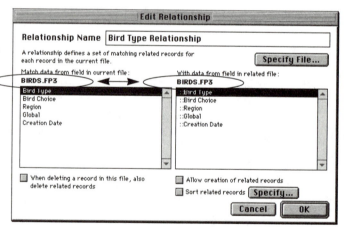

Updating Relationships

Knowing all the nuances about how FileMaker Pro features work can differentiate a good database from a

REFRESH.FP3

Technique File:
Refreshing Relationships

professional solution. All relational databases support the relational structure to different degrees. In FileMaker Pro, however, relationships update automatically through one level only.

A good example of this limitation is a calculation field that includes a reference to a related field. If this calculation is used as the match field for another relationship, it's possible the relationship will not update properly. In order to remedy this refresh problem, the match field must be set to itself using a Set Field step. In this example, you must set a field that the calculation is based upon since you can't modify a calculation. By doing this the relationship is updated and any new calculated values are refreshed in the portal.

There are hundreds of situations where a relationship will not be updated automatically. Whenever you notice that a portal doesn't refresh or a calculation based on relationship is not recalculating when a change is made, you will need to offer a way of updating the match field via a script.

Referential Integrity

Open this file and follow along

18_E.FP3

Chapter File:
Referential Integrity

Many relational database systems support referential integrity. This is something you don't currently need to worry about with FileMaker Pro. However, it is something you should become familiar with in order to become more proficient at database design. To understand what referential integrity is, follow this example.

A record with a Customer ID value of 101 relates to an Invoice file that also has a value of 101 in the Customer ID field. This relationship allows you to display all the invoices for customer 101 in a portal.

When you change the CustomerID value from 101 to 102, the items in the portal disappear because the Customer ID on the invoices has remained the same.

This does not mean the data in the Invoice file for that customer no longer exists. What it means is, FileMaker Pro did not update the relationship key in the Invoice file when you changed it in the Customer file. This is what is meant by referential integrity. In some database products, the integrity of the relationship would be maintained even if the relationship key was changed or updated. In other words, the 101 would be changed to a 102 in the Invoice file as soon as it was changed in the Customer file.

Picture 18.2.3
It is possible to script a pseudo method of referential integrity into a FileMaker Pro file. See file 18_E.FP3 for the specifics.

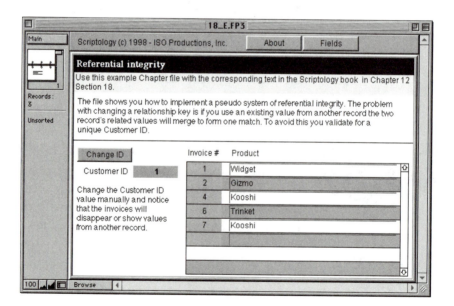

While FileMaker Pro does not directly support referential integrity, it is possible to simulate this feature using a script. Clicking a button next to the key field would cause FileMaker Pro to find the related records using the Go to Related Record script step. After the new key value is entered, the script would change the found records in the related file using the Replace feature.

Referential integrity is an essential part of a database system, because the people using your solution don't necessarily understand relational database concepts. Any system that prevents users from making mistakes improves your database design.

Creating new records using Set Field

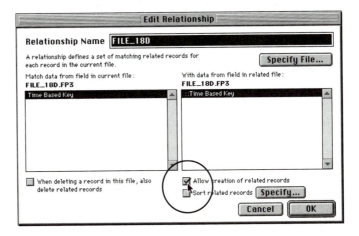

RRECORDS.FP3

Technique File:
New Related Records

Another FileMaker Pro nuance is how records are created through relationships. A single Set Field step can create a new record in a related file. The only prerequisite is the check box allowing record creation must be checked in the Edit Relationship dialog box (see Picture 18.2.4).

Picture 18.2.4
When the option to create related records is checked, a new record will be created if there is no match in the related database.

New related records will only be created if there are no currently related records. This little known technique can generate whole sets of records using a single Set Field script step inside a loop. Open the file named RRECORDS.FP3 from the CD ROM for a hands-on example.

Try this experiment. Create two files related to each other via a match field of type number. Define a second field of type text in the secondary file. Set the relationship to allow creation of related records. Create a new record in the primary file and make sure there is a value in the number field. Next, define a script in the primary file with a single Set Field step. In the options for the Set Field step, choose the related text field with the Specify Field option (e.g Secondary File::Text Field) and use the Specify button to enter the number field as the formula for the calculation:

```
Set Field ["Secondary File::Text Field", "Number
Field"]
```

Running the script the first time will create a new record in the related file because there is no match. FileMaker Pro expects a match, but does not find one, so it creates a new related record to hold the data from the number field. If the script is run a second time, no related record will be created unless the number field in the primary file is changed to a value that does not exist in the secondary file. Knowing this little tidbit about relationships could eliminate the alternative of creating a new record in a related database using the Perform Script step. This route requires ScriptMaker to bounce between both files running two scripts to accomplish what one Set Field in a single script can do.

18.3 Advanced Relational Techniques

Creating a basic relationship is easy. If you want to move beyond a database and into a solution, these advanced techniques will allow you to create some powerful features.

Calculated relationships

Calculated relationships are a unique approach to creating match fields. They allow you to combine fields to generate a **unique key**. While the field on the left hand side of the relationship can be any type of calculation, if you want to create related records through the relationship, the field on the right must be a regular FileMaker Pro field (i.e. text, number, date or time). This is necessary since you cannot enter data into a calculation field. However, it is possible to have a stored calculation on the right hand side of a relationship, as long as records aren't going to be created through the relationship.

Consider the process of creating related records through a relationship. If you enter data into a related field, FileMaker Pro compares the match field value on the record in the primary file with that in the secondary file. If no match is present, FileMaker Pro will attempt to make a new related record to store the information being input. In order for this new record to be created in the secondary file, the new match data must be entered. Since the match field in the secondary file is calculated and cannot be modified, FileMaker Pro returns an error message.

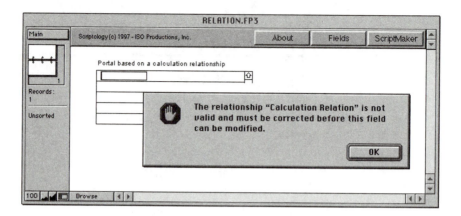

Picture 18.3
An error will occur when creating a new related record if the match field in the related file is a calculation field.

There are many examples of calculated match fields on the CD ROM. Look to the end of this chapter and in the Techniques file Index for examples (INDEX.FP3).

Global relationships

Open this file and follow along

18_A.FP3
Chapter File:
Global Relationships

CLAIRVOY.FP3
Technique File:
Clairvoyance

GLOB_REL.FP3
Technique File:
Global Relationships

By using a global match field in a relationship, you can vary the related information displayed in a portal. No matter what record you're on, the contents of the portal will be the same because the global match field is the same on every record. On the CD ROM there is an example of this technique (18_A.FP3). It's recommended that you look at this file before moving on to the next section. Pay attention to how the values for the pop-up list on the global match field are derived. Use Field Format to reveal that they are based on the values found in the related file.

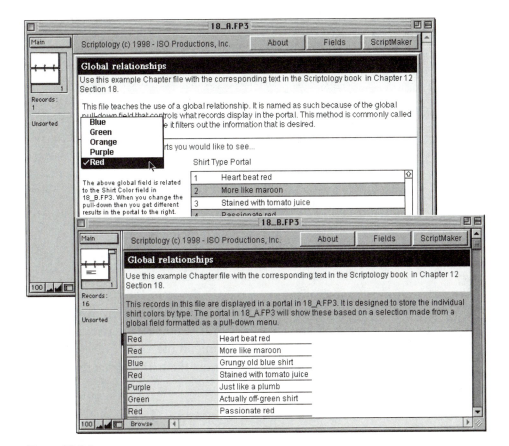

Picture 18.3.1
When the global value in file 18_A is changed, the portal displays the new match values from file 18_B. This is known as a filter.

Concatenated keys

A concatenated key is derived by combining two or more pieces of data using the ampersand "&" character. Think of the ampersand (shift-7 on your keyboard) as the glue that holds two items together. The intention of concatenating two fields together is to generate something unique out of two or more fields that are not unique by themselves.

An example use for concatenated keys is showing filtered information in a portal. Assume you want to show all items sold within a given month (find this example in the DATEPORT.FP3 file). It is possible to find these items with a search, but showing them in a portal is more convenient. Starting in the Line Items file, parse out the month in which an item was sold from the Purchase Date field. This can be done using the MonthName () function. Concatenating this information with the Item ID field will give us the following calculation:

```
MonthName(Purchase Date) & Item ID
```

In the primary file, use a global field formatted as a pop-up menu. When defining the value list for the pop-up menu, select the "Use values from a field" radio button and specify the Item ID field from the Line Items file. This will create a pop-up menu with all the Item IDs. You can also mark the check box "Also display value from:" in the Define Value Lists dialog box. This will show the name of the product matching the Item ID.

The next step is to create a calculation in the primary file that concatenates the global field with the current month name:

```
MonthName(Status(CurrentDate)) & Item ID
```

Now all you need is a relationship based on the two calculations and a portal to display the related information. The data for that month will be filtered depending on the Item ID choice made from the global pop-up menu.

This method does not require using a global field as part of the match calculation in the primary file. For instance, you might want to use this technique to display the monthly sales for each product on each record of your Product database.

Time-based relationships

Open this file and follow along

◎ **18_C.FP3**

Chapter File:
Time based keys

Time is the most definitive system for defining unique keys. The second you just took to read this sentence was spent, and it will never come back. If you had created a record in a related file based on that specific second, it would be unique to the whole database system for the rest of time.

The way to implement a time-based key is to use the Set Field step with a formula that concatenates the Status(CurrentDate) with the Status(CurrentTime). This will create a unique number representative of the date and time. An added advantage to using this type of key is being able to eliminate Creation Date and Creation Time fields. At any time, you can extract that information from the time-based key. For example, the number 72930663013 represents October 9, 1997 at 5:30:13 to FileMaker Pro. If you break the number up into two parts, the date being the first 6 digits and the time being the last 5, you get 729306 as 10/9/97 and 63013 as 5:30:13. These values are the number of days since January 1st, 0001 and the number of seconds since the beginning of the current day – 12:00 AM midnight.

◎ **REMINDER.FP3**

Technique File:
Reminders

There are several situations where this technique will not work. For instance, if more than one record is created in the same second as can happen with looping scripts, if the database is used in a multi-user environment and two users create a record at the same time, and if clocks are not synchronized in a multi-user scenario or the clock on a computer is accidentally set back or forward in time. A solution to

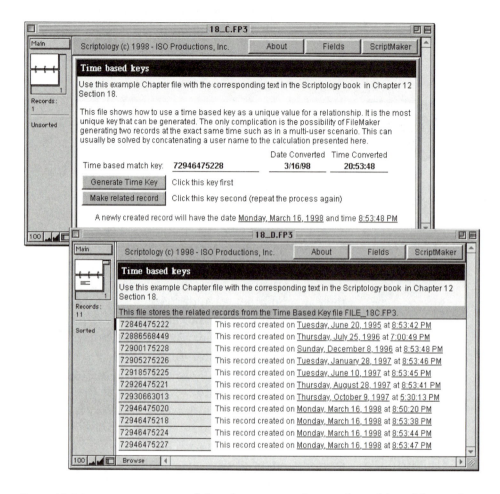

Picture 18.3.2
Files 18_C and 18_D show how a time based key is unique for all of time.

most of the above scenarios can be achieved by making the time based key even more unique. Just concatenate the User Name to the time key and it will be unique by time and user. In the case of the looping script, there is not much that can be done if it creates more than one record per second. The best solution in this scenario, is to add the record ID to the time and date using the new FileMaker Pro 4.0 Status(CurrentRecordID) function.

18.4 Related Finds

When the Find in Progress dialog box comes up, (see
Picture 18.4) a search is being performed for data
both in the current file and a related file. FileMaker
Pro is creating a cross-table index of two separate files
on the fly. Each FileMaker Pro file contains the index
of its own fields, but there is no index holding the
values of two or more files. When multiple files are
searched, FileMaker Pro must create an index derived
from all files being searched. This intense process
slows down the search significantly. For this reason, it
is best to design your database so you don't have to
search related fields.

Picture 18.4
When searching related fields,
FileMaker Pro must create an
ad hoc index.

Designing your database properly involves mapping
out the user process. Consider how users will be
searching the database and even test it out in a real
life scenario. With careful preparation, you won't be
surprised by a multi-user system that takes minutes to
search a database. See the Technique file titled
Related Finds (REL_FIND.FP3) for tricks on how to
get around a problem that cannot be avoided.

REL_FIND.FP3

Technique File:
Related Finds

Test yourself to see what you've learned.

1. Lookups are best used for which type of data?
- ○ Dynamic
- ○ Flexible
- ○ Historical
- ○ All of the above

2. A relationship uses what type of field?
- ○ Text
- ○ Number
- ○ Calculation
- ○ All of the above

3. Another name for a match field in a related database is?
- ○ Primary Key
- ○ Master Key
- ○ Parent Key
- ○ None of the above

4. A many-to-many relationship in FileMaker Pro uses?
- ○ A found set match record
- ○ Return delimited data in a field
- ○ A same-file relationship key
- ○ All of the above

5. Same-file relationships are limited to?
- ○ Constant field match keys
- ○ Using globals with dynamic value lists
- ○ Using an indexed field in the same file
- ○ All of the above

6. In order to create a record using Set Field, the value used...
- ○ Must not exist in the related database
- ○ Must have been used before
- ○ Must be a static value
- ○ All of the above

7. Calculated relationships can be used?
- ○ On the left side
- ○ On the right side
- ○ On both the left and right side
- ○ All of the above

8. Searching a related field creates?
- ○ A database search table
- ○ A temporary index
- ○ A temp file
- ○ All of the above

9. Referential integrity...
- ○ Is not supported by FileMaker Pro
- ○ Can be simulated with scripts
- ○ Is an essential part of a database
- ○ All of the above

Answers:

Answers: 1. Historical 2. All of the above 3. None of the above 4. Return delimited data in a field 5. Using an indexed field in the same file 6. Must not exist in the related database 7. All of the above 8. A temporary index. 9. All of the above

What you should have learned
- The fundamental difference between a lookup and relationship
- Where and when a lookup is useful in your database
- How to use a relationship and when it is useful
- Advanced relational techniques
- How finds on related fields work

More technique files about relationships...

SERIAL.FP3
Cycling Serial Numbers

Adds serial numbers that increment to a point and then start over.

ZIP.FP3
Next Lower Value

Uses the advanced lookup options of next lower value to optimize the assignment of shipping costs.

HIDE.FP3
Hide Records

Uses a relationship to prevent a user from seeing records he did not create. Eliminates the need for additional fields or layouts.

SERIALIZ.FP3
Serialize by Category

Shows how to use lookups to create serial numbers by category.

MATCH.FP3
Related Match Field

Highlights the default behavior of FileMaker Pro that creates related records without a match key.

MESSAGE.FP3
Messaging

Allows users to leave messages for each other in a multi-user database. Messages for each user are filtered by a calculated match field.

PREVIOUS.FP3
Previous Record

Shows how to locate the previous record using a lookup and copy data from it.

Portal Power

19.0 Using Portals Effectively

Manipulating data from a related file is done by placing related fields on your layout. This allows you to change one related record at a time. Portals allow you to work with the data from more than one related record.

Quite simply, portals are windows that look into another file. A window with a view into the building next door is a good analogy. The building you're in right now can be considered your master file and the building next to you is a related file. If you use a pair of binoculars, you can see inside each office in the other building. Each window presents you with a different view.

Once you understand how portals are used with relationships, you'll find a number of ways to use them. Just using them to show and interact with data in the layout is limiting. In the following sections you'll gain insight into the many different uses of a portal.

Picture 19.0
There are four options for portals. Allowing for deletion of related records, the number of portal rows to show, whether a scroll bar should be visible and what color to use for alternating, if any.

19.1 Hidden portals

DBINDB.FP3

Technique File:
Database in a
Database

One of the best tricks with portals is hiding them on the layout. If you need to interact with data in a related file, but don't want it to be visible to the user, you can hide the portal. The trick to hiding a portal is to make it the same color as the background in both line and fill color. You also need to set it to show one row only and include a scroll bar. Lastly, shrink the portal to 25 x 25 pixels or less using the Size palette under the Show menu. There is no need for the portal to contain fields unless you need to copy and paste from related fields; the Set Field step works just fine in most situations.

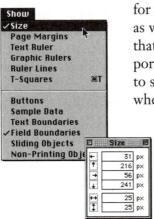

There may be a few instances for making a portal hidden, such as when using a looping script that goes from row to row in a portal and the user doesn't need to see the portal. A general rule when deciding whether or not to hide a portal is to determine if it is required for direct interaction by the user. If no user interaction is necessary, there is no reason to waste layout space.

Making a portal hidden on a layout

Things to do
- Set portal fill and line color to same color as background.
- Set to show one row only.
- Set so that scroll bar is showing.
- Using the size palette, shrink to 25 by 25 pixels or smaller.
- There is no need for the portal to contain fields.

19.2 Embellishing portals

Making portals appealing in your user interface is important. There is no reason you have to stick with the limited interface options offered by FileMaker Pro. By combining good interface design with functionality, a portal can add a new dimension to your current database.

Buttons in portals

Open this file and follow along

19_A.FP3

Chapter File:
Go to Related Record

Within each row of a portal, you can have buttons that perform a number of actions like deleting or creating related records. Clicking a button in a particular row will act on the related record represented by that portal row. When placing buttons, fields or graphics into a portal, you need to be very careful. If elements are not fully contained within the first row of the portal, they will not display on every row. The boundaries of the first portal row are the surrounding lines. Even one pixel beyond the outline will cause problems.

HILIGHT2.FP3

Technique File:
Highlighting Portal
Rows

DOUBLE_P.FP3

Technique File:
Double-Clicking in
Portals

One of the coolest techniques for portals is defining a transparent button that utilizes a Go to Related Record step. Start by resizing the button so it spans the entire portal row. Next, set the button to transparent using the pen and fill pattern pop-up menus. The button is invisible, but still displays the related database when clicked. This allows you to use the portal row to show a limited amount of data before making a selection. After clicking on a portal row, the related database will show the details of the record in the other file (see Picture 19.2).

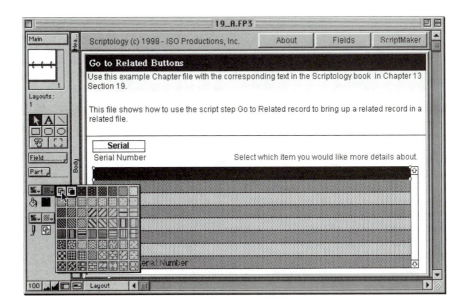

Picture 19.2
You only need to define the button on the first portal row and then set it to transparent fill and line.

This technique can also be used with list view and form view layouts. Place a transparent button that activates a Go to Layout step on a list view layout, making sure it does not extend beyond the boundaries of the body part. If the object extends beyond the boundaries, it will not repeat on every record. Whenever a record in list view is clicked, the layout that appears will be a form view layout displaying more information.

3-dimensional portals

⚠ Power Tip

When you overlay graphics on a scroll bar in a regular field, the graphics don't have to be offset.

Portals can be very bland when using just the standard options of fill, pen and alternating background color. You can overlay graphic scroll bars and outline the portal, so it looks 3-dimensional. However, you can't just place lines and other graphic elements on top of a portal without knowing how it works with objects. As pointed out in the previous section, objects contained completely within the first row, will

Picture 19.2.1

Graphics can be placed on a portal scroll bar but they must be offset by one pixel in order to display correctly.

display in each row of the portal. In this section, objects will be placed in a portal so as not to repeat on every row.

Let's start with scroll bars. Use some of the scroll bar graphics from the GPXLIB.FP3 Reference file on the CD ROM, and place them directly over the portal scroll bars. When you enter Browse mode, part of the graphic scroll bars will disappear. This happens with any graphic that is completely contained within a portal scroll bar. To solve this, all you need to do is move the scroll bar graphics one pixel to the right, so they extend outside the portal scroll bar. This is easily accomplished with the arrow keys, since they allow you to move objects one pixel at a time.

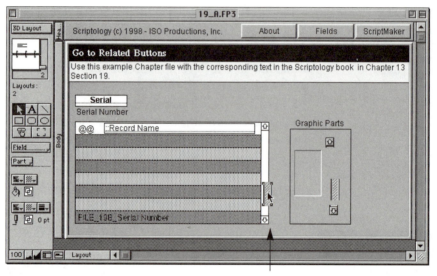

When dragging a scrollbar graphic on top of a portal make sure it offsets the portal by one pixel to the right.

This technique can also be applied to any graphic that should be included in the first row of a portal, but not repeated on every subsequent row. For instance, let's say you wanted to make a 3-dimensional outline for your portal. The horizontal line at the top of the portal needs to be contained within the first row, but not repeated on every row. By dragging it one pixel wider so it extends outside the portal, it will not repeat.

19.3 Performing AND searches on portals

If you enter find mode on a layout that contains a portal, you will notice that you can't move beyond the first row. This prevents you from performing an AND search that would allow you to find a record containing two different items in the same portal. For instance, let's say you had a database of invoices and you wanted to find all the people who purchased two different products on the same invoice. This would be impossible performing the find on a portal, but not with the technique discussed in this section.

The solution is quite simple and only requires one modification. The related field showing in the portal needs to be redefined as repeating. This design is not used to store data in the repetitions. The purpose for turning the repetitions on is to allow FileMaker Pro to accept more values when entering find mode. A special search layout, using the repeating field instead of the portal, is created. The best interface for this solution is to use a script for performing a find, rather than letting users manually enter find mode. The script will take users to the search layout containing the repeating field. If you disguise the repeating field well enough, they'll never know you switched to a special find layout. Open the technique file FIND-PORT.FP3 to grasp a better understanding of how to implement this technique.

FINDPORT.FP3

Technique File:
Find in a Portal

19.4 Portal printing dilemmas demystified

Open this file and follow along

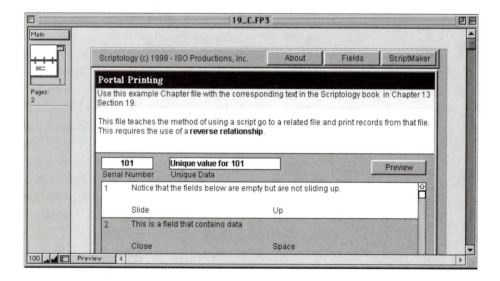

19_C.FP3

Chapter File:
Portal Printing

Portals were not designed to be printed. They will print, but there are serious limitations. The problem is that portals only print as many rows as are showing on the layout. If you have a portal that displays five rows, but this particular record has eight rows in the portal, the last three will never print. You could make a separate layout with a portal that has enough rows to satisfy the largest number of rows. Even then, fields within portal rows will not slide up through unused portal space (see Picture 19.4). In addition, if a portal crosses a page break, it will not break elegantly.

```
┌─────────────────────── 19_C.FP3 ────────────────────────┐
│ Main                                                      │
│  ┌──┐                                                     │
│  │  │    Scriptology (c) 1998 - ISO Productions, Inc.  [About] [Fields] [ScriptMaker] │
│  └──┘                                                     │
│         Portal Printing                                   │
│ Pages:  Use this example Chapter file with the corresponding text in the Scriptology book in Chapter 13 │
│ 2       Section 19.                                       │
│                                                           │
│         This file teaches the method of using a script go to a related file and print records from that file. │
│         This requires the use of a reverse relationship.  │
│                                                           │
│         ┌─────────┐ ┌──────────────────────┐    ┌─────────┐ │
│         │   101   │ │ Unique value for 101 │    │ Preview │ │
│         └─────────┘ └──────────────────────┘    └─────────┘ │
│         Serial Number   Unique Data                       │
│         1    Notice that the fields below are empty but are not sliding up. │
│                                                           │
│              Slide                          Up            │
│         2    This is a field that contains data           │
│                                                           │
│              Close                          Space         │
│ [100]  Preview                                            │
└───────────────────────────────────────────────────────────┘
```

Picture 19.4
This picture shows a portal in Preview mode. Even if a portal is set to slide up during printing, open portal rows and unused space will not close up.

To get the best results, you'll need to use a sub-summary report in the related file. The sub-summary part is sorted by the match field from the related file (the match field on the right side of the relationship). For

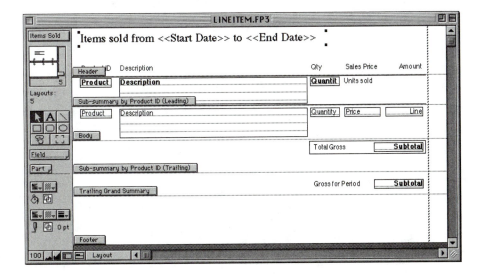

PRNTPORT.FP3

Technique File:
Printing Portals

instance, let's say you have an invoicing solution. One of the reports you may need is a gross sales report based on a specified period of time that breaks down the total number of units sold.

This report can be initiated from the Invoices file as might be expected. To get the totals for the items sold, you'll need to create a summary field that adds the line item prices. Place this summary field in the sub-summary part.

Picture 19.4.1
A better solution for printing portals is to use a script to print a sub-summary report in the related file.

Once the sub-summary report is complete, you'll need a script to print the report. The script will perform a series of steps. To start, the script will prompt for a starting and ending date and search the invoices database for this range of records. It would then create a return delimited list of related invoice numbers using the Copy All Records on a special layout that contained only the invoice number field. It would then paste this list into a match field. Next it would use the Go to Related Record step with the Show option to create a found set of records in the related Line Items file. Next, a script in the related file is called using the Perform Script step. The script in the related file will sort the database by the field used in the sub-summary part and print. If the script is designed like this, the user will never know they left the original Invoices file.

Picture 19.4.2
If printing multiple invoices or reports containing sub-summary parts, use the Page break options in the Part Definition to print each form out separately.

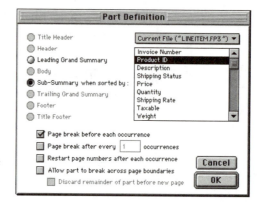

A **reverse-relationship** may be required to achieve the same kind of printed form as the master file displaying the portal. Using the Products Sold Report example again. The sales date exists in a field in the Invoices file. If you want to include this in the sub-summary layout in the related file, you'll need to create another relationship. This reverse-relationship originates from the related file and points to the main file. It is handled the same way as the original relationship with the same match key, but in reverse. It is this reverse-relationship that allows you access to the fields originating from the main file.

19.5 Sorting portals

The ability to sort portals has been a common request since the release of FileMaker Pro 3.0. FileMaker Pro 4.0 introduces portal sorting as a built-in feature, but it has limitations. In order to make a portal sort, you have to define the relationship as sorted. If you want to display the portal as sorted in one layout and unsorted in another layout, you need to use two relationships. Another limitation is the inability to sort in different orders. Once a sort order has been established, there is no way to modify it on the fly via a script.

Picture 19.5
The new sorting feature for portals is tied to the relationship.

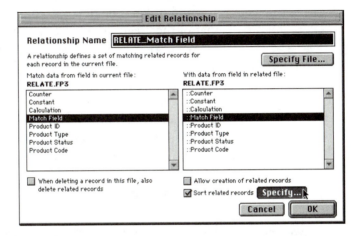

Even if you are content with the way FileMaker Pro 4.0 sorts portals, users of your solution may only own FileMaker Pro 3.0. Solutions created in FileMaker Pro 4.0 can be used in 3.0 without modification, but are limited to 3.0 features. Using one of the first three solutions discussed here, you won't have to worry which version they own. In addition, working through these solutions will give you insight into how FileMaker Pro works, which will assist you when coming up with solutions for other problems.

The following sections discuss four methods for sorting portals. Each technique has advantages and disadvantages, so learn them all. The discussion covers the theory and is complimented by the examples on the CD ROM. Use them both to gain a full understanding of how these sorts work.

Overview

A portal displays records based on creation order. Most sorting portal techniques change the creation order by removing the records and recreating them in a sorted order. The new sorted order will now equal that of the creation order. Some methods rearrange the data, so it displays in sorted order, even though the creation order of the records has not changed. All methods require some type of script to initiate the process. Since most portal sorting methods can take a significant amount of time to process, it is better to limit the sort to the related records contained in the portal on the current record.

Import method

SORTPORT.FP3

Technique File:
Sorting Portals

Method one uses importing to accomplish a sorted portal. The found set of records to be sorted is first imported into a separate FileMaker Pro database. Once the records are sorted, they are imported back into the related file. The original found set of related records is replaced by the new set in sorted order. Another FileMaker Pro file is used, rather than exporting to a text file, because it's much faster. In addition, pictures and sound would be lost in a text file.

The biggest advantage to the import method, on larger found sets of records, is speed. In most tests, the import method easily defeats all other methods. However, the import process can be slower where more fields and greater amounts of text are involved.

One way to speed up the import process is to leave the fields unindexed. Turning off the indexing increases speed because fields are indexed during the import process.

Duplicate/delete method

SORTPORT.FP3

Technique File:
Sorting Portals

Method two is by far the easiest technique to implement. It sorts the related records, using a looping script to duplicate each record and delete the original. By duplicating each record in the sorted order, the new creation order is the sorted order.

This technique is very fast on small sets of records, very easy to implement and does not require the addition of any files. One disadvantage for this method is that auto-enter values will replace any data in a duplicated record (e.g. auto-enter serial numbers), but this can be accounted for with a script.

Lookup method

SORTPORT.FP3

Technique File:
Sorting Portals

Method three relies on a lookup to create a new sorted order, rather than actually changing the creation order of the records. This method is more complex than the previous techniques, but it does provide insight into how lookups work. Understanding this solution may help you solve future problems using lookups.

This solution requires that you add several new fields to your related database. Start by adding a number field that will hold serial numbers. You'll need to add a second number field that will also contain serial numbers. The first number field holds sequential values when sorted and the second number field holds sequential values when unsorted.

Finally, you'll need to define a new field for every field you have displayed in the portal. Each of these fields will be defined as a lookup based on a **same-file relationship.** Use the first number field on the left side and the second serial number on the right side. Once you have tested the lookups and verified they work, you can create the sorting script. This script sorts the database and replaces the second serial number field with sequential numbers. Performing a Relookup moves all the data from the original fields to the lookup counterparts. When you unsort the database, you'll see that the data in the lookup fields is in sorted order (see the Lookup reserialization picture below). This is the basic premise of the method. The technique file on the CD ROM (SORTPORT.FP3) takes this method one step further. It adds an additional lookup, so the data is copied back into the original fields. Otherwise, you would have to display the lookup fields in the portal

Lookup reserialization

Sorting a portal using a lookup

Using two sets of serial numbers and lookups, field values can be copied into sorted order. Arrows represent lookups.

ORIGINAL DATA UNSORTED	SERIAL #1 UNSORTED	SERIAL #1 SORTED	SERIAL #2 SORTED	ORIGINAL DATA SORTED
F	1	6	1	A
A	2	1	2	B
D	3	4	3	C
B	4	2	4	D
E	5	5	5	E
C	6	3	6	F

in order for it to be sorted. This would prevent editing in the display portal and require a duplicate layout, displaying the original fields, for editing purposes.

4.0 Only

Multiple fields method

The biggest hole in the new FileMaker Pro 4.0 portal sorting feature is the inability to change the sorted field on the fly with a script. Method four demonstrates how to add this functionality with the addition of two fields. Start by adding a global number field to your database. This field acts as a control to designate which field to use for sorting. A calculation field looks at this global field to determine what field value to return. The example below provides three different options for a sort based on the value in the global field:

```
Case(
Global Field = 1, First Name,
Global Field = 2, Last Name,
State
)
```

MULTSORT.FP3

Technique File:
Sort Portal
Multiple Fields

This calculation is used as the sorting field for the relationship. Whenever the global field changes, the result of the calculation changes to return the contents of a different field. All you need is an easy way to change the global value. Use a simple script that sets the global field to a number from 1 to 3. The example file on the CD ROM (MULTSORT.FP3) shows an excellent technique for incorporating the buttons into the interface of your solution.

Test yourself to see what you've learned.

1. **Portals can be hidden on a layout by?**
   - ○ Making them the same color as the background
   - ○ Shrinking them down
   - ○ Adding a scrollbar
   - ○ All of the above

2. **Adding a transparent button to a portal must?**
   - ○ Extend outside the portal
   - ○ Be contained within the first portal row
   - ○ The same size as the portal row
   - ○ All of the above

3. **Performing an AND search within a portal requires?**
   - ○ The searched field to be repeating
   - ○ The related database to be frontmost
   - ○ Multiple search requests to be made
   - ○ All of the above

4. **The best method to print the contents of a portal is to?**
   - ○ Increase the number of rows showing
   - ○ Put it on its own print layout
   - ○ Print from the related file
   - ○ All of the above

5. **Creating a reverse-relationships depends on?**
   - ○ A new secondary key
   - ○ The same match key
   - ○ A custom calculation
   - ○ All of the above

6. **Sorting portals can be accomplished with?**
   - ○ Scripts
   - ○ A relationship
   - ○ Calculations
   - ○ All of the above

Answers:

Answers: 1. All of the above 2. Be contained within the first portal row 3. The searched field to be repeating 4. Print from the related file 5. The same match key 6. All of the above

What you should have learned
- What portals are and how they are used
- Techniques for hiding portals
- Interface tricks for portals
- Printing portals
- Methods for sorting portals

More technique files about portals...

CLAIRVOY.FP3
Clairvoyance

Better known as type ahead or smart typing shows how you can accomplish this in FileMaker Pro.

DATEPORT.FP3
Date Range Portals

How to filter portals based on a date range.

DOUBLE_P.FP3
Double-Clicking in Portals

A user interface technique that first highlights a portal on click one and then does something on click two.

DUP_PORT.FP3
Duplicating Portals

How to duplicate all the related records showing in the portal on the current record.

PORT_SUM.FP3
Sub-Summarizing Portals

Demonstrates how to total by category within a portal.

RETURN.FP3
Return to Portal Row

Once a script leaves a portal, the current row is lost. This technique shows you how to remember the portal row.

PORTPORT.FP3
Portal Row Movement

How to move data from one portal to another.

SORTPRT2.FP3
Sorting Portals 2

Yet another method for sorting portals.

Relationship Debugging

20.0 Debugging your relationships

There are many reasons why a relationship may not function properly. The best troubleshooting technique is to go step-by-step, making sure that each part of the puzzle is in the right place. This may seem basic, but walking through each step of the process really helps. The following sections cover more in-depth techniques for troubleshooting relationships.

20.1 Making sure both match fields are the same type

Incorrect field types can cause a relationship to either show incorrect data or show nothing at all. The match field on the left and right side of the relationship need to be of the same field type. If the field on one side is a number field and on the other is a text field, you may run into problems. As far as FileMaker Pro is concerned, when a field is of a type number, the only characters it sees in the field are numbers, any extra text characters are ignored. The first place

Picture 20.1

An example of a relationship where the fields are not the same type.

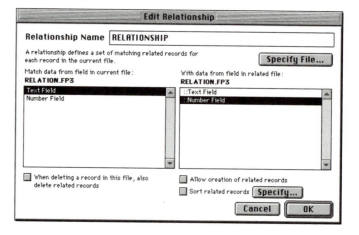

you should go to check when the relationship is not working is the Define Fields of each file (the same file if it is a same-file relationship) and check to make sure the field types match each other. This problem can happen with any field type mismatch, not just text and number.

If you are using calculations as the match fields in your relationship, make sure the result type is the same. For instance, if you have a calculation field on the left side of the relationship and a text field on the right side, the result of the calculation must be in text format.

Picture 20.1.1

Specifying an incorrect result type for a calculation used as a match field could cause a relationship to fail.

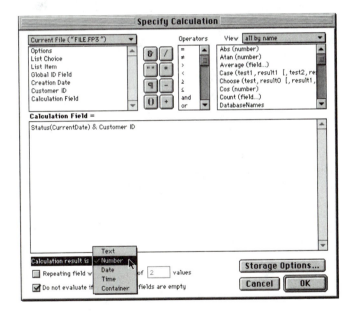

21.0 The right field for the right portal

In many cases there is nothing wrong with the relationship you are using for your portal. Rather, the problem lies in how the layout is set up to display the data. One common problem occurs when placing a non-related field in a portal. When you enter browse mode, the same data will be repeated on every row in the portal.

Picture 21.0
When adding a field to a portal make, sure the field is not from the current file.

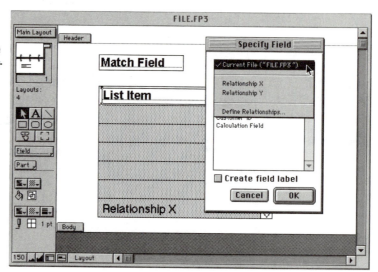

This often happens with a same file relationship. A case might be where you have a portal that should display the Name field from three related records (e.g. Bob, Susie and Judy), but you accidentally place a regular field rather than a field from the relationship in the portal. This is easy to do since a same file relationship relates to itself. Instead of displaying different names in the three rows of the portal, "Bob"

will be repeated on each row. This problem can also happen when a separate file is used in the relationship. Quite often, the same field names will be used in both files for a variety of reasons. To avoid this problem, make sure only related fields are placed in a portal. You can identify related fields by the double colon before the field name.

A similar problem can occur, even if you have a related field in a portal. If the relationship attached to the field is not the same as that defined in the portal, no data will appear in the portal. Let's say you have file A related to file B and file C. If you create a portal using the relationship from file A to B, but accidentally place a field from the A to C relationship, empty rows will show equalling the number of related records in file B, but no data will appear.

Picture 21.1
If a portal does not show the proper data, it is possible that the portal and the field contained in the portal are from different relationships. Notice the field being specified is from Relationship Y, while the portal is set to show information from Relationship X.

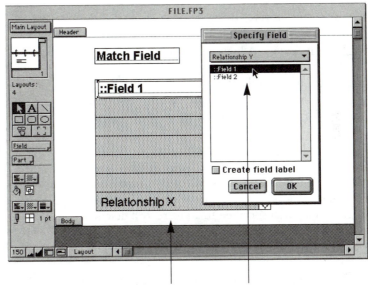

The Portal based on Relationship X will not display Field 1 from Relationship Y.

The quickest way to check if a portal has the right field in it, is to compare the name of the portal to the name of the field. The portal, in Layout mode, will show the name of the relationship that it is using. Double-clicking the field will present the name of the field. This allows you to see what relationship it's using.

The following list is a good way to troubleshoot portals and relationships that may not be working properly.

Troubleshooting Portals

Portal settings for various actions

I want to create records in the portal:

- ❏ Is the option "Allow creation of related records" checked in the Edit Relationship dialog?
- ❏ Am I using a related field?
- ❏ Am I using a field from the correct relationship?
- ❏ Is the right relationship attached to the portal?

I want to delete records in the portal:

- ❏ Have I checked "Allow deletion of portal records" in the settings of the portal?
- ❏ Is the portal specified to allow record deletion?

I want all related records deleted when I delete in the main file:

- ❏ Is the option "When deleting a record in this file, also delete related records" checked in the Edit Relationship dialog?

Troubleshooting

Portal/Relationship checking

❑ Are the field types on both sides of the relationship the same?
❑ Is the field in the portal coming from the database that portal opens into?
❑ Is the portal you are working with coming from the right relationship?
❑ Are the options set correctly in the relationship?
❑ Are the portal settings allowing you to do what you want?

Chapter 14 Overview & Quiz

Test yourself to see what you've learned.

1. Related records will only delete from a portal when?
   ○ They are deleted from the related file via a script
   ○ The whole portal is selected
   ○ Both the relationship and portal are set to allow deletions
   ○ All of the above

2. The first thing to check when a relationship is not working is?
   ○ The calculation storage
   ○ The field types of the match fields
   ○ The field formatting
   ○ All of the above

3. The first thing to check when a portal is not working is?
   ○ The portal options
   ○ The field formatting of portal fields
   ○ Where the fields in the portal originate
   ○ All of the above

4. All related records will be deleted when?
   ○ The relationship is set to delete all related records
   ○ The portal has all related records selected
   ○ A script deletes the found set in the related file
   ○ All of the above

Answers:

Answers: 1. Both the relationship and portal are set to allow deletions 2. The field types of the match fields 3. Where the fields in the portal originate 4. The relationship is set to delete all related records

What you should have learned

- Basic troubleshooting skills for relationships
- Matching the field types of match fields
- What fields can exist in portals
- What to check for when a relationship is not working

More technique files about relationships...

REFRESH.FP3

Refreshing Relationships

Technique for updating relationships that do not refresh properly.

Chapter 15

Going Cross-Platform

22.0 Cross-platform adventures

One of the most appealing aspects of FileMaker Pro is its cross-platform capability. There are many ways to share a FileMaker Pro solution. By setting the networking protocol to either IPX/SPX or TCP/IP, a FileMaker Pro database on Windows can be shared with a computer running FileMaker Pro on a Macintosh. If you don't need the solution to be multi-user, you can share it simply by giving anyone a copy on a disk or as an e-mail attachment. The details about copying files cross-platform can be found on the CD ROM in a reference file called XPLAT.FP3.

XPLAT.FP3

Reference File:
Cross-Platform
Considerations

Even though FileMaker Pro files can be transferred cross-platform easily, the differences between the platforms can change the appearance of the database. By adhering to a few fundamentals, results can be improved dramatically.

22.1 Font conversion

! Power Tip

For Macintosh users, it's possible to use Microsoft TrueType versions of the Windows fonts. The fonts can be obtained directly from the Microsoft web page at no cost (www.microsoft.com). Last we checked the fonts were at this URL (www.microsoft.com/true-type/fontpack/mac.htm).

When developing cross-platform files, there are issues that crop up when moving from the Macintosh OS to the Windows OS and vice versa. The biggest issue involves fonts. The following sections will enable you to approach a cross-platform solution with confidence. No matter what development platform you choose, you will be able to create files that look like works of art on any platform.

Font substitution

When moving files from one platform to another, the same fonts may not be available. When this happens, FileMaker Pro will substitute a font that is available

on the current platform. Here is the table that
FileMaker Pro uses when substituting fonts:

Cross-platform font conversion

What happens to fonts when files are opened on the other platform?

Macintosh		Windows
Helvetica	converts to	Arial
Monaco	converts to	Courier New
Times	converts to	Times New Roman
Courier	converts to	Courier

The above fonts are the most common but there may be other substitutions
that affect your files.

Information courtesy of FileMaker, Inc. Technical support cross-platform documentation.

On Windows, the font substitution is driven by the
FontSubstitutes section of FileMaker Pro in the
Windows registry:

Picture 22.1
The Windows registry is
where the font substitution is
handled under the Windows
operating system.

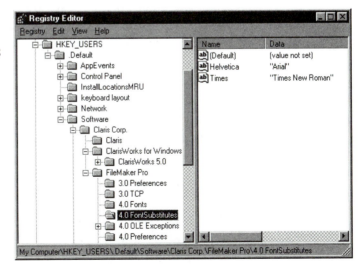

Even though custom fonts can enhance an interface, using standard fonts is a safer bet. This ensures that a user will have them installed. The best fonts to use for visibility are Helvetica on the Macintosh and Arial for Windows or Times for Macintosh and Times New Roman for Windows. Use font sizes of 10 point or higher for better visibility. The only situation where non-standard fonts should be considered is when they can be licensed and distributed with the solution.

Field and text block tricks

Knowing how fonts substitute cross-platform does not ensure a clean cross-platform user interface. Windows fonts are generally larger than their Macintosh counterparts. This can lead to the descenders in certain letters being cut off at the bottom (e.g. g, j, p and q) and text not fitting within the specified boundaries of the field or text block.

The most basic solution to cross-platform font changes is to make the field larger. Increase the width and height so the field or text block is large enough to handle any font size adjustments. This won't be necessary for fields with scroll bars, but can significantly reduce the time spent moving a solution back and forth between Macintosh and Windows to make small adjustments. No matter how much knowledge you have about cross-platform issues, you won't be able to design a flawless solution, but you can reduce the amount of time needed to create a working cross-platform layout.

Single line text blocks and fields are very common in database systems. Rather than enlarging the field more than is needed, there is a general rule that can be followed so descenders are not cut by the bottom margin of a text block or field. Adding an additional 2 pixels to the vertical height of a text block or field will prevent this problem. For example, 12 point Helvetica type will default to a vertical height of 16 pixels. Increasing the vertical height of fields to 18 pixels ensures full visibility of the font on both platforms.

Picture 22.1.1
By adding both pixel height and width to text and fields you can ensure a clean cross-platform look.

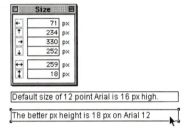

Power Tip

Clicking on the measurement system in the size palette will toggle between the different available systems of inches, centimeters and pixels. Working in pixels is the best system for accuracy.

The best way to add a few pixels to each text block or field is to use the Size palette. Select the field or text block, type a value two pixels larger in the last entry area of the size palette and type the Tab or Enter key to initiate the changes. If you need to add many single line fields to a layout, it's best to place the first field, adjust the height and then option-drag (Macintosh) or control-drag (Windows) the first field to make copies. When you let go of the mouse button, the Specify Field dialog will appear allowing you to choose a new field. Whatever field you select will have the same characteristics as the field that was dragged.

Beyond adding the two pixels, there is also the alignment of the text. Any vertical alignment of text other than Center will force a text block back to its original size after being edited. In many cases this is not desired, especially if the text block has been purposely resized to account for cross-platform font size changes. By setting the Align Text setting to Center, it is possible to edit the text block and have it retain its custom size setting. This will enable you to size the text block or field to any height or width while retaining the ability to edit the text within.

Picture 22.1.2
Setting the vertical alignment of text to Center will retain any custom size dimensions set to text blocks.

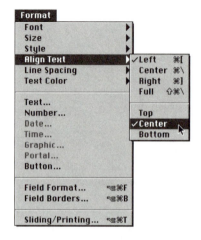

Avoiding font substitution

On the Macintosh, it is possible to use True Type versions of the Windows fonts Arial and New Times Roman. Using these fonts on the Macintosh creates a very close approximation of what the interface will look like on Windows. If your customers are willing to download these fonts, it is possible to create a nearly seamless cross-platform solution.

Another approach to cross-platform design is to use separate files for Macintosh and Windows. Let's say you are designing on the Macintosh. Create your solution using a readable font, like Chicago for System 7 or Charcoal for System 8. When you are done with the solution, duplicate the file and modify all the layouts to use standard Windows fonts. The best font for readability under the Windows operating system is MS Sans Serif in 11 point.

This approach has distinct advantages and disadvantages. It allows you to create an interface that will work flawlessly no matter what platform is used. However, it causes problems in distribution, since you need to ship platform specific versions of your solution instead of one for all customers. It also prevents the solution from being used in a multi-user scenario. One way around this problem is to use a single file with two sets of layouts; one set for Macintosh and the other for Windows. All you need to do is check the platform on startup using the Status(CurrentPlatform) function and show the correct platform layout. The biggest problem with this approach is modifying scripts to be platform sensitive. The best solution is to create a conditional script that goes to one of two layouts based on the platform. Given all the extra work creating file specific or layout specific solutions it is best to avoid this unless necessary.

High-ASCII characters

⊚ ASCII.FP3

Reference File:
ASCII Characters

Other font issues occur when using the high-ASCII characters. Both platforms have the same number of ASCII characters, but some of the higher ASCII values result in different characters. There are characters available on the Macintosh that are not available on Windows and vice versa. Some of these characters on the Macintosh include the ≠, ≥, ≤, √ and other specialized characters such as and fl. Characters available on Windows that won't show properly on the Macintosh are: 1/4, 1/2 and 3/4. High-ASCII characters such as ™, ©, ® and others can be used cross-platform. Every font is different, so always test the character sets of the fonts you will be using. On the Macintosh, they can be accessed using Key Caps and on Windows using Character Map. There is also a reference file on the CD ROM called ASCII.FP3 which lists all of the available ASCII characters.

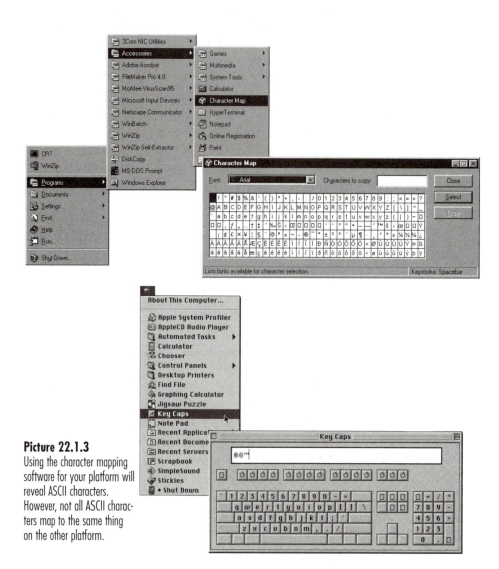

Picture 22.1.3
Using the character mapping software for your platform will reveal ASCII characters. However, not all ASCII characters map to the same thing on the other platform.

Font Style

Yet another font issue is the style. On the Macintosh, there are two styles with no counterparts under the Windows operating system; outline and shadowed text. They should not be used in a cross-platform situation. They won't cause problems, but the style will be removed. A technique file on the CD ROM called SHADOW.FP3 shows methods for emphasizing text without using platform specific font styles.

SHADOW.FP3

Technique File:
Shadowed Text

Graphic fonts

One way to get around the problem of cross-platform font differences is to use a graphic version of the font. This solution won't work for fields but it can help with button text, field labels and anywhere else text is static.

There are many ways to convert fonts to graphics. Text entered into a paint program is automatically converted into a graphic. There is a list of paint products below that can do the job. It is also possible to make custom screen shots within FileMaker Pro. Just type in the text, set the size and style and use the keyboard command to take a screen shot (see below for the steps). Another solution is to paste text into a container field and then copy it out of the same field after it has been pasted. These techniques should be used sparingly since graphics add significantly to the file size of your database solution.

The built-in screen capture utilities on Macintosh and Windows are very limited. Third party products have features that can make screen capture easier (e.g. taking a screen shot of the current window instead of the whole screen).

Steps to use FileMaker Pro to convert font text into graphic text

The quickest method for converting fonts within FileMaker Pro depends on the knowledge that, when text is pasted into a container field FileMaker Pro will convert that text into a graphic representation of the text. This makes it possible to use any font you have installed on your computer and make sure that it will look the same on the Windows platform.

Step 1: While in layout mode enter your text and set size, style and other attributes.

Step 2: Copy the text block (not the text itself).

Step 3: Enter Browse mode and paste the copied text block into a container field.

Step 4: Copy the contents of the container field.

Step 5: Enter Layout mode and paste your newly converted font text into the layout.

Note: Font conversion from Windows to Mac using this method will cause text to become anti-aliased and will not render exactly the same as it does going from Macintosh to Windows. The reason for this is Windows bitmaps are converted to Macintosh PICT. The option of Store Compatible Graphics must also be selected in the document's preferences for it to work.

Screen capture with the Macintosh OS

Steps for ensuring good looking fonts with cross-platform files

Step 1: Take a screen shot with the Command-Shift-3 key combination.

Step 2: Locate the screen capture file on your root hard drive (it is named Picture X, where X is the number of the picture).

Step 3: Double-click or open the picture with SimpleText.

Step 4: Marquee the area of the picture that you would like to paste into your FileMaker Pro layout and copy it.

Step 5: Paste the copied graphic into your FileMaker Pro layout.

Listed below are a few screen capture utilities for the Macintosh:

- Snapz Pro by Ambrosia Software (www.ambrosiasw.com)
- ScreenShot by Beale Street Group (www.beale.com)
- Captivate from Mainstay Software (www.mstay.com)

Third party software for screen capture manipulation: Macintosh

Software packages that offer a broad range of editing tools

- ClarisWorks® from Apple Computer (www.apple.com)
  (name may change to AppleWorks)
- Photoshop™ from Adobe Systems Incorporated (www.adobe.com)
- Color It™ from MicroFrontier (www.microfrontier.com)
- Canvas™ from Deneba Systems, Inc. (www.deneba.com)

Screen capture with the Windows OS

Steps for ensuring good looking fonts with cross-platform files

Step 1: While in Browse mode of your FileMaker Pro file hold down the Alt key and hit the Print Screen F13 key.

Step 2: Open the Paint program that comes with Windows, usually found in the Accessories folder in the Start menu.

Step 3: Paste the screen capture into the Paint program.

Step 4: Marquee the area of the picture that you would like to paste into your FileMaker Pro layout. Make special notice of the size that you are selecting as indicated in the lower right hand corner of the window.

Step 5: Go back to the FileMaker Pro file and paste the copied object into your layout. In most cases FileMaker Pro will reduce the image from its original size.

Step 6: Using the Size palette you will need to set the dimensions of the pasted graphic to the original settings as remembered from the Paint program.

Listed below are a few screen capture utilities for Windows:

- SnagIt/32 (www.techsmith.com)
- Snap View (www.bayimage.com)
- Capture Professional (www.creativesoftworx.com)
- Print Screen Deluxe (www.americansys.com)
- HyperSnap-DX (www.hyperionics.com).

Third party software for screen capture manipulation: Windows

Software packages that offer a broad range of editing tools
- Photoshop™ from Adobe Systems Incorporated (www.adobe.com)
- Microsoft Works from Microsoft (www.microsoft.com)
- Corel Photo-Paint from Corel (www.corel.com)
- Paint Shop Pro from Jasc (www.jasc.com)

22.2 Graphics

The second major issue with cross-platform development is graphics. The color values from the Macintosh OS to Windows vary. Because of this, it is best to use colors that work well on both platforms.

Storing graphics

When graphics are imported into FileMaker Pro for Macintosh, they are converted into PICT format. FileMaker Pro for Windows can display these graphics without any modification. Conversely, FileMaker Pro for Windows requires that a preference be checked in order for it to store a Macintosh version of a graphic. It is turned off by default since this setting stores a Windows and a Macintosh version of the

Picture 22.2

The store compatible graphics feature is now found on both Macintosh and Windows in version 4.0 of FileMaker Pro. This option should be checked if a solution is going to be used cross-platform or needs to be backward compatible with FileMaker Pro 3.0 for GIF and JPEG graphics.

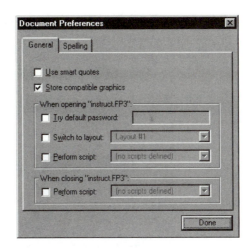

graphic, which increases the size of your database. If you are designing a cross-platform solution under the Windows operating system, it is necessary that you turn on this preference option.

Color and grayscale shades

COLORS.FP3

Reference File:
FileMaker Native Palettes

Colors on Windows tend to be a few shades darker than on the Macintosh when using FileMaker Pro. In fact, the top row of colors in the FileMaker Pro color palette should be avoided if the database will be cross-platform. A deep color from the top row, that looks great on the Macintosh, could look almost black on Windows. It is also important to remember the shade

Picture 22.2.1

Because of the Gamma conversion from Macintosh to Windows, the top row of colors will appear very dark under the Windows OS.

Avoid top row colors when developing cross-platform.

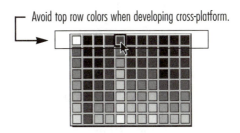

Picture 22.2.2
When developing on a
Macintosh computer, set the
Gamma value in the Monitors
& Sound control panel to
approximate what the colors
will look like under the
Windows operating system.

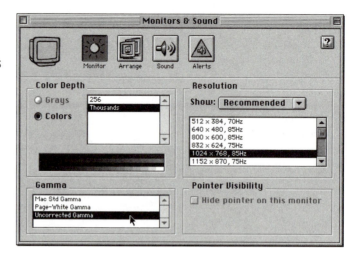

variation from Macintosh to Windows when working
with the grayscale. If developing on Windows, a
medium shade of gray will become several shades
lighter on a Macintosh computer.

The best solution when working with colors is to test
them before deciding on a color scheme. Make a sample database with the colors you plan to use and test
them on the other platform. If working on a
Macintosh (without access to a Windows computer),
setting the Gamma to Uncorrected closely approxi-
mates the screen gamma of a Windows computer.
When developing on a Windows computer, increasing the brightness and contrast of the monitor will
approximate the colors on a Macintosh computer.

Even though the colors may look different cross-platform, it is very likely you will be able to decide on
colors that work well in various shades on both platforms. It is also possible to use some of the tricks
from the previous section to solve cross-platform
color changes. Consider different files or layouts for

each platform, but also remember the extra work involved. Most likely, a happy medium can be reached so that colors and grayscales look good on both platforms.

Custom Colors

◎ **COLORS.FP3**

Reference File: FileMaker Native Palettes

Single color objects created within the FileMaker Pro architecture are stored as hexadecimal values. This allows FileMaker Pro to store native layout objects with a minimum of overhead. When you copy colored (bitmap) graphics from outside of FileMaker Pro, they are stored in FileMaker Pro with each pixel assigned a color value. This adds a significant amount of overhead, making files grow larger and interfaces display more slowly. When colors are applied to objects with FileMaker Pro tools, the whole object has a color value rather than each pixel. To get more native colors than are available from the 88 color FileMaker Pro palette with minimum overhead, use the COLORS.FP3 Reference file. Each object within this Reference file is a native FileMaker Pro object. Even when database files using these custom colors are opened over the network or distributed to others, the color values are retained as hexadecimal values.

To use these custom colors, enter layout mode and drag or copy and paste a color square from the COLORS.FP3 file to your solution. Next, make sure no objects are selected on the layout. To do this, click anywhere on the layout where there is white space and no objects. After all objects have been deselected, hold down the Command key (Macintosh) or Control key (Windows) while clicking the color square. The color from the object will now become the default for any new object. Even though the color will not appear in the FileMaker Pro color palette, it is stored as a hexadecimal value. Any new object you create will draw significantly faster and use less storage space.

Setting the default color value for FileMaker objects

Neat trick for using colors from COLOR.FP3

There is a unique trick that can be performed in FileMaker Pro that sets any color to the default color for any newly created FileMaker Pro objects.

Step 1: Make sure no objects are selected in the layout. To deselect all objects click into the gray area underneath the last layout part.

Step 2: Holding down the Command key on Macintosh or Control key for Windows, click on the object with the desired color.

Step 3: The color for both fill and line of the clicked object will be inherited by the default color value for FileMaker Pro to use. Any subsequent layout object created will have that fill and line.

22.3 Printing issues

Power Tip

A single Page Setup script step can store individual Macintosh and Windows settings. Create the script on one platform, open the script on the other platform and choose to replace the Page/Print Setup setting when exiting the script.

When it comes to forms that will be printed in a cross-platform environment, always use 0.5 inch margins. Most printers can print to within 0.25 inches of the edge of the paper, but many ink jet printers need 0.5 inch margins. Because of the various printer drivers on both Windows and Macintosh, there are no guarantees that the page will print properly if margins are less than 0.5 inches.

One alternative is to create one layout for each printer type being used. This would allow laser printers to print closer to the edge of the paper with 0.25 inch margins and prevent the right edge of ink jet printers from being cut. Use the Status(CurrentPrinterName) to gather information regarding the currently selected printer, so the user doesn't have to make the choice about which print button to click.

Another important printing issue regards internationalization. While the United States is standardized on U.S. Letter, many countries use A4 paper size. U.S. Letter is slightly wider than A4. If you create a form that extends to the edge of a U.S. Letter size, it is very likely, even with 0.5 inch margins, for the text to be cut off on the right. Therefore, it is best to design all forms with regards to the A4 paper size, unless this paper size will never be used.

22.4 Screen sizes

Picture 22.4
The Status Area occupies 70 pixels wide.

When designing a cross-platform solution, it is necessary to consider the different interface elements on Macintosh and Windows and how they affect window size. There is an area in the FileMaker Pro window on the Windows OS called Status Line Help (called Status Bar in FileMaker Pro 4.0). It can be turned on and off in the preferences section of FileMaker Pro (see Picture 22.4.1). When this option is turned on, the screen is significantly smaller than on the Macintosh. Unfortunately, this option cannot be controlled by a script and is left to each user and his individual preferences. If the user has a lower resolution screen, it is possible that the Status Line Help will force a portion of the layout off the screen, requiring the user to scroll to see the bottom of the layout. Therefore, it is best to design the window size of your solution with the expectation that this option is turned on.

Another consideration is screen size. If your solution will be used at a single location, you can design the window for the lowest resolution screen. However, if your solution is to be distributed worldwide, you need to assume the lowest common denominator.

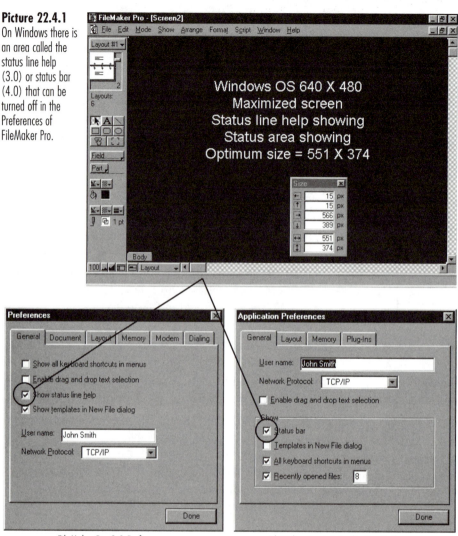

Picture 22.4.1
On Windows there is an area called the status line help (3.0) or status bar (4.0) that can be turned off in the Preferences of FileMaker Pro.

FileMaker Pro 3.0 Preferences   FileMaker Pro 4.0 Application Preferences

It is best to design for a 640 x 480 screen. Even though this will make the working area of the window much smaller, it is better than making users on lower resolution screens scroll down to see data entry fields. One way to reclaim screen real estate is to hide the

STATAREA.FP3

Technique File:
Recreating the Status
Area

Status Area. While it provides feedback regarding the status of the database and enables the user to navigate the database, almost all of the functionality can be recreated using graphics and Status functions. There is a technique file on the CD ROM that demonstrates how to simulate the Status Area.

Optimum screen sizes for different computer platforms

Best screen sizes for 640 x 480 screens

The sizes specified here are based on the assumption that the lowest common denominator of a computer screen sizes is a 15" 640 x 480 pixel screen.

	Status Area	Status Line Help	Maximized	Best Size
Macintosh	YES	N/A	YES	541 x 415
Macintosh	NO	N/A	YES	610 x 415
Windows	YES	YES	YES	551 x 374
Windows	YES	NO	YES	551 x 393
Windows	NO	NO	YES	620 x 393
Windows	NO	NO	NO	607 x 362
Windows	NO	YES	NO	607 x 343
Hybrid	YES	YES	YES	541 x 343
Hybrid	NO	YES	YES	607 x 343

Chapter 15 Overview & Quiz

Test yourself to see what you've learned.

1. **The best thing to do to fields and text blocks for cross-platform files is?**
   - ○ Make them transparent
   - ○ Add size in both width and height
   - ○ Use a non standard font
   - ○ All of the above

2. **The safest fonts for cross-platform are?**
   - ○ Helvetica/Times or Arial/New Times Roman
   - ○ Courier/Monaco or MSSans
   - ○ Chicago/Geneva or Impact/Arial
   - ○ All of the above

3. **Setting the default color for objects is done by?**
   - ○ Command/Ctrl clicking an object with nothing else selected
   - ○ Command/Ctrl clicking an object after selecting the color in the palette
   - ○ Selecting it from the Status Area with an object selected
   - ○ All of the above

4. **Which colors should be avoided in cross-platform files?**
   - ○ Non primary colors
   - ○ The second row of grays
   - ○ The top row in the FileMaker Pro palette
   - ○ All of the above

5. **Cross-platform printed forms should?**
   - ○ Use margins no smaller than .5"/1.27cm
   - ○ Adjust for various printer drivers
   - ○ Always be set to use A4
   - ○ All of the above

6. **If it's unknown what size screen the database will be used on, you can use?**
   - ○ A script to determine the size
   - ○ One minimum sized layout
   - ○ Multiple layouts
   - ○ All of the above

Answers:

Answers: 1. Add size in both width and height 2. Helvetica/Times or Arial/New Times Roman 3. Command/Ctrl clicking an object with nothing else selected 4. The top row in the FileMaker Pro palette 5. Use margins no smaller than .5"/1.27cm 6. All of the above

What you should have learned

- What issues surround cross-platform development
- Issues surrounding fonts, colors and screen graphics
- Cool tools and techniques for working with screen graphics

More technique files about cross-platform issues...

 RADIO.FP3

Technique File:
Radio Buttons

Shows how to create radio buttons that look good on both Windows and Macintosh.

User Interface Issues

23.0 FileMaker Pro Interface Design

The user interface is one of the most important aspects of your database. It's almost as important to your database as the data itself. A good interface also makes a database appealing, especially if you are staring at it all day long.

Good interface design involves much more than pretty graphics. The following sections don't tell you how to design good looking graphics. For that you'll need to purchase a book that focuses on design. What this chapter discusses are FileMaker techniques for optimizing interface design.

23.1 Global Repeating Containers

With the release of FileMaker Pro 3.0 and its relational capabilities, repeating fields have become less important for repetitive data storage. However, repeating fields still have significant value. A global repeating container field can store all your graphics in one field, rather than using one field for each graphic element.

TIP.FP3
Technique File:
Storing Graphics

MULTI.FP3
Technique File:
Multi-State Buttons

Let's say you have a button that changes depending on the state of your database. For instance, you might want a sort button to display a graphic representing the current sort order; ascending or descending. When the sorting script is performed, all you need to do is set the container field, overlaying the button, to the repeating field repetition storing the appropriate sort graphic. Rather than using one global container field for every graphic, you can store all of the graphics for your entire database solution in a single global repeating container field. In this example, the ascending sort graphic could be stored in repetition one and the descending sort graphic could be stored in repetition two.

Picture 23.1
In the CONTACTS.FP3 file there are repeating global fields that store various icons and variables. See chapter 24 for information on the developer layout.

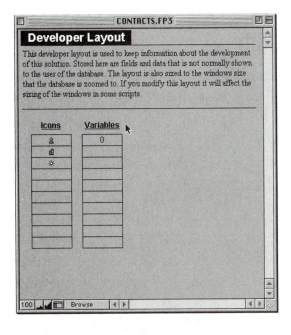

CONTACT.FP3

Chapter File:
Contacts Database

⚠ Power Tip

If a database is saved as a clone, all the values stored in global fields will be cleared. Conversely, if all records in a database are deleted, the global values will remain.

A good analogy is that of a pencil holder. If you didn't have a central location to store all your pens and pencils, they would create a mess on your desk. The concept behind using global repeating containers is not much different. If you store each graphic in a separate global container field, the number of fields in Define Fields becomes unmanageable with large projects. It is much more efficient to create a single global repeating container field and track the contents of each repetition in a developer layout. If you have a single global repeating container named "Icons", it is apparent upon entering Define Fields which field stores icons for the entire file. This makes it easier for you when you come back a month later to make modifications to the solution.

23.2 Progress bars and motion graphics

Open this file and follow along

23_A.FP3

Chapter File:
Progress Bars &
Dialog Boxes

Storing graphics in global repeating container fields enables you to accomplish many user interface tasks, such as providing visual feedback during long operations. Progress bars should be used whenever a process takes more than a few seconds. If there is no visual feedback, the user may think your solution has crashed and force quit, possibly corrupting the database. For instance, let's say you have a solution with twenty files. When you launch the solution, it can take a while for all twenty files to open. Your best bet is to provide visual feedback using a progress bar so the user knows to wait.

Picture 23.2
Each step of a 9 step progress bar is stored in an individual repetition of a global repeating container field.

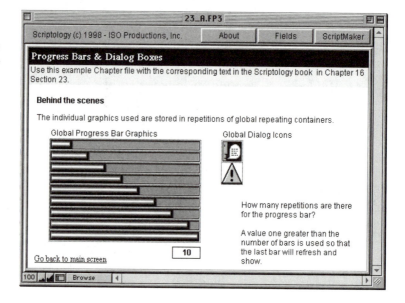

It's possible to simulate the motion of a progress bar in FileMaker Pro by storing bars of different lengths in a global repeating container field. The progress bar can be advanced in many ways. If you take the example of opening twenty different files, add a Set Field step after each Open step. Each Set Field step will set the progress bar display field to the next repetition in the global repeating field. The string of Set Field steps will simulate a moving progress bar.

Another way to advance a progress bar is to use a looping script. Each time the loop cycles, a global counter field is incremented. This counter will be used in the GetRepetition function in a Set Field step to designate the repetition parameter:

```
GetRepetition(Global Repeating Container, Counter)
```

PROGRESS.FP3

Technique File:
Progress Bars

As the counter changes, so will the repetition that the Set Field step uses. See the Chapter file 23_A.FP3 for the details on how this looping method works.

The same looping script technique can also be used to create animation in FileMaker Pro. Animation is good for splash screens that show upon launch of a solution. Animation is not an essential part of a user interface, but it can give a product a more polished look. There is a good technique file on the CD ROM called ANIMATE.FP3 that shows how to implement an animation sequence.

ANIMATE.FP3

Technique File:
Animation

23.3 Layout/Portal ID storage

One of the most valuable features in a programming languages is the ability to declare variables. Variables allow you to assign a value to a storage space that is available to the rest of the program. FileMaker Pro lacks a **variable** feature, but this does not preclude you from creating a similar system. Storing control values and flags in global repeating text fields simulates the storage of variables in an **array**.

Let's say you have a portal that contains a button. The script attached to the button needs to leave the portal row to copy a value from another field. In order to return to the portal row that was selected when the script was initiated, it is necessary to store the row number using the Status(CurrentPortalRow) function. This number could be stored in a global field or in a repetition of a global repeating field. Most likely you have values to track from other scripts, so a repeating global field makes more sense.

Picture 23.3
A repeating global field can store the last location in a tabbed interface so you can return to it anytime. Find this in file 23_B.FP3

Another example of how to use the variable field technique is when creating tabbed interfaces. The idea behind tabbed interfaces in a FileMaker Pro solution is to use multiple layouts to simulate it.

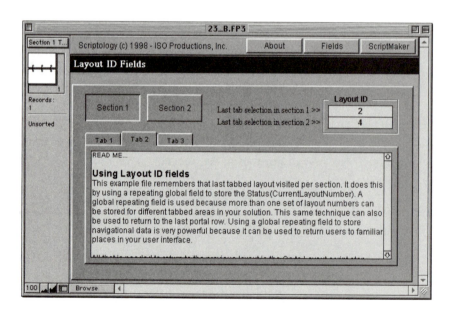

Clicking on a tab changes the layout. If you design the different layouts well, it will seem as if only certain pieces of the layout have changed. See the Technique file titled Remember Layout for an example of a tabbed layout.

When the user navigates to another location in the solution, the tab order layout that was active should be remembered. When they return to the tabbed set of layouts, the tab order they last used should show rather than the first layout in the tabbed interface. In order to track the tabbed layouts, set the Status(CurrentLayoutNumber) function to a global repeating field. When the user returns to the tabbed layout, specify the option for "layout number from field" in the Go to Layout script step. Again, it makes sense to store this value in a global repeating field. It is likely there will be many tabbed layout sets you will want to track, along with tons of variables about the status of your solution all dependant on user interaction.

A problem occurs with global variable fields when a clone of the database is saved. Saving a clone removes all data from global fields. The solution is to create a script, called "Initialize Variables", that uses a sequence of Set Field steps to set each repetition of your Variables field to a default value. The only time this script would run at startup would be if there were no records in the database. You can check for no records using the Status(CurrentRecordCount). This Status function will return the total number of records in the database regardless of the found set. If you're storing interface elements in global container fields then there's no solution if the database is saved as a clone.

Using Set Field to set a value to a repetition of a field is very simple, but elusive if you have not done it before. When selecting the target field, there is an entry field just above the OK and Cancel buttons named Repetition. It's in this field that you specify which repetition you want the Set Field, or other script step, to manipulate (see Picture 23.3.1).

Picture 23.3.1
By changing the Repetition value in the Specify Field dialog, you can adjust which repetition of a repeating field is manipulated.

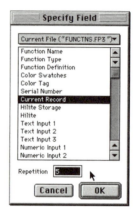

23.4 Sorting Controls

Open this file and follow along

23_C.FP3

Chapter File:
Sorting Visuals

If you offer buttons that sort, it is important to provide feedback as to the current sort order. One method was already discussed in a previous section. The technique demonstrated in this section is slightly different because it indicates which field is sorted rather than the sort order. This method also shows how to approach the task using different tools. Rather than a script, a calculation is used to change the sort graphics.

The 23_C.FP3 Chapter file on the CD ROM is shown in Picture 23.4. It indicates the sort by showing a green dot on the button that last sorted the

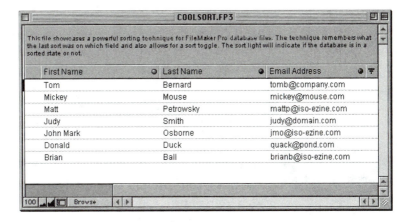

Picture 23.4

Using a combination of scripts and global fields, it is possible to provide the user with visual feedback regarding the current sort status. Take a look at the chapter file 23_C.FP3 for details.

database. Red dots indicate which buttons were not used for the last sort. You could use a script to set a green dot graphic into a container field overlaying the button attached to the script and a red dot to all other buttons. However, the dots would not update whenever the database was unsorted (e.g. after a find). It is better to track the sort status in a calculation field. Use the Status(CurrentSortStatus) function to check whether the database is sorted by a particular field or not.

Here is the formula for displaying a green dot if the file is sorted by the First Name field:

```
Case(
GetRepetition(Variables, 3) = "First Name"
and Status(CurrentSortStatus) = 1,
GetRepetition(Icons, 3),
GetRepetition(Icons, 4)
)
```

Notice the Case statement checks to see if the Variables field contains "First Name", but also requires the database to be sorted. When the database becomes unsorted due to a find, the calculation will remove the green dot even though the First Name field contains a value. Also, notice that the calculations in the Chapter file are unstored. If they are set to stored, Status functions will not update.

23.5 Dimmed buttons

Open this file and follow along

23_D.FP3

Chapter File:
Dimmed Buttons

One of the best feedback systems that can be implemented in a user interface is button states. Much like the power on/off light on electronic products, the state of a button can provide the user with feedback about its current options. An example is a database that tracks sales leads. It's desirable to dim a button that uses the Open URL step when a lead does not have a URL. You can use the IsEmpty() function to determine the contents of the URL field and display the appropriate button state. Take a look at the Chapter file 23_D.FP3 and follow along.

Method one

Method 1 uses a global container field to store graphics representing the dimmed state of each button. To create the dimmed button graphic, use a paint program. Most paint programs have a feature for lightening graphics. When the dimmed state of your buttons are complete, paste them into a global repeating container field for storage.

The example in picture 23.5 shows navigation arrows. These are popular buttons to use when controlling user navigation, because they indicate where the user is in the database. The buttons are controlled by unstored calculations that dim the button when the first or last record in the found set is reached. The first calculation checks if the current record equals one:

```
Case(
Status(CurrentRecordNumber) = 1,
GetRepetition(Navigation Icons,1),
""
)
```

The second calculation determines if the last record has been reached:

```
Case(
Status(CurrentRecordNumber) =
Status(CurrentFoundCount),
GetRepetition(Navigation Icons,2),
""
)
```

Picture 23.5
Making buttons dimmed is only a matter of controlling them with calculation fields.

The calculation fields are overlaid on top of the regular copies of the buttons. Only when the first record or last record is active will the calculation return a value for the first or second calculation, masking the regular button behind.

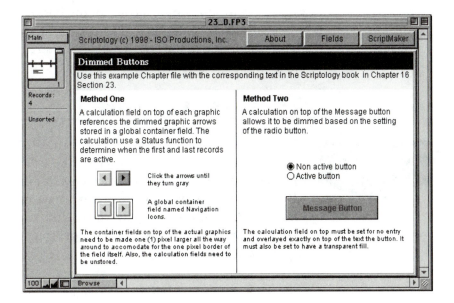

There are, however, caveats when using a system of storing buttons in global container fields. There is a possibility that a user could save the database as a clone and wipe out all data in the fields. To remedy the problem of graphics and other global values being cleared out when a database is saved as a clone, try using a preferences file (outlined in Chapter 17). It's possible to reference stored graphics through a relationship to a preferences file so they are less likely to be cleared out.

Method two

The second method for creating dimmed buttons or non-active state buttons, is to use a calculation field that returns gray colored text (shown in Picture 23.5). When the calculation field is placed on top of the button, it will seem as though the button becomes gray because the text in the calculation masks the text on the button. Place the calculation field carefully so, when the button dims, the text on top of the actual button masks the original color of the button text. The advantage of this technique is that no graphics need to be stored, thus reducing the file size of your solution.

23.6 Cover techniques

Open this file and follow along

23_E.FP3

Chapter File:
Cover Techniques

"Cover techniques" sounds very cosmetic. To get right down to it, that's exactly what they are - techniques that cover up different elements in FileMaker Pro. This section describes methods for number formatting (**field filters**) and covering up the parts of your user interface depending upon the state of your database.

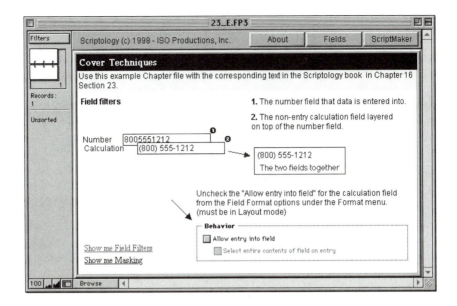

Formatting fields

Picture 23.6
Formatting numbers and text can be accomplished with calculation fields.

FileMaker Pro offers formatting for dates and times via the Field Format dialog. Missing from Field Format are options for social security, phone numbers and custom settings. There is a solution for simulating field formatting that allows you to format any text entry. The solution is very practical, since it only requires the addition of a single calculation field. The calculation field will display the number or text in the format you specify according to the calculation settings. Turning off the storage of the calculation field saves storage space and, therefore, requires very little overhead.

⊙ FILTER.FP3
Technique File:
Field Filters

Picture 23.6.1
Setting objects to transparent in the pattern menu allows you to overlay objects defined as buttons on top of other objects in the layout.

Incorporating the calculation field into the user interface, so it works just like field formatting via Field Format, is very simple. Make the calculation field opaque and disallow entry via Field Format. Next, place the calculation directly over the field it is formatting. When the user clicks into the field area, it will click-through the calculation field and enter the data entry field. When the field is not being edited, the calculation will mask the data entry field below.

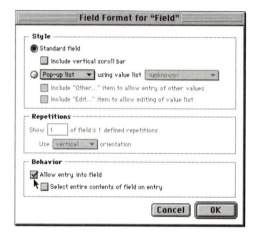

Masking

The information covered here is intended for visual feedback and is not very effective if used to cover fields intended for data entry. If you place a layout object on top of fields, the user can still enter the fields. This reveals the field you want to be hidden. Therefore, masked fields are usually set to non-entry via Field Format. An example is an option in a pulldown menu that, when selected, hides part of your user interface. Start by storing a very small swatch, that's the same color as the background, in a global container field. The size is not that important, as you'll see later, but let's say five by five pixels. Next, create a calculation field that results in the global container field when a certain value is selected from the pop-up menu. You'll need to adjust the graphic settings of the calculation so that it enlarges the graphic (see Picture 23.6.3). Choose to enlarge the graphic and deselect the "Maintain original proportions" option. This will enlarge the swatch to the size of the calculation field when the pop-up menu contains the correct value. See the 23_E.FP3 Chapter file on the CD ROM for an example of this technique.

Picture 23.6.3
Setting the graphic options of a container field, whether calculation or not, allows you to use a small graphic and stretch it out to become a large graphic that covers portions of the user interface.

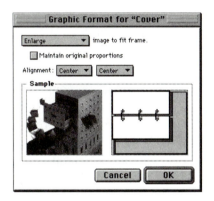

INDEX.FP3

Technique Files Index
Find Button

There is a variation of this method in the INDEX.FP3 file on the CD ROM. When you click the Find button, a data entry field seems to appear out of nowhere. The field is hidden using a layout object that's the same color as the background. The Find script uses the Go to Field script step to enter the field. Activating the field forces FileMaker to bring it to the front temporarily. Users are prevented from entering the field accidentally by deselecting the field entry check box in the Field Format dialog, but the Go to Field script step overrides this option.

HILIGHT.FP3

Technique File:
Highlighting Records

HILIGHT2.FP3

Technique File:
Highlighting Portal
Rows

There's a technique using this same method to create a highlight color in the background of records in list view and portal rows. The files HILIGHT.FP3 and HILIGHT2.FP3 explore these techniques.

23.7 Colored Text

Open this file and follow along

23_F.FP3

Chapter File:
Using colored labels

In FileMaker Pro, it always seems like magic when text changes color based on the choices in a field. This is because there are no default options that have a calculation change the color of text based on a condition. All that's needed are multiple calculation fields. Placing the calculation fields on top of a data entry field allows you to change the color of the text depending on the entry.

Here's an example. You have a field called Customer Status. You could have three calculation fields named Status Label Red, Status Label Blue and Status Label Yellow. Each of the Status Label fields would have a slightly different calculation formula that watches for different conditions in the Customer Status field. If, for example, the Customer Status field has the value of "Hot", the calculation for the Status Label Hot field will result in the value from the Customer Status field. The other calculation fields will result in nothing because they do not look to see if the customer field is "Hot". Here is the Status Label Hot calculation:

```
Case(
Customer Status = GetRepetition(Color Labels, 1),
"Hot",
""
)
```

By layering the fields on top of each other, it is possible to simulate the effect of colored text. Make sure to set the calculation fields to not allow data entry via Field Format or you will not be able to click into the Customer Status field.

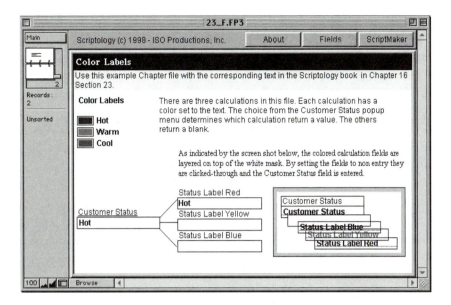

Picture 23.7
By layering individual colored calculation fields on
top of an original data
entry field it is possible to
simulate colored text.

23.8 Modifier Keys

4.0 Only

Modifier keys have been a requested feature for quite some time and FileMaker Pro 4.0 finally introduces them. Modifier keys are the Command Key, Option Key, Control Key and Shift Key on Macintosh and the Alt Key, Control Key and Shift Key on Windows. This feature is easy to implement. However, a little math is needed to make the modifier keys work. Depending on which keys are held down at the time a script is initiated, FileMaker Pro attaches a number equalling the total of all the keys depressed.

Open this file and follow along

23_G.FP3

Chapter File:
Modifier Delete

The best example is a delete button. The option on the Delete Record/Request script step allows you to delete with or without the warning dialog. You want to have the warning for beginners, but power users will be annoyed by it. By using the modifier keys, it's

MODIFIER.FP3

Technique File:
Modifier Keys

possible to bypass this dialog when a modifier key is held down. In the example provided, holding down the Option key (Macintosh) or Alt key (Windows) while clicking the delete button bypasses the warning dialog.

Modifier Keys

Key values for using the Status(CurrentModifierKeys)

FileMaker Pro uses the total of all the keys pressed on the keyboard to make use of the Status(CurrentModifierKeys)

Macintosh	Windows
Shift Key = 1	Shift Key = 1
Caps Lock = 2	Caps Lock = 2
Control Key = 4	Ctrl Key = 4
Option Key = 8	Alt Key = 8
Command/Apple Key = 16	

Example, when both the Shift Key and Control Key are depressed the total value would be 5 (4+1).

Modifier Script Example

Example of using Status(CurrentModifierKeys)

This script detects whether the control key is held down. Any other key combination is ignored. The steps after the Else step are run if the control key is not held down when the button associated with this script is clicked.

```
If ["Status(CurrentModifierKeys) = 4"]
      Show Message ["Because you held down the control key I will
      run the first part of the If statement."]
Else
      Show Message ["The control key was not held down when this
      button was clicked so I will run a different part of this
      script."]
End If
```

Using a modifier key to bypass delete prompt

This script watches to see if the Alt (Windows) or Option (Macintosh) key is depressed to bypass the dialog prompt associated with deleting a record.

```
Set Error Capture [On]
If ["Status(CurrentModifierKeys) = 8"]
      Delete Record/Request [No dialog]
Else
      Delete Record/Request []
End If
```

Using a modifier key to offer instant help

One of the best advantages of modifier keys is offering the user context-sensitive help. When a user clicks a button in the user interface with a modifier key held down, a help dialog associated with that interface item is presented.

23.9 Dialog boxes

Open this file and follow along

23_A.FP3

Chapter File:
Progress Bars &
Dialog Boxes

Because FileMaker Pro doesn't allow you to create dialog windows, you need to use a FileMaker layout to simulate one. Many FileMaker Pro beginners limit what they do with their layouts, thinking they are only good for printed forms, finds or data entry. If you expand the use of FileMaker Pro features beyond what they were designed to accomplish, you can create the illusion that FileMaker has an ability not inherent in it's design.

Creating your own dialogs, whether they are password access dialogs, warning dialogs or progress dialogs, is just a matter of taking the user to a layout that has been formatted to look like a dialog box. You can either have a simulated dialog graphic (**floating dialog box**) above the other layout items or you can turn the whole window into what looks like a dialog box (**window dialog box**).

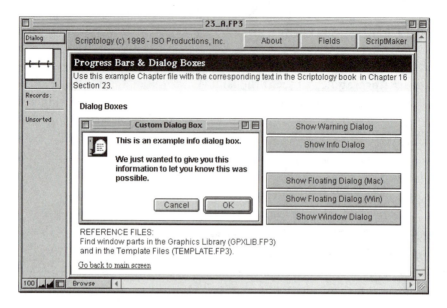

Scriptology (c) 1998 - ISO Productions, Inc. | About | Fields | ScriptMaker

Progress Bars & Dialog Boxes

Use this example Chapter file with the corresponding text in the Scriptology book in Chapter 16 Section 23.

Dialog Boxes

Custom Dialog Box

This is an example info dialog box.

We just wanted to give you this information to let you know this was possible.

Cancel | OK

Show Warning Dialog
Show Info Dialog

Show Floating Dialog (Mac)
Show Floating Dialog (Win)
Show Window Dialog

REFERENCE FILES:
Find window parts in the Graphics Library (GPXLIB.FP3) and in the Template Files (TEMPLATE.FP3).

Go back to main screen

Picture 23.9

Creating your own dialog boxes is only a matter of a couple of fields and a layout.

Floating dialog boxes

In FileMaker Pro, a floating dialog box doesn't actually float; it appears to be floating because of how it is included on the layout. Start by making an exact duplicate of the layout you want the dialog box to appear above. Set all the fields on the layout to not allow data entry via Field Format and remove all the scripts from the buttons. Next, add a graphic object or a composite of a dialog box on top of all of the other layout items. When a script switches to the dialog layout, it appears as if the dialog box is floating above the original layout. Few users will realize they have been taken to another layout, since the user interface trick is so clean. File 23_A.FP3 contains example implementations.

Picture 23.9.1

Making a field non-entry is done in the Behavior settings of the Field Format found under the Format menu while in Layout mode.

There is a good trick to make this technique work even better. If you lighten the items underneath the dialog box, it looks like the rest of the database is inactive until the dialog box is dismissed. There are two methods for lightening the background. You can either set all text blocks and objects to be a lighter shade using FileMaker Pro tools or you can take a screen shot of the window and fade the graphic with a paint program. Replace the faded screen shot for all the objects on the layout. Another idea to keep in mind is that the dialog box cannot be moved by the user. Therefore, it is best to design a dialog box that looks like it can't be moved.

Window dialog boxes

The cleanest look for dialog boxes are those that show in their own windows (see Picture 23.9.2). The dialog floats above the other windows, is moveable and takes up much less file space. The process is also fairly simple to implement. Create a new layout with just a Body part on it. Design your dialog box and you are ready to go. Simply add a script that goes to the dialog layout, hides the **status area** and zooms the window. Although the user won't see the previous layout behind the dialog, the zooming of the layout will be enough to make it appear as if a real dialog has appeared.

Picture 23.9.2
Using an actual FileMaker Pro window as a dialog box offers a lot of power for user feedback.

If you need to display many different dialogs, create a single universal layout. All you need to add is a global text and global container field. Each time the dialog layout is called from a script, the global text and container fields will be set to the message and icons you want. This saves time and keeps the size of your file down. The Chapter file 23_A.FP3 shows examples of how to repurpose a dialog box.

If you have a multi-file solution, you might want to consider using a single database for all your dialogs. The advantage is that the database with the dialogs floats above the other database windows. A disadvantage is that the dialog can be dismissed simply by clicking on the window behind it. Fortunately, there is an easy way around the problem. If you turn on Allow User Abort when you open the dialog and pause the database, the window behind cannot be accessed. The user will be forced to answer the dialog before he can continue. The steps for this procedure are demonstrated in the Technique file called Custom Dialogs (DIALOG.FP3).

DIALOG.FP3

Technique File:
Custom Dialogs

If you don't want the windows to be seen behind the dialog, use the Toggle Window script step to hide the window prior to going to the dialog box layout. Under the Windows operating system, windows are minimized rather than hidden. The best way to cover minimized windows is to use the Toggle Window script step to maximize the windows in your solution. The problem with this technique is the extra space surrounding your layout that will show on larger monitors.

23.10 Power layout techniques

Optimizing your layout design is one of the keys to creating databases more quickly. The following techniques will teach you tricks, shortcuts and other ideas in order to create your layouts more efficiently.

Grid on or grid off?

If you are intending to do any level of detail work, you need to get used to working with the grid off. The grid, while useful in a few situations, gets in the way of detail work. Often times, you will need to shift layout objects by a pixel at a time, which is not possible using the mouse with the grid turned on. You can turn the grid off by selecting it in the Arrange menu in Layout mode. If you find yourself switching the grid on and off all the time, consider using a power key to bypass the grid. On the Macintosh, hold down the Option key while dragging an object. Under the Windows operating system, hold down the Alt key. Another way to bypass the grid without turning it off, is to use the arrow keys on the keyboard to nudge graphics one pixel at a time. Choose the technique that works best for your work style.

Power Tip

The arrow keys on your keyboard will still move objects one pixel at a time, even while the grid is turned on.

Picture 23.10
Turning the AutoGrid off allows you to perform pixel perfect layout manipulation.

Finding your ideal environment

If you're putting effort into your user interface, it is important to become familiar with the different options you have when working in Layout mode. If you are working on a database that will be commercialized or used by others on a network, a clean interface is crucial. This means that half your time, if not more, will be spent designing the user interface in Layout mode. Spend time testing out the Show menu and determine what options suit your style. Setting up layout mode to work the way you do is very important in creating an efficient environment.

Picture 23.10.1
The Show menu in Layout mode offers many options. Become familiar with them so you can design your own working environment.

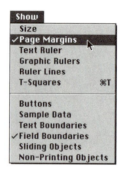

Getting a closer picture

If you design a good interface for your solution, you'll spend time adjusting the location of layout objects. Many times, you'll move objects just a few pixels to align them or increase the spacing. These minute detail adjustments are much easier at a view scale of 400%. Clicking the mountain icons in the lower left corner of the FileMaker Pro window decreases and increases the zoom percentages. Clicking the zoom percentage number will toggle you between the 100% and the last zoom percentage. Knowing this, you can quickly switch to 400% zoom to make some minute changes and flip back to 100% to see the overall change to the layout.

Advantages of the Size palette

The Size palette is one of the best friends to a FileMaker Pro layout designer. It provides you with precise measurements, so you can make objects the same size or move them to an exact location on the layout. Before you start working with it, toggle the measurement system by clicking on the text to the right of the values showing in the Size palette. Keep changing till the palette shows "px" which stands for pixels. This is the most accurate measurement system, since it accurately represents the screen resolution.

If you have a button that needs to go in the same exact position on several different layouts, you can use the Size palette to place the objects. Select the objects in the first layout and take note of the top four alignment values. You can use either the Left and Top settings or Right and Bottom settings to position the object on the new layout.

Picture 23.10.2
The size palette facilitates exact object placement from layout to layout. Sizing objects to exact dimensions is one of its other primary uses.

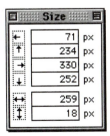

GPXLIB.FP3

Reference File:
Graphics Library

Another beneficial use of the size palette is that of adjusting the size of layout objects. A good example is when creating buttons. In the Graphic Library Resource file on the CD ROM (GPXLIB.FP3), you will find many custom buttons. After one of these has been selected, you need to add a label to the button. This is done by placing a text block on top of the button. The trick is getting the label in the exact same location for every button based on the same graphic. Set the text to Center both vertically and horizontally via the Align Text menu. Now the text is centered in the text block. Select the button and remember, width and height, the last two numbers in the Size palette. Select the label with the arrow tool and type the same two numbers into the Size palette.

Chapter 16 Overview & Quiz

Test yourself to see what you've learned.

1. **Global repeating fields are useful for?**
   - ⃝ Storing Layout ID values
   - ⃝ Storing icons and graphics
   - ⃝ Storing control data
   - ⃝ All of the above

2. **Controlling the states of buttons is done using?**
   - ⃝ Calculation and container fields
   - ⃝ Calculation fields alone
   - ⃝ Status functions
   - ⃝ All of the above

3. **Colored text can be created in FileMaker Pro using?**
   - ⃝ Special color functions
   - ⃝ Multiple calculation fields
   - ⃝ Status functions alone
   - ⃝ All of the above

4. **Modifier keys are useful for?**
   - ⃝ Adding power functions to buttons
   - ⃝ Creating tool tip help systems
   - ⃝ Modifying buttons
   - ⃝ All of the above

5. **Custom window dialog boxes require?**
   - ⃝ Many fields and layouts
   - ⃝ Two fields and one layout
   - ⃝ The Show Message script step
   - ⃝ All of the above

6. **The size palette can be used to?**
   - ⃝ Move objects to specific locations
   - ⃝ Adjust objects to perfect dimensions
   - ⃝ Align objects from layout to layout
   - ⃝ All of the above

Answers:

Answers: 1. All of the above 2. All of the above 3. Multiple calculation fields 4. Adding power functions to buttons 5. Two fields and one layout 6. All of the above

What you should have learned

- The value of global repeating fields
- How to create dialog boxes, progress bars, colored text and dimmed buttons
- Dynamic scripted sorting processes
- Key interface techniques for user feedback
- How to make working in layout mode as efficient as possible
- Using modifier keys
- Filtering and masking fields
- Uses of the Size palette

More technique files about user interface issues...

3D.FP3
Technique File:
3D Tips

How to create 3D recessed and raised boxes that are resizeable to any object.

BUTTON.FP3
Technique File:
Button Tips

A file that highlights how to properly define irregularly shaped buttons.

ALTERNAT.FP3
Technique File:
Alternating Background Color

Using an alternating background color in your list views.

DOUBLE.FP3
Technique File:
Double-Clicking

How to simulate a double-click in the user interface of a FileMaker Pro database.

MULTIPLE.FP3
Technique File:
Multi-Function Buttons

Using scripts to cause buttons to have more than one function in your user interface.

HILIGHT.FP3
Technique File:
Highlighting Records

How to highlight a record based on its selection by the user.

HELP3.FP3
Technique File:
Context Sensitive Help 3

A help system that uses the Status(CurrentModifierKey) function to show interactive help.

Chapter 17

Intermediate/Advanced

Advice – Making it Easy

24.0 Suggestions worth reading

Some of the best advice from this book, will come from this section. After reading this book and using the CD ROM, you might need to know where to go for more information. Scriptology doesn't teach you everything there is to know about FileMaker Pro. You need to surround yourself with many resources to complete your knowledge.

Where to go & what to look for

⊙ **TOPRSRCS.FP3**

Reference File:
Top Resources

Aside from this book, there are many other places that you can go for information. Depending on your current level, there are various places to go for information on the World Wide Web. Many of these are outlined in the Top Resources Reference file (TOPRSRCS.FP3) on the CD ROM. Read the following section along with the Reference file for a list of the best resources. The URL's included here were added as of March, 1998. If the actual URL has been updated or changed you can always visit the root domain (e.g. www.filemaker.com).

Third party resources

When it comes to outside sources of FileMaker Pro information, there is no shortage. From daily mailing lists to high-end development courses, you can find all kinds of information for learning and using FileMaker Pro. Whether creating a small contacts database or a corporate, mission critical information management system, use the following list of items to find more information on FileMaker Pro.

Creating a stand-alone run-time FileMaker Pro solution:

FileMaker, Inc.
FileMaker Pro SDK
Web: http://www.filemaker.com/products
Phone: 1-800-325-2747 or 408-727-8227

Commercializing a FileMaker Pro solution:

ISO Productions, Inc.
Web: http://www.isoproductions.com/
Specialty training for FileMaker Pro. Courses on a variety of subjects are available. Call for more information.
Phone: (925) 454-0187
Email: iso@isoproductions.com

Joining the FileMaker Pro Developer's association:

FileMaker, Inc. FSA Organization
Web: http://www.claris.com/partners/csa/

Daily mailing lists about FileMaker Pro:

FileMaker Pro Web discussion list
Web: http://www.isoproductions.com/res-fmwebtalk.phtml

FileMaker Pro Talk discussion list
Web: http://www.blueworld.com/lists/fmpro/

Training courses for FileMaker Pro:

FileMaker, Inc.
Web: http://www.claris.com/support/training/trngprodserv.html

Chris Moyer Consulting
Web: http://www.mindspring.com/~fmpro/
239 Kenlock Place N.E.
Atlanta, GA 30305
United States
Phone: 404-467-9301
Fax: 404-467-9416

Bowman Software
Web: http://www.bowmansoftware.com
2025 Vista Crest Drive
Carrollton, TX 75007
United States
Phone: 972-783-3411
Training: 800-287-0845
Fax: 972-394-9945

Information Specialists
Web: http://www.info-specialists.com/Training.html
2727 Walsh Avenue, Suite 105
Santa Clara, CA 95051
United States
Phone: 408-986-8802
Fax: 408-986-8905

The Support Group
Web: http://www.supportgroup.com/fmserve.htm
2344 Washington Street
Newton Lower Falls, MA 02162
United States
Phone: 617-965-0300
Fax: 617-965-0301

Robin Consulting Services
Web: http://www.robinconsulting.com/
Phone: 602-759-4844

CoreSolutions Development Inc.
Web: http://www.coresolutions.on.ca/
209-747 Hyde Park Road
London, ON Canada N6H 3S3
Tel: London: 519-641-7727
Toronto: 416-410-8649
Fax: 519-641-7728

Training materials for FileMaker Pro:

MacAcademy/Windows Academy Training
Web: http://www.macacademy.com/

Personal Training Systems
Web: http://www.ptst.com/macintosh/claris/filemaker.html

Announcements about FileMaker Pro products:

FileMaker Pro Announce
Web: http://www2.claris.com/forms/sub-announce.html

Searching for FileMaker Pro products:

ISO's ProductMart.com
Web: http://www.productmart.com/

FileMaker Solutions Guide
Web: http://www2.claris.com/forms/solutionsearch.html

FileVille
Web: http://www.ecxs.com/filemaker/index.html

ClickWorld
Web: http://www.clickworld.com/

Everything CD for FileMaker Pro
Web: http://www.everythingcd.com/

Online Technical Support:

FileMaker, Inc. TechInfo
Web: http://www2.claris.com/forms/techinfo-search.html

FileMaker Pro User Groups:

FileMaker Pro User Group of Colorado
Web: http://www.webwrks.com/FMPROUG/FileMakerProUG.html

DIGFM User Group
Web: http://www.digfm.org/
Web: http://www.pc-mac.com/index.shtml

MIT FileMaker User Group
Web: http://web.mit.edu/mugs/www/fmug.htm/

BMUG FileMaker Pro SIG
Web: http://www.bmug.org/Services/SIGs/ClarisSIG.html

FileMaker Pro Magazine Publications:

ISO FileMaker Magazine
Web: http://www.filemakermagazine.com/
4049 First Street, Suite 215
Livermore, CA 94550
United States
Phone: 925-454-0187
Fax: 925-454-9877
Email: iso@isoproductions.com

FileMaker Pro Advisor Magazine
Web: http://www.advisor.com/
5675 Ruffin Road
San Diego, CA 92123
United States

FileMaker Pro Advisor Magazine (cont.)
Phone: 800-336-6060
Phone: 619-278-5600
Fax: 619-278-0300
Email: order@advisor.com

Inside FileMaker Pro Newsletter
by The Cobb Group
Web: http://www.cobb.com/fmp/freevvr6.htm

FileMaker Pro Books:

FileMaker Pro for Dummies
Author: Tom Maremaa
Publisher: IDG
ISBN: 0764502107

Database Design and Publishing with FileMaker Pro 4
Author: Don Crabb and Jeff Gagne
Publisher: IDG
ISBN: 1558515143

Database Publishing with FileMaker on the Web
Author: Maria Langer
Publisher: Peachpit
ISBN: 0201696657

FileMaker Pro 4 (Visual Quickstart Guide series)
Publisher: Peachpit
ISBN: 0201696649

FileMaker Pro and the World Wide Web
Author: Jesse Feiler
Publisher: AP Professional
ISBN: 0126380554

24.1 Most common fields to add

Deciding what fields are common to all database projects is a personal preference related to the way you design databases. This section covers how to approach database design in a general format. After reading this section, spend some time thinking about how you can use the ideas presented. What you'll come up with is your own development process. You can also use the TEMPLATE.FP3 Resource file on the CD ROM as a template for starting all your database projects. The Resource file covers most all of the techniques described in the following sections.

TEMPLATE.FP3

Reference File:
Template Resource
File

Fields

There are fields that always seem to be added at some point in the life of a database. These include the following standard auto-entry fields:

```
Creation Date
Creation Time
Modification Date
Modification Time
```

Then there are those fields that add value to the database. These include the following:

```
Found Count [calculation, number]
Marked [standard, number]
Serial Number [standard, number, auto-enter]
Constant [calculation, number] = 1
Counter [global, text or number]
Icons [global repeating, container]
Variables [global repeating, text]
Messages [global, text]
```

Each of the above provides a unique feature. The following sections describe the importance of each.

A Found Count field

Open this file and follow along

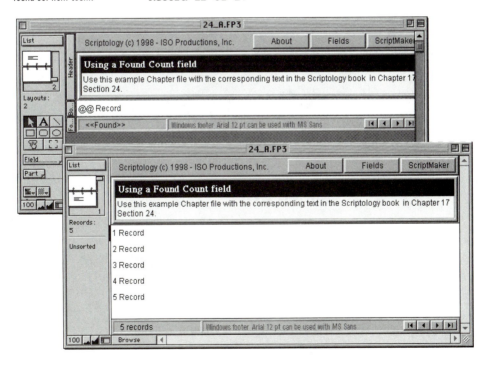

The Found Count field provides the user with a count of the records in the current found set. While this information is provided in the Status Area, there are many situations where it is hidden. The main reason to hide the Status Area is to reclaim unused screen real estate.

24_A.FP3

Chapter File:
Found Count field

The Found Count field is created using the Status(CurrentFoundCount) function. Make sure to set this field to unstored, so it refreshes every time the found count changes. The Found Count is best displayed as a merge field (see Picture 24.1). This enables you to add the total record count in a format like this:

Picture 24.1
Using a merge field in the footer of a list view provides the user with a found set item count.

    Record 12 of 27

Status Area

The Status Area uses valuable screen real estate, so it is often hidden and recreated using Status functions.

If you were to use regular fields, it would be nearly impossible to space them to accommodate all record number lengths. Merge fields shrink and enlarge according to the values available. Think of merge fields as having the ability to slide through unused space.

There is a Technique file called Recreating the Status Area (STATAREA.FP3) on the CD ROM that covers how to recreate the Status Area with calculations.

Found Count Calculation

Clean code for a smart found count

Going the extra mile in the user interface means that you account for all possible situations. The following calculation will result in a properly displayed found count field. Don't forget to set the calculation to be unstored so it refreshes properly.

```
Case(
Status(CurrentFoundCount) < 1, "0 records",
Status(CurrentFoundCount) = 1, "1 record",
Status(CurrentFoundCount) > 1, Status(CurrentFoundCount) & " records"
)
```

Note: The word "records" can be changed to whatever your database is storing (e.g. items, messages, invoices, customers, etc.).

 STATAREA.FP3

Reference File:
Recreating the
Status Area

A Marked field

Part of the value of a database is being able to isolate records by performing finds. Many times, a database query returns a found set of records that you may want to access later. One way to accomplish the task is to create a script that will restore the Find requests. However, what if the found set of records was not

Open this file and follow along

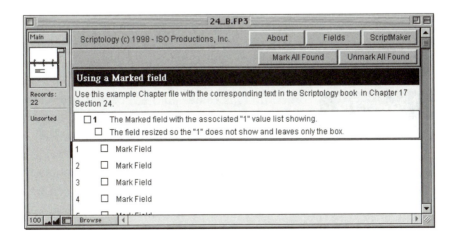

24_B.FP3

Chapter File:
Marking records

BOOKMARK.FP3

Technique File:
Bookmark

MARK.FP3

Technique File:
Marking Records by Category

Picture 24.1.1
Using a standard number field formatted as a check box provides users with marking capabilities on a record-by-record basis.

created just using Find mode, but the Omit option as well. One way to remember this found set is to mark the records. Using file 29_B.FP3 will shed some light on how to use a marked field.

Creating a marked field is very simple. All you need is a single number field and a script that performs a Replace. The Replace command places the value of one (1) on every record. In order to retrieve the marked records, add a script that performs a find for the number one (1) in the Marked field.

If you want to be able to mark records as you browse them, add a check box with a single value of one (1). Shrink the check box so all you can see is the box (see picture 24.1.1). This will enable users to perform the steps manually.

One problem that can occur with record marking is clearing marked records. If you start marking records before the previous set of records is cleared, the found set will be incorrect. To resolve this problem, create a script that locates all the marked records and clears the data in the Marked field using the Replace script command.

A more sophisiticated method for marking records for retrieval is setting a global field to the Status(CurrentTime) and then replacing the mark field with that time value. Since the current time is unique, a find by the value in the global field will return the most recently marked records. This eliminates the need to clear the previously marked records. Passing information from a gloabl field to a field in Find mode only requires a Set Field script step and a few others. Here is an example:

```
Set Field ["Global", "Status(CurrentTime)"]
Replace [No dialog, "Mark Field", "Global"]
Enter Find Mode []
Set Field ["Mark Field", "Global"]
Perform Find []
```

A Serial Number field

An auto-enter serial number field is the most common method for creating relationships between files. It also provides an effective way to uniquely identify each record in the database. In fact, a good percentage of the Technique files on the CD ROM incorporate the use of a serial number. Without serial numbers, many advanced FileMaker Pro techniques would not be possible.

4.0 Only

⚠ Power Tip

FileMaker Pro 4.0 introduces the Status(CurrentRecordID) function which uniquely identifies each record in the database. This decreases the need to use an auto-enter serial number field.

In FileMaker Pro 4.0, a new Status function was added that returns the unique ID value for each record. This value can often be substituted for a serial number field. However, there is a stability issue to consider when using the Status(CurrentRecordID) as a match value for a relationship. If the records from your database need to be transferred to a new shell, the ID on each record will change, which will invalidate all of your relationships. In this case, a serial number will work better since the values can be imported into the new FilcMakcr database. However, other situations could benefit from the Status(CurrentRecordID) function.

A Constant field

A constant field allows you to create a **data channel** from one file to another. By including a calculation field with a number result of one (1), you are able to create a relationship that acts as a channel for passing data back and forth between two files. See Chapter 5 for more information regarding data channels.

A Counter field

If you ever plan on using any sort of looping script in your database, you'll probably need a global counter field. The most common method for exiting a loop is incrementing a counter field each time the script loops and checking to see if it has reached a limit. See Chapter 5 for more information regarding looping scripts.

An Icons field

Storing all your graphics and icons in a global repeating container field reduces the clutter in Define Fields. It also gives you a single reference location for graphics. By maintaining this field on a **developer layout**, you can quickly reference each repetition of the repeating field. If you are unfamiliar with the developer layout and its use, you'll find more information in an upcoming section. Global repeating container fields are covered in more detail in Chapter 16.

A Variables field

Chapter 16 also covers the use of a global repeating text field to store variables. Using this technique provides a high level of flexibility to your database while keeping the field count to a minimum. A **developer layout** is also used to keep track of which repetition corresponds to which variable. Open the file TEMPLATE.FP3 reference file to see how the variables field is used.

TEMPLATE.FP3
Reference File:
Developer Template

A Messages field

In both Windows and Macintosh environments, users have come to expect some type of online interactive help system. While the addition of a Messages field does not directly implement that functionality, it does offer many unique solutions for getting information to the users of the database. A Messages field is a global field of type text. It is used as a universal field for conveying information to the user. This can be in the form of a dialog box (see Chapter 16) or a help system.

In the case of key based help, it is possible to use a combination of the new FileMaker Pro 4.0 Status(CurrentModifierKeys) to adjust your scripts to provide context sensitive help. When the Control key is held down, a button could place information in the Messages field instead of performing it's normal operation.

HELP.FP3
Technique File:
Context Sensitive Help

24.2 Using a developer layout

Many chapters in this book have references to a **developer layout**. The premise behind using a

TEMPLATE.FP3

Resource File:
Developer Template

developer layout is straightforward. You create a layout used for documentation, field storage, data storage, graphic storage and other tasks that the user does not need to see. The developer layout is much like a personal tool box. In this tool box you can keep whatever information and objects you need to develop your solution.

If you plan on doing a lot of development in your database, having this layout will help you test your ideas. You can place test fields on it and if you decide to use them, transfer them to the user layouts. You can also document what you are doing with the different fields in your database. This really helps when you need to change something you created months or years before. The developer layout is also where you will access variable and graphic fields.

Picture 24.2
Hiding layouts from users while in Browse mode is as easy as unchecking the Include in layouts menu option from the Layout Setup dialog box.

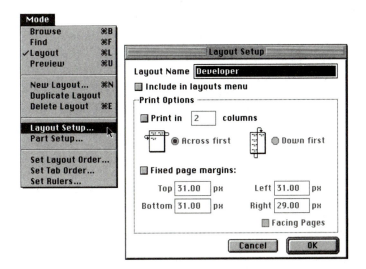

The best example of a developer layout is found in the TEMPLATE.FP3 Reference file on the CD ROM. The developer layout is often the very first layout in the database. It can be accessed using a script that jumps to that layout when you need to work with fields and information not available in the standard interface of your solution. Creating the layout is as simple as making a new layout in layout mode and giving it a name of "Developer". It is important to uncheck the Include in layouts menu option, so the layout is not accessible in Browse mode.

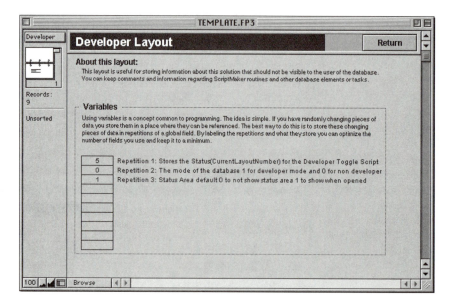

Picture 24.2.1
A developer layout provides you, the database creator, with a workspace that users cannot access.

Another development tool that helps you create databases more efficiently is a set of developer scripts. You can make these scripts available under the Script menu as you develop a solution and uncheck them, making them unavailable in the Script menu, just before releasing the database. This will give you quick access via keyboard commands. An example of a developer script is one that takes you to the developer layout. To prevent users from accessing the developer

Picture 24.2.1
Creating your own Toolbox
scripts and associating them
to the keyboard commands
creates a highly productive
development environment.

layout manually, it should not be available from the
layout menu. This works when you need a quick way
to access the developer layout without entering layout
mode to access the expanded layout menu. Another
idea for a developer script is one that unlocks the
Status Area. It is very common for a database to lock
the Status Area to increase the screen real estate and
prevent users from manually controlling the database.
You'll notice the first script in the INDEX.FP3 file
on the CD ROM unlocks the Status Area.

24.3   Using a preferences file

A common practice of database developers is to use a
preferences file. When you know the number of files
in a solution will be more than a few, a preferences
file increases the flexibility of your database system.
One of the biggest advantages is centralizing the storage of information specific to the operations of your

Picture 24.3
The INVOICER solution found
in the Chapter Files folder on
the CD ROM uses a preference
file.

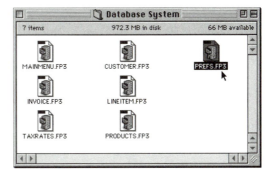

database system. A good analogy is a desk, which is the center of operations for an office. Like the desk, a preferences file is a central repository for the information and tools necessary to run a business. An example use is a logo that displays on every file in a solution. Rather than import the graphic into every file, a preferences file could store the graphic once, and through the use of **data channels**, could be displayed in every file in your solution.

Most solutions are created for more than one person. You may be distributing a solution as freeware, shareware through commercial channels, or even making it network accessible. In the case of a distributed solution, the advantage of a preferences file is the ability to update the other database files separately from your preferences file. When you release a new version of your solution and want to allow current users to upgrade, you can retain the current preference settings by replacing all the files except the Preferences file.

Test yourself to see what you've learned.

1. **A found count field is best incorporated into the layout using?**
   - ○ A formatted field
   - ○ A merge field
   - ○ Raw text
   - ○ All of the above

2. **A marked field is...**
   - ○ A number field formatted as a check box
   - ○ Boolean
   - ○ Useful for maintaining sub-sets of data
   - ○ All of the above

3. **The developer layout can be seen by?**
   - ○ All users of the database
   - ○ Anyone with access to layout mode
   - ○ Only the developer
   - ○ All of the above

4. **A variables field is useful for?**
   - ○ Preferences
   - ○ Storing manipulated data
   - ○ Storing multiple pieces of control data
   - ○ All of the above

5. **The purpose of a preferences file is to?**
   - ○ Make icons redraw faster
   - ○ Isolate preference data from the database
   - ○ Store frequently accessed data
   - ○ All of the above

Chapter 17 Highlights

What you should have learned
- Supplementary sources for FileMaker Pro information
- The common fields to have in a FileMaker Pro file and why
- Why a preferences file is useful

Answers:

Answers: 1. A merge field 2. All of the above 3. Anyone with access to layout mode 4. All of the above 5. Isolate preference data from the database

FileMaker Pro Power Keys

Documented and Undocumented Power Keys
    Macintosh Power Keys
    Windows Power Keys

Learning the power keys for any software package can increase productivity. Contained in this appendix is every keyboard command and mouse shortcut possible in FileMaker Pro. Included are both documented and undocumented keys.

The list of keys are broken down by the mode they are available in. These include Browse mode, Dialog Boxes, Find Mode, Layout Mode, Text Formatting/Editing and Universal Power Keys. The first group of keys are Macintosh and the second set is Windows.

Browse Mode

Cancel running script/default cancel button . . . . .Command-(period) Browse
  Cancels either an operation or a dialog box.

Copy all records . . . . .Command-Option-C Browse
  Copies each and every record in the found set. The records will be copied to a tab-separated format. Make sure no
  fields are selected or the keyboard command will not work.

Copy record/text . . . . .Command-C Browse
  Using Command-C, the Copy command, while no fields are selected or active will copy the ENTIRE RECORD. If there
  are multiple fields then they will be separated by tab characters. See Command-Option-C. Otherwise, the selected
  text will be copied.

Correct spelling . . . . .Command-Shift-Y Browse
  Corrects the currently selected word if spell as you type is turned on.

Create new record . . . . .Command-N Browse

Cut text . . . . .Command-X Browse

Delete record . . . . .Command-E Browse

Delete record without confirmation . . . . .Command-Option-E Browse

Duplicate record . . . . .Command-D Browse
  Duplicates a layout object, record or search request. Duplicating a layout object will offset it 6 pixels by 6 pixels. Use
  the arrow keys to move it up 5 and over 5 for a perfect 1 pixel offset.

Exit record . . . . .Enter Browse

Find all records . . . . .Command-J Browse

Hide pop-up list . . . . .Esc Browse
  When in a pop-up menu field hitting Esc will hide the list values and remain in the current field.

Jump to book . . . . .Esc Browse
  A handy little key that is often overlooked. Hitting Escape will jump to what is called 'the book'. This is the number
  under the cards in the status area to the left. In order for it to work there must be no active fields selected.

Next field . . . . .Tab Browse

Omit multiple . . . . .Command-Shift-M Browse

Omit record . . . . .Command-M Browse

Open host (bypass open dialog) . . . . .Command-Option-O Browse

Paste . . . . .Command-V Browse

Paste current date	.Command-(hyphen)	Browse
Paste current time	.Command-;	Browse
Paste from field index	.Command-I	Browse
Paste from last record	.Command-'	Browse
Paste from last record/move one field	.Command-Shift-'	Browse
Paste user name	.Command-Shift-N	Browse
Paste without style	.Command-Option-V	Browse
Play/record sound	.Space Bar	Browse
Previous field	.Shift-Tab	Browse
Print (bypass dialog box)	.Command-Option-P	Browse
Refind	.Command-R	Browse
Replace current contents in found set	.Command-=	Browse
Select all	.Command-A	Browse
Select multiple radio buttons	.Shift-Click-[radio button]	Browse
Select multiples in list	.Shift-Click-[pop-up menu]	Browse
Sort records	.Command-S	Browse

Dialog Boxes

Force show password dialog	.Option-Launch File	Dialog Box

Having FileMaker use a default password via Preferences is a great interface enhancement if most of the time the same password is being used by your users. If you need to enter a different password then hold down the Option key while launching the file.

Increase host search timeout	.Option-Click-[hosts button]	Dialog Box

Makes FileMaker Pro search longer for networked files. Works well when you are running over TCP/IP and need to increase the timeout.

Move item down in list	.Command-Down Arrow	Dialog Box

Moves the selected item in a list down. Works in the Layout Reordering, ScriptMaker, Sort, and Export/Import Order dialogs.

Move item up in list	.Command-Up Arrow	Dialog Box

Moves the selected item in a list up. Works in the Layout Reordering, ScriptMaker, Sort, and Export/Import Order dialogs.

Rebuild options	.Option-Click-[new button]	Dialog Box

Rebuilds the list of fields. Sometimes fields will disappear from the list of export choices. If that happens, hold down the Option key while clicking on the New button. Keep the Option key down until the list of fields for export appear.

Find Mode

Delete request	.Command-E	Find
Paste current date	.Command-(hyphen)	Find
Paste current time	.Command-;	Find
Paste from field index	.Command-I	Find
Paste from last record	.Command-'	Find

Paste user name	.Command-Shift-N	Find
Toggle omit request check box	.Command-M	Find
Adjust layout part (ignoring layout objects)	.Option-Drag-[layout part]	Layout
Align objects using current settings	.Command-K	Layout
Alignment dialog box	.Command-Shift-K	Layout
Constrain line	.Option-[line tool]	Layout
Constrain object movement	.Shift-Drag-[object]	Layout
Constrain oval	.Option-[oval tool]	Layout
Constrain rectangle (create square)	.Option-Drag-[rectangle tool]	Layout
Constrain resizing	.Shift-Drag-[resizing object]	Layout
Context-sensitive pop-up menu	.Control-Click-[layout object]	Layout
Copy layout object/text	.Command-C	Layout
Create a new layout	.Command-N	Layout
Cut layout object/text	.Command-X	Layout
Define part setting	.Double Click-[layout part]	Layout
Delete layout	.Command-E	Layout
Duplicate layout object	.Command-D	Layout

Duplicates a layout object, record or search request. Duplicating a layout object will offset it 6 pixels by 6 pixels. Use the arrow keys to move it up 5 and over 5 for a perfect 1 pixel offset.

Duplicate object	.Option-Drag-[layout object]	Layout
Field borders	.Command-Option-B	Layout
Field format	.Command-Option-F	Layout
Group objects	.Command-G	Layout
Lock layout tool	.Double Click-[tool]	Layout
Lock object(s)	.Command-H	Layout
Marquee partial objects	.Command-Drag	Layout

Selects any items touching the marquee rectangle. Normally, an object needs to be completely contained within the selection marquee for it to be selected.

Move layout object one pixel down	.Down Arrow	Layout
Move layout object one pixel left	.Left Arrow	Layout
Move layout object one pixel right	.Right Arrow	Layout
Move layout object one pixel up	.Up Arrow	Layout
Move object (ignoring grid)	.Command-Drag-[object]	Layout
New Break	.Option-[layout setup]	Layout

Displays the New Break check box. This feature is normally hidden. Only use it if text is being cut across page breaks. Just choose Layout Setup from the Mode menu while holding down the Option key.

Paste current date	.Command-(hyphen)	Layout
Paste current time	.Command-;	Layout
Paste from clipboard	.Command-V	Layout
Paste merge field	.Command-M	Layout

Paste user name . . . . .Command-Shift-N Layout

Paste without style . . . . .Command-Option-V Layout

Print (bypass dialog box) . . . . .Command-Option-P Layout

Reorder layout part . . . . .Shift-Drag-[layout part] Layout

Resize (ignoring grid) . . . . .Command-[resize object] Layout

Rotate object . . . . .Command-Option-R Layout

Select all . . . . .Command-A Layout

Select all (same object type) . . . . .Command-Option-A Layout

  When in Layout mode, selecting a particular object TYPE (e.g. box or line) and then performing this keyboard command will select all objects of the same type.

Send object(s) backward . . . . .Command-Shift-J Layout

Send object(s) forward . . . . .Command-Shift-F Layout

Send object(s) to back . . . . .Command-Option-Shift-J Layout

Send object(s) to front . . . . .Command-Shift-Option-F Layout

Set default object attributes . . . . .Command-Click-[layout object] Layout

  Sets whatever is clicked to the default setting for the next object. For example, if the default setting is for 14 point
  Helvetica, but you want new fields to be set to 12 point Times, Command-click a field or text block that is already in
  12 point Times.

Sliding/Printing . . . . .Command-Option-T Layout

Specify button . . . . .Double Click-[button] Layout

Specify field . . . . .Double Click-[field] Layout

Text format dialog box . . . . .Option-Double Click-[text/field] Layout

Toggle AutoGrid . . . . .Command-Y Layout

Toggle layout part . . . . .Command-Click-[layout part] Layout

  Toggles part labels between horizontal and vertical configuration.

Toggle previous layout tool . . . . .Enter Layout

Toggle T-square . . . . .Command-T Layout

Ungroup selection . . . . .Command-Shift-G Layout

Unlock selection(s) . . . . .Command-Shift-H Layout

Text Formatting/Editing

Align text center . . . . .Command-\ Text

  Aligns text to the center. Command-Shift-C can also be used to center text.

Align text full justify . . . . .Command-Shift-\ Text

Align text left . . . . .Command-[Text

  Aligns text to the left. Command-Shift-L can also be used to left justify text.

Align text right . . . . .Command-] Text

  Aligns text to the right. Command-Shift-R can also be used to right justify text.

Bypass WYSIWYG fonts . . . . .Option-[font menu] Text

Delete character to right . . . . .Del Text

Delete line left . . . . .Command-Del Text

Delete paragraph left	.Command-Option-Del	Text
Delete word left	.Option-Delete	Text
Delete word right	.Option-Del	Text
Extend text selection by line	.Shift-Up Arrow	Text
Extend text selection one line	.Shift-Down Arrow	Text
Extend text selection to end	.Command-Shift-Down Arrow	Text
Extend text selection to line end	.Command-Shift-Right Arrow	Text
Extend text selection to line start	.Command-Shift-Left Arrow	Text
Extend text selection to next character	.Shift-Right Arrow	Text
Extend text selection to next word	.Shift-Option-Right Arrow	Text
Extend text selection to start	.Command-Shift-Up Arrow	Text
Extend text selection to previous character	.Shift-Left Arrow	Text
Extend text selection to previous word	.Shift-Option-Left Arrow	Text
Increase font size (by point)	.Command-Shift-Option->	Text
Increase font size (preset range)	.Command-Shift->	Text
Insert tab	.Option-Tab	Text
Move text cursor one word left	.Option-Left Arrow	Text
Move text cursor one word right	.Option-Right Arrow	Text
Move text cursor to beginning	.Command-Left Arrow	Text
Move text cursor to end	.Command-Down Arrow	Text
Move text cursor to end of line	.Command-Right Arrow	Text
Move text cursor to paragraph start	.Command-Up Arrow	Text
Reduce font size (by point)	.Command-Shift-Option-<	Text
Reduce font size (preset range)	.Command-Shift-<	Text
Select line	.Triple Click	Text
Select paragraph	.Quadruple Click	Text
Select whole text block	.Quintuple Click	Text
Select word	.Double Click-[word]	Text
Toggle text style bold	.Command-Shift-B	Text
Toggle text style italic	.Command-Shift-I	Text
Toggle text style outline	.Command-Shift-O	Text
Toggle text style plain	.Command-Shift-P	Text
Toggle text style shadow	.Command-Shift-S	Text
Toggle text style subscript	.Command-Shift-(hyphen)	Text
Toggle text style superscript	.Command-Shift-+	Text
Toggle text style underline	.Command-Shift-U	Text

Close window . . . . .Command-W   Universal
> Closes the current window. Will even close files that are hidden under the Window menu. Great way to close all hidden files.

Define fields dialog box . . . . .Command-Shift-D   Universal

Enter browse mode . . . . .Command-B   Universal

Enter find mode . . . . .Command-F   Universal

Enter layout mode . . . . .Command-L   Universal

Enter preview mode . . . . .Command-U   Universal

Force window to main monitor (maximize) .Option-Click-[resize box]   Universal

Forward record/layout/request navigation . . . . .Command-Tab   Universal
> Jumps to the next record, layout, page or find request. Will also work using the keyboard equivalent Control-Down Arrow or Command-Down Arrow. See Command-Shift-Tab.

Launch FileMaker Pro help . . . . .Command-?   Universal

Open file . . . . .Command-O   Universal

Print . . . . .Command-P   Universal

Quit . . . . .Command-Q   Universal

Reverse record/layout/request navigation . . . . .Command-Shift-Tab   Universal
> Jumps to the previous record, layout, page or find request. Will also work using the keyboard equivalent Control-Up Arrow. See Command-Tab.

Scroll window page view down . . . . .Page Down   Universal

Scroll window page view up . . . . .Page Up   Universal

Toggle status area . . . . .Command-Option-S   Universal

Undo . . . . .Command-Z   Universal

Zoom window . . . . .Command-Shift-Z   Universal

FileMaker Pro Keyboard Commands (Windows)

Activate layout pop-up in status area . . . . .F2   Browse
> Activates the layout selection pop-up found at the top of the status area.

Cancel running script/default cancel button . . . . .Esc   Browse

Copy all records . . . . .Control-Shift-C   Browse
> Copies each and every record in the found set. The records will be copied to a tab-separated format. Make sure no fields are selected or the keyboard command will not work.

Copy record/text . . . . .Control-C   Browse
> Using Command-C, the Copy command, while no fields are selected or active will copy the ENTIRE RECORD. If there are multiple fields then they will be separated by tab characters. See Command-Option-C. Otherwise, the selected text will be copied.

Correct spelling . . . . .Control-Shift-Y   Browse
> Corrects the currently selected word if spell as you type is turned on.

Create new record . . . . .Control-N   Browse
Cut text . . . . .Control-X   Browse
Delete record . . . . .Control-E   Browse
Delete record without confirmation . . . . .Control-Shift-E   Browse
Duplicate record . . . . .Control-D   Browse
Exit record . . . . .Enter (on keypad)   Browse
Find all records . . . . .Control-J   Browse
Jump to book . . . . .Esc   Browse
      A handy little key that is often overlooked. Hitting Escape will jump to what is called 'the book'. This is the number
      under the cards in the status area to the left. In order for it to work there must be no active fields selected.
Next field . . . . .Tab   Browse
Omit multiple . . . . .Control-Shift-M   Browse
Omit record . . . . .Control-M   Browse
Open host (bypass open dialog) . . . . .Control-Shift-O   Browse
Paste current date . . . . .Control-(hyphen)   Browse
Paste current time . . . . .Control-;   Browse
Paste from field index . . . . .Control-I   Browse
Paste from last record . . . . .Control-'   Browse
Paste from last record/move one field . . . . .Control-Shift-'   Browse
Paste text . . . . .Control-V   Browse
Paste user name . . . . .Control-Shift-N   Browse
Paste without style . . . . .Control-Shift-V   Browse
Play/record sound . . . . .Space Bar   Browse
Previous field . . . . .Shift-Tab   Browse
Print (bypass dialog box) . . . . .Control-Shift-T   Browse
Refind . . . . .Control-R   Browse
Replace current contents in found set . . . . .Control-=   Browse
Select all . . . . .Control-A   Browse
Select multiple radio buttons . . . . .Shift-Click-[radio button]   Browse
Select multiples in list . . . . .Shift-Click-[pop-up menu]   Browse
Sort records . . . . .Control-S   Browse

Dialog Boxes

Force show password dialog . . . . .Shift-Launch File   Dialog Box
      Having FileMaker use a default password via Preferences is a great interface enhancement if most of the time the
      same password is being used by your users. If you need to enter a different password then hold down the Shift key
      while launching the file.
Increase host search timeout . . . . .Control-Click-[hosts button]   Dialog Box
      Makes FileMaker Pro search longer for networked files. Works well when you are running over TCP/IP and need to
      increase the timeout.

Move item down in list . . . . .Control-Down Arrow   Dialog Box
> Moves the selected item in a list down. Works in the Layout Reordering, ScriptMaker, Sort, and Export/Import Order
> dialogs.

Move item up in list . . . . .Control-Up Arrow   Dialog Box
> Moves the selected item in a list up. Works in the Layout Reordering, ScriptMaker, Sort, and Export/Import Order
> dialogs.

Rebuild options . . . . .Control-Click-[okay button]   Dialog Box
> Rebuilds the list of fields. Sometimes fields will disappear from the list of export choices. If that happens, hold down
> the Control key while clicking on the New button. Keep the Control key down until the list of fields for export appear.

Find Mode

Activate search options pop-up . . . . .Alt-B   Find
Delete request . . . . .Control-E   Find
Paste current date . . . . .Control-(hyphen)   Find
Paste current time . . . . .Control-;   Find
Paste from field index . . . . .Control-I   Find
Paste from last record . . . . .Control-'   Find
Paste user name . . . . .Control-Shift-N   Find
Toggle omit request check box . . . . .Alt-O   Find

Layout Mode

Adjust layout part (ignoring layout objects) . . . . .Alt-Drag-[layout part]   Layout
Align objects using current settings . . . . .Control-K   Layout
Alignment dialog box . . . . .Control-Shift-K   Layout
Constrain line . . . . .Control-[line tool]   Layout
Constrain object movement . . . . .Shift-Drag-[object]   Layout
Constrain oval . . . . .Control-[oval tool]   Layout
Constrain rectangle (create square) . . . . .Control-Drag-[rectangle tool]   Layout
Constrain resizing . . . . .Shift-Drag-[resizing object]   Layout
Context-sensitive pop-up menu . . . . .Right Mouse Click   Layout
Copy layout object/text . . . . .Control-C   Layout
Create a new layout . . . . .Control-N   Layout
Cut layout object/text . . . . .Control-X   Layout
Define part setting . . . . .Double Click-[layout part]   Layout
Delete layout . . . . .Control-E   Layout
Duplicate layout object . . . . .Control-D   Layout
> Duplicates a layout object, record or search request. Duplicating a layout object will offset it 6 pixels by 6 pixels. Use
> the arrow keys to move it up 5 and over 5 for a perfect 1 pixel offset.

Duplicate object . . . . .Control-Drag-[layout object]   Layout
Field borders . . . . .Alt-T then R   Layout

Field format . . . . .Alt-T then O   Layout

Group objects . . . . .Control-G   Layout

Lock layout tool . . . . .Double Click-[tool]   Layout

Lock object(s) . . . . .Control-H   Layout

Marquee partial objects . . . . .Control-Drag   Layout

> Selects any items touching the selection rectangle. Normally, an object needs to be completely contained within the selection marquee for it to be selected.

Move layout object one pixel down . . . . .Down Arrow   Layout

Move layout object one pixel left . . . . .Left Arrow   Layout

Move layout object one pixel right . . . . .Right Arrow   Layout

Move layout object one pixel up . . . . .Up Arrow   Layout

Move object (ignoring grid) . . . . .Alt-Drag-[object]   Layout

New Break . . . . .Shift-[layout setup]   Layout

> Displays the New Break check box. This feature is normally hidden. Only use it if text is being cut across page breaks. Just choose Layout Setup from the Mode menu while holding down the Shift key.

Paste current date . . . . .Control-(hyphen)   Layout

Paste current time . . . . .Control-;   Layout

Paste from clipboard . . . . .Control-V   Layout

Paste merge field . . . . .Control-M   Layout

Paste user name . . . . .Control-Shift-N   Layout

Paste without style . . . . .Control-Shift-V   Layout

Print (bypass dialog box) . . . . .Control-Shift-T   Layout

Reorder layout part . . . . .Shift-Drag-[layout part]   Layout

Resize (ignoring grid) . . . . .Alt-[resize object]   Layout

Rotate object . . . . .Alt-A then R   Layout

Select all . . . . .Control-A   Layout

Select all (same object type) . . . . .Control-Shift-A   Layout

> When in Layout mode, selecting a particular object TYPE (e.g. box or line) and then performing this keyboard command will select all objects of the same type.

Send object(s) backward . . . . .Control-Shift-J   Layout

Send object(s) forward . . . . .Control-Shift-F   Layout

Send object(s) to back . . . . .Alt-A then B   Layout

Send object(s) to front . . . . .Alt-A then F   Layout

Set default object attributes . . . . .Control-Click-[layout object]   Layout

> Sets whatever is clicked to the default setting for the next object. For example, if the default setting is for 14 point Helvetica, but you want new fields to be set to 12 point Times, Command-click a field or text block that is already in 12 point Times.

Sliding/Printing . . . . .Alt-T then I   Layout

Specify button . . . . .Double Click-[button]   Layout

Specify field . . . . .Double Click-[field]   Layout

Text format dialog box . . . . .Control-Double Click-[field]   Layout

Toggle AutoGrid . . . . .Control-Y   Layout

Layout Mode (cont.)

Toggle layout part	Control-Click-[layout part]	Layout
Toggle previous layout tool	Enter (on keypad)	Layout
Toggle T-square	Control-T	Layout
Ungroup selection	Control-Shift-G	Layout
Unlock selection(s)	Control-Shift-H	Layout

Text Formatting/Editing

Align text center	Control-\	Text
Align text left	Control-[	Text
Align text right	Control-]	Text
Delete character to right	Delete	Text
Delete word left	Control-Backspace	Text
Delete word right	Control-Delete	Text
Extend text selection by line	Shift-Up Arrow	Text
Extend text selection one line	Shift-Down Arrow	Text
Extend text selection to end	Control-Shift-End	Text
Extend text selection to line end	Shift-End	Text
Extend text selection to line start	Shift-Home	Text
Extend text selection to next character	Shift-Right Arrow	Text
Extend text selection to next word	Shift-Control-Right Arrow	Text
Extend text selection to paragraph start	Control-Shift-Home	Text
Extend text selection to previous character	Shift-Left Arrow	Text
Extend text selection to previous word	Shift-Control-Left Arrow	Text
Increase font size (by point)	Control-Shift->	Text
Increase font size (preset range)	Control-[period]	Text
Insert tab	Control-Tab	Text
Move text cursor one word left	Control-Left Arrow	Text
Move text cursor one word right	Control-Right Arrow	Text
Move text cursor to beginning	Home	Text
Move text cursor to end	Control-End	Text
Move text cursor to end of line	End	Text
Move text cursor to paragraph start	Control-Home	Text
Reduce font size (by point)	Control-Shift-<	Text
Reduce font size (preset range)	Control-[comma]	Text
Select line	Triple Click	Text
Select paragraph	Quadruple Click	Text
Select whole text block	Quintuple Click	Text
Select word	Double Click-[word]	Text
Toggle text style bold	Control-Shift-B	Text

Text Formatting/Editing (cont.)

Toggle text style italic . . . . .Control-Shift-I   Text
Toggle text style plain . . . . .Control-Shift-P   Text
Toggle text style underline . . . . .Control-Shift-U   Text

Universal Power Keys

Cancel paused script . . . . .Alt-N   Universal
Cascade windows . . . . .Shift-F5   Universal
Close window . . . . .Control-W   Universal

> Closes the current window. Will even close files that are hidden under the Window menu. Great way to close all those related files that keep opening up every time a related field shows on the screen. Ctrl + F4 will also perform the same function.

Context-sensitive help . . . . .Shift-F1   Universal

> Opens Quick Info. After using this keyboard equivalent, the FileMaker Help program will launch with information about whatever interface element is clicked next.

Cycle to next window . . . . .Control-F6   Universal
Cycle to previous window . . . . .Control-Shift-F6   Universal
Define fields dialog box . . . . .Control-Shift-D   Universal
Enter browse mode . . . . .Control-B   Universal
Enter find mode . . . . .Control-F   Universal
Enter layout mode . . . . .Control-L   Universal
Enter preview mode . . . . .Control-U   Universal
Forward record/layout/request navigation . . . . .Control-Down Arrow   Universal

> Alternate key is Shift-Page Down.

Increase view percentage . . . . .F3   Universal
Launch FileMaker Pro help . . . . .F1   Universal
Open file . . . . .Control-O   Universal
Print . . . . .Control-P   Universal
Quit . . . . .Control-Q   Universal

> Alternate key is Alt + F4.

Reduce view percentage . . . . .Shift-F3   Universal
Reverse record/layout/request navigation . . . . .Control-Up Arrow   Universal

> Alternate key is Shift-Page Up.

Scroll window left . . . . .Control-Page Up   Universal
Scroll window page view down . . . . .Page Down   Universal
Scroll window page view up . . . . .Page Up   Universal
Scroll window right . . . . .Control-Page Down   Universal
Tile windows . . . . .Shift-F4   Universal
Toggle status area . . . . .Control-Shift-S   Universal
Undo . . . . .Control-Z   Universal
Zoom window . . . . .Control-Shift-Z   Universal

FileMaker Pro Functions

Functions listed by type

At the heart of what makes a FileMaker Pro database useful as a data storage and retrieval system are the functions that can be used in both calculations and scripts. It is the universal implementation of these functions that make FileMaker Pro an extensive development tool.

Text Functions	Type	Result

Exact (original text, comparison text) ....Text — Boolean

Returns a value of 1 for an exact match between original text and comparison text returns 0 if there is no exact match. Function is case sensitive.

Example 1: Exact(Status,"Active") = 1
presuming the Status field contains the word "Active"
Example 2: Exact("Some Text","some text") = 0

Left (text, number) ....Text — Text

Starting from the left of the "text" string, returns the first "number" of characters. Spaces count as a valid character.

Example 1: Left(Notes,3) = The
presuming the Notes field contains the words "The field"
Example 2: Left("Some Text",4) = Some

LeftWords (text, number of words) ....Text — Text

Starting from the left, selects the "number of words" in "text". Commas and other punctuation are not considered words or parts of words.

Example 1: LeftWords(Notes,2) = On September
presuming the Notes field contains the words "On September second"
Example 2: LeftWords("Some Text",1) = Some

Length (text) ....Text — Number

Returns the length in number of characters found in "text". Spaces and punctuation count.

Example 1: Length(My Field) = 10
presuming My Field contains the words "The fields"
Example 2: Length("Some Text") = 9

Lower (text) ....Text   Text

Converts all characters in "text" to lower case.

Example 1:   Lower(Field X) = the field
> *presuming Field X contains the words "The field"*

Example 2:   Lower("Some Text") = some text

Middle (text, start, size) ....Text   Text

Returns characters of "text" determined by "size", beginning at "start".

Example 1:   Middle(Field X,6,3) = Due
> *presuming Field X contains the words "Past Due Today"*

Example 2:   Middle("Some Text",3,2) = me

MiddleWords (text, starting word, number of words) ....Text   Text

Returns words, beginning at "starting word", for "number of words" specified.

Example 1: MiddleWords(Field X,2,1) = Due
> *presuming Field X contains the words "Past Due Today"*

Example 2: MiddleWords("Some Literal Text",2,1) = Literal

PatternCount (text, search string) ....Text   Number

Returns the number of occurrences of a "search string" in "text". Case insensitive. How many times does the *search string* appear in the *text*?

Example 1:   PatternCount(Notes,"the") = 2
> *presuming the Notes field contains the text "The document was the best evidence."*

Example 2:   PatternCount("ABCDEFGHIJKLMNOPQRSTUV","ABC") = 1

Position (text, search string, start, occurrence) ....Text   Number

Returns the position of "search string" in "text", beginning at "start", for the *n* "occurrence" – where *n* is equal to a number. *Starting* at the *first* occurrence, what is the position of the *search string* in the *text*?

Example 1:   Position(Notes,"the",1,2) = 18
> *presuming the Notes field contains the text "The document was the best evidence."*

Example 2:   Position("ABCDEFGHIJKLMNOPQRSTUV","E",1,1) = 5

Proper (text) . . . . .Text   Text
Capitalizes the first character of each word in "text".

Example 1:   `Proper(Notes) = The Document Was The`
               `Best Evidence.`
               presuming the Notes field contains the text "The document was the best evidence."
Example 2:   `Proper("abcdef ghijkl") = Abcdef Ghijkl`

Replace (text, start, size, replacement text) . . . . .Text   Text
Replaces the replacement string in "text" beginning at "start" for the num-
ber of characters in "size" and results in the new text with the replaced
characters.

Example 1:   `Replace(Notes,5,8,"knife") = The knife was`
               `the best evidence`
               presuming the Notes field contains the text "The document was the best evidence."
Example 2:   `Replace("ABCDEFGH",1,3,"123") = 123DEFGH`

Right (text, number) . . . . .Text   Text
Starting at the right, returns the first "number" of characters in "text".
Spaces count as one character.

Example 1:   `Right(Notes,14) = best evidence.`
               presuming the Notes field contains the text "The document was the best evidence."
Example 2:   `Right("Some Text",4) = Text`

RightWords (text, number of words) . . . . .Text   Text
Starting at the right, returns the first "number" of words in "text". Commas
and other punctuation are not considered words or parts of words.

Example 1:   `RightWords(Notes,2) = best evidence`
               presuming the Notes field contains the text "The document was the best evidence."
Example 2:   `RightWords("Some Text",1) = Text`

Substitute (text, search string, replace string) . . . . .Text   Text
Replaces the "search string" in "text" with "replace string". Case sensitive.

Example 1:   `Substitute(Notes,"cat","dog") = The dog was in`
               `the tree.`

presuming the Notes field contains the text "The cat was in the tree."

Example 2:   `Substitute("Some Text","Some","Extra") =`
                       `Extra Text`

TextToDate (text) . . . . Text   Date

Converts a "text" string to a date so that date calculations can be applied.

Example 1:   `TextToDate(Text Field) = 11/12/98`
                presuming Text Field contains the text "11/12/98"
Example 2:   `TextToDate("10/23/71") = 10/23/71`

TextToNum (text) . . . . Text   Number

Converts "text" to a number. FileMaker Pro will only see valid numeric characters and ignore all other text characters.

Example 1:   `TextToNum(Text Field) = 15.238`
                presuming Text Field contains the text "MSP15.238"
Example 2:   `TextToNum("67843") = 67843`

TextToTime (text) . . . . Text   Time

Converts "text" to a time. Text must be in time (hh:mm:ss) format.

Example 1:   `TextToTime(Text Field) = 1:46:00`
                presuming Text Field contains the text "1:46 AM"
Example 2:   `TextToTime("12:34:40") = 12:34:40`

Trim (text) . . . . Text   Text

Strips leading and trailing spaces from "text". Disregards spaces between words.

Example 1:   `Trim(Some Field) = Hello`
                presuming Some Field contains the text " Hello "
Example 2:   `Trim("   Extra Spaces   ") = Extra Spaces`

Upper (text) . . . . Text   Text

Converts all characters in "text" to uppercase.

Example 1:   `Upper(Some Field) = THIS IS TEXT`
                presuming Some Field contains the text "This is text"
Example 2:   `Upper("lower case?") = LOWER CASE?`

WordCount (text) . . . . .Text   Text

Returns the number of words in "text". No entry required.

Example 1: Upper(Some Field) = THIS IS TEXT
                presuming the field Some Field contains the text "This is text"
Example 2: Upper("lower case?") = LOWER CASE?

Number Functions   **Type**   **Result**

Abs (number) . . . . .Number   Number

Returns the absolute or positive value of "number".

Example 1:   Abs(Number Field) = 5
                presuming the field Number Field contains the number -5
Example 2:   Abs(-75.8) = 75.8

Exp (number) . . . . .Number   Number

Returns the value of the constant "e" (the base of the natural logarithm, equal to 2.7182818) raised to the power you specify. The Exp function is the inverse of the Ln function.

Example 1:   Exp(Number Field) = 2.71828182845905
                presuming the field Number Field contains the number 1
Example 2:   Exp(Ln(2)) = 2

Int (number) . . . . .Number   Number

Returns the integer or whole portion of the "number". Any numbers trailing the decimal point are truncated.

Example 1:   Int(Number Field) = 2
                presuming the field Number Field contains the number 2.865
Example 2:   Int(-56.32159) = -56

Mod (number,divisor) . . . . .Number   Number

Returns the remainder after the "number" is divided by the "divisor" (e.g. 2 divides into 5, two times equaling 4, leaving a remainder of 1).

Example 1:   Mod(Number1,Number2) = 1
                presuming the field Number1 is 5 and Number2 is 2
Example 2:   Mod(20,6) = 2

NumToText (number) . . . . .Number   Text

Converts the "number" to text. Once converted, numeric functions will no longer work on a text value.

Example 1:   NumToText(Number Field) = "234"
                     presuming the field Number Field contains 234)

Example 2:   NumToText(82) = "82"

Random . . . . .Number   Number

Returns a random value between 0 and 1. Using a multiple of ten (10, 100, 1000, etc.) will move the decimal point of the random number. Using the Int function will remove all numbers after the decimal point.

Example 1:   Random = .5236

Example 2:   Random * 100 = 33.4870370260845

Round (number, precision) . . . . .Number   Number

Returns a number rounded to the value provided by the "precision" value. Negative precision drops digits to the right of the decimal and rounds left tens, hundreds, etc. Round uses 5 as the value to round up.

Example 1:   Round(Number Field,2) = 2.56
                     presuming the field Number Field contains 2.56984

Example 2:   Round(8543.42586,-1) = 8540

Sign (number) . . . . .Number   Number

Returns -1 when "number" is negative; 0 when "number" is zero; 1 when "number" is positive. Enter value in Numeric 1.

Example 1:   Sign(Number Field) = 1
                     presuming the field Number Field contains 8965.54

Example 2:   Sign(-5654) = -1

Sqrt (number) . . . . .Number   Number

Returns the square root of "number".

Example 1:   Sqrt(Number Field) = 5
                     presuming the field Number Field contains 25

Example 2:   Sqrt(81) = 9

Truncate (number, precision) . . . . .Number   Number

Returns the supplied "number" truncated to the specified number of decimal places.

Example 1:   Truncate(Number Field,3) = 86.523
                 presuming the field Number Field contains 86.52361

Example 2:   Truncate(8857.425,1) = 8857.4

* All date functions will only work properly on date fields or values converted into a date.

Date (month, day, year) . . . . .Date   Date

Returns calendar date for mm,dd,yyyy (Format will vary depending on current date formatting for specified country). Dates start at January 1, 0001 in FileMaker Pro and it is suggested that you use the full four digits for the year. Format for date display depends on the field formatting.

Example 1:   Date(Month Field,Day Field,Year Field) =
            10/23/1971
            presuming the fields Month, Day and Year contain 10, 23 and 1971 respectively

Example 2:   Date(Month(Field X),Day(Field Y),Year(Field Z)) =
            xx/xx/xxxx

DateToText (date) . . . . .Date   Text

Converts a "date" to text.

Example 1:   DateToText(Date Field) = "5/6/97"
            presuming the field Date Field contains a valid date

Example 2:   "Today is " & DateToText(Status(CurrentDate)) =
            Today is 3/14/98

Day (date) . . . . .Date   Number

Returns a number representing the day part of the "date".

Example 1:   Day(Scorpio Start) = 23
            presuming the field Scorpio Start contains the date 10/23/1998

Example 2:   Day(TextToDate("08/10/1952")) = 10

DayName (date) ....Date   Text

Returns the day of the week (text) for the "date" value supplied.

Example 1:   DayName(`Birthdate`) = "Thursday"
                presuming the field Birthdate contains the date 04/24/1998

Example 2:   DayName(`TextToDate("09/25/1991")`) = "Wednesday"

DayofWeek (date) ....Date   Number

Returns a number representing the day of the week based on the "date" value.
Sun = 1, Mon = 2, Tue = 3, Wed = 4, Thur = 5, Fri = 6, Sat = 7.

Example 1:   DayofWeek(`Paid Date`) = 5
                presuming the field Paid Date contains the date 2/20/1975

Example 2:   If(DayofWeek(`Status(CurrentDate)`) = 6,
                "It's Friday!","More work.")

DayofYear (date) ....Date   Number

Returns the number of days elapsed since January 1 of the current year for the "date" value.

Example 1:   DayofYear(`Invoice Date`) = 320
                presuming the field Invoice Date contains the date 11/16/1997

Example 2:   If(DayofYear(`Field X`) > 358,"Last week of the
                year.","")

Month (date) ....Date   Number

Returns the month part of the "date" value as a number.

Example 1:   Month(`Subscription Date`) = 3
                presuming the field Subscription Date contains the date 3/25/1998

Example 2:   Month(`TextToDate("01/18/1945")`) = 1

MonthName (date) ....Date   Text

Returns the month name (text) of the "date" provided.

Example 1:   MonthName(`Pay Period`) = March
                presuming the field Pay Period contains the date 3/25/1998

Example 2:   MonthName(`Date(10,19,1973)` = October

Today . . . . .Date   Date

Returns the current date (as a date value).

Example 1:   Today = 5/16/98
                 presuming Today was 5/16/1998

Example 2:   Case(Today = TextToDate("1/1/2000"),"Yeah! New
                 Years Day 2000!","")

WeekofYear (date) . . . . .Date   Number

Returns the number of weeks elapsed since January 1 of the year in "date"
counting fractions of weeks as whole weeks.

Example 1:   WeekofYear(Starting Date) = 2
                 presuming the field Starting Date contains 1/7/1997

Example 2:   Case(WeekofYear(TextToDate ("03/03/1998")) =
                 10,"First week of March 1998","")

WeekofYearFiscal (date, starting day) . . . . .Date   Number

Returns the number of the week (1 - 53) in the year of "date" using starting
day (1-7). Sun = 1 through Sat = 7. The first week of the year is a week that
contains four or more days of that year.

Example 1:   WeekofYearFiscal(Incorp Date,3) = 20
                 presuming the field Incorp Date contains the valid date 5/16/1998

Example 2:   Case(WeekofYearFiscal(Date(4,15,1998),2) = 16,
                 "Hope you filed!","")

Year (date) . . . . .Date   Number

Returns the year part of the "date" provided.

Example 1:   Year(Posting Date) = 1975
                 presuming the field Posting Date contains the date 8/16/1975

Example 2:   Year(TextToDate("12/20/1945")) = 1945

Hour (time) ....Time   Number

Returns the hour portion of the value in "time" as a number. FileMaker
Pro works in 24 hour mode so conversions to 12 hour mode will be needed.
(e.g. using 9:05 PM will result in 21)

Example 1:   Hour(Time In) = 9
              presuming the field Time In contains the time 9:05 AM
Example 2:   "It's " & Hour(Status(CurrentTime)) & " o'clock."

Minute (time) ....Time   Number

Returns the Minute portion of the value in "time" as a number.

Example 1:   Minute(Time In) = 5
              presuming the field Time In contains the time 9:05 AM
Example 2:   Case(Minute(Status(CurrentTime)) > 30,"It's the
              downside of the hour.","")

Seconds (time) ....Time   Number

Returns the Seconds portion of the value in "time" as a number. If no seconds value is provided in the time value FileMaker Pro defaults to 00 seconds.

Example 1:   Seconds(Track Time) = 45
              presuming the field Track Time contains the time 00:00:45
Example 2:   Seconds(TextToTime("16:40:21"))

Time (hours, minutes, seconds) ....Time   Time

Returns the time using the "hours", "minutes" and "seconds" values. Time
counts up in seconds from 12:00:00 AM (midnight) each day.

Example 1:   Time(14,34,45) = 14:34:45

Example 2:   Time(Hour(Field X),Minute(Field Y),
              Seconds(Field Z))

TimeToText (time) ....Time   Text

Converts the "time" value to a text string.

Example 1:   TextToTime(Clocked Time) = "17:45:00"
              presuming the field Clocked Time contains the time 5:45 PM
Example 2:   "You arrived at " & TimeToText(Clock In)

Average (field...) ....Aggregate   Number

Returns the average of all non blank values in a repeating field, the average
of all referenced number fields or the average of a relationship. Possible
variations of the Average function are Average (field), Average
(field1,field2,...), Average (relationship::field).

Example 1:   `Average(Line Items File::Price Paid) = 33`
    presuming the field Price Paid in the Line Items file contains various prices paid
Example 2:   `Average(Subtotal Pretax,Subtotal Aftertax)`

Count (field...) ....Aggregate   Number

Returns count of number of all non blank values in a field, repeating fields
or relationship (e.g. How many fields are there that have information in
them?). Possible variations of the Count function are Count (field), Count
(field1,field2,...), Count (relationship::field).

Example 1:   `Count(Line Items File::Product Code) = 45`
    presuming the field Product Code in the Line Items file contains data
Example 2:   `Count(Subparts 1,Subparts 2) = Total number of`
    `parts for assembly`

Max (field...) ....Aggregate   Number

Returns the highest non blank value in a field, sequence of fields, a repeating field or relationship (e.g. What is the highest value of all of these
fields?). Possible variations of the Max function are Max (field), Max
(field1,field2,...), Max (relationship::field).

Example 1:   `Max(Line Items File::Price Paid) = 1250`
    presuming the field Price Paid in the Line Items file contains various prices paid
    Result would be the higest price paid for an item
Example 2:   `Max(Repeating Price Field)`

Min (field...) ....Aggregate   Number

Returns the lowest non blank value in a field(s), repeating field or relationship (e.g. What is the lowest value of all of these fields?). Possible variation
of the Min function are Min (field), Min (field1,field2,...), Min (relationship::field).

Example 1:   `Min(Line Items File::Price Paid) = 5`
    presuming the field Price Paid in the Line Items file contains various prices paid
    Result would be the lowest price paid for an item.
Example 2:   `Min(Repeating Price Field)`

StDev (field…) . . . . .Aggregate   Number

Returns standard deviation of the sample in a series of non-blank field(s),
repetition field(s) or related field(s). Possible variation of the StdDev function are StDev (field), StdDev (field1,field2,...), StDev (relationship::field).

Example 1:   StDev(Voting File::Question 1) = 2.82842712474619
                presuming the field Question 1 in Voting file contains various ratings from 1-10
Example 2:   StDev(Repeating Field)

StDevP (field…) . . . . .Aggregate   Number

Returns standard deviation of population in series of non-blank field(s) or
repetition field(s) or related field(s). Possible variation of the StdDevP function are StDevP (field), StdDev (field1,field2,...), StdDevP
(relationship::field).

Example 1:   StDevP(Geographic Areas::People Count) =
             205954.042408737
                presuming the field People Count in Geographic file contains various counts
Example 2:   StDevP(Repeating Field)

Sum (field…) . . . . .Aggregate   Number

Returns the total of all values in the referenced field(s), repeating field(s) or
related field(s) (e.g. What is the total of all of the values in the fields I
include?). Possible variation of the Sum function are Sum (N1,N2,...), Sum
(RepeatField), Sum (relationship::field).

Example 1:   Sum(Line Items::Line Amount) = 352.45
                presuming the field Line Amount in Line Items file contains various prices
Example 2:   Sum(Repeating Field)

Summary Functions   **Type**   **Result**

GetSummary (summary field, break field) . . . . .Summary   Variable

A field that contains the results of a summary calculation of values across a
group of records. The "break field" is a field used to group values together
so that you can obtain summary values for a subset of records (instead of
one summary value for all the records in the found set). Break field can be a
text, number, date, time, or calculation field and is grouped according to
the sorted order of records.

Example 1:   GetSummary(Total Summary,Customer Name)
                presuming the field Total Summary is a summary field in the Invoices file
Example 2:   GetSummary(Count of People,Voting District)

Extend (non-repeating field) . . . . .Repeating   Variable

Allows a non-repeating field to be used in calculations involving repeating fields.

Example 1:   `Extend(Tax Field)*Line Items`
                  presuming the field Tax Field stores a tax value to be
                  applied to a repeating amount field

Example 2:   `Extend(Prime Rate)*Loan Amounts`

GetRepetition (repeating field, number) . . . . .Repeating   Variable

Returns the contents of the repetition number of the "repeating field".

Example 1:   `GetRepetition(Graphic Icons,3)`
                  presuming the field Graphic Icons stores icons in their repetitions

Example 2:   `GetRepetition(Variables,6)`

Last (repeating field) . . . . .Repeating   Variable

Returns the last valid, non blank value in a "repeating field" or a relationship.

Example 1:   `Last(Frequency)`
                  presuming the field Frequency contains data in its repetitions

Example 2:   `Last(Title Text)`

FV (payment, interest rate, periods) . . . . .Financial   Number

Future Value of an initial investment, based on "interest rate", "payment", for "periods". (e.g. $50 per month at a fixed interest rate of 7% – usually divided by 12 – for a number of months, 36 = 3 years)

Example 1:   `FV(Monthly Payment,Interest Rate/12,MonthDuration)`
                  `= 2760.46`
                  presuming fields Monthly Payment, Interest Rate and Month Duration
                  had number values of 50, 7 and 48

Example 2:   `FV(Monthly Payment,Interest Rate/12,Years*12)`

NPV (payment, interest rate) . . . . .Financial   Number

Returns the Net Present Value of a series of unequal payments made at
regular intervals, assuming a fixed rate per interval. Resulting value is the
profit in current days dollars. First value will often be negative. Payment =
Repeating Field contains -2000 (the initial payment) & 2500. Interest Rate
= the fixed interest rate percentage.

Example 1:   NPV(Repeating Payment Field, Interest Rate)
                *presuming the field Repeating Payment contains negative loan value and
                unequal subsequent payments*
Example 2:   NPV(Payments, Prime Rate + 1)

PMT (principal, interest rate, term) . . . . .Financial   Number

Payment for the "term", "interest rate", and "principal". A common calculation for what a payment book on a loan would be. Principal = the principal amount of a loan – $24,000 car, Interest rate = the fixed interest rate at
7% – usually divided by 12 – for the Term = number of months, 48 = 4
years.

Example 1:   PMT(Loan Amount, Interest Rate/12, Payment Months)
                = 574.70...
                *presuming fields Loan Amount, Interest Rate and Payment Months contain
                24000, .07 and 48*
Example 2:   PMT(Loan, Prime Rate + 1, Years*12)

PV (payment, interest rate, periods) . . . . .Financial   Number

Present value of a series of equal payments made at regular intervals (periods), assuming a fixed interest rate per interval. Payment = how much is
being paid on a loan – $500 being paid at Interest rate = fixed interest rate
at 5% for Periods = number of years – 5 years.

Example 1:   PV(Payment Amount, Interest Rate, Years)= 2164.73...
                *presuming the fields Payment Amount, Interest Rate and Years
                contain 500, .05 and 5*
Example 2:   PV(Payment Amount, Prime Rate, Years)

Atan (number) . . . . .Trigonometric   Number
Returns the trigonometric arc tangent (inverse tangent) of the "number"
supplied. The arc tangent is the angle, in radians, whose tangent is equal to
"number".

Example 1: Atan(.90)= .7328151017865

Cos (number) . . . . .Trigonometric   Number
Returns the cosine of the angle supplied. The supplied "number" must be
represented in radians. Convert degrees to radians with the Radians function.

Example 1: Cos(Radians(Angle Field)) = 0
              presuming the field Angle Field contains the value of 90 representing degrees
Example 2: Cos(Radians(60) = .5

Degrees (number) . . . . .Trigonometric   Number
Converts the supplied "number" from radians to degrees. A radian is equal
to 180/Pi degrees.

Example 1: Degrees(3.1416) = 180.000420918299

Example 2: Degrees(Radians(90)) = 90

Ln (number) . . . . .Trigonometric   Number
Returns the base-e (natural) logarithm of the supplied "number". The Exp
function is the inverse of the Ln function.

Example 1: Ln(2.7182818) = .9999999895305

Example 2: Ln(Exp(90)) = 90

Log (number) . . . . .Trigonometric   Number
Calculates the common logarithm (base 10) of the supplied "number",
which can be any positive value.

Example 1: Log(1) = 0

Example 2: Round(Log(100), 1) = 2

PI . . . . .Trigonometric   Number

Calculates the value of the constant Pi, which is approximately 3.14159.

Example 1: `PI*15 = 47.124`

Radians (number) . . . . .Trigonometric   Number

Converts the degrees supplied in a "number" to radians. Trigonometric
functions must be expressed in radians. A degree is equal to Pi/180 radians.

Example 1:   `Radians(Angle Field) = .7853…`
               presuming the field Angle Field contains the value of 45 representing degrees
Example 2:   `Radians(60) = 1.0471975511966`

Sin (number) . . . . .Trigonometric   Number

Returns a number that is the sine of an angle expressed in radians.

Example 1:   `Sin(Radians(Angle Field) = .70710…`
               presuming the field Angle Field contains the value of 45 representing degrees
Example 2:   `Sin(.610865) = .57357624123063`

Tan (number) . . . . .Trigonometric   Number

Returns a number that is the tangent of an angle. With Tan, you cannot use
values exactly equal to 90 degrees (Pi/2 radians), or multiples thereof.
Tan(Radians(34)) returns .6745085.

Example 1:   `Tan(Radians(Angle Field) = .26794919243112`
               presuming the field Angle Field contains the value of 15 representing degrees
Example 2:   `Tan(60) = .32004038937956`

Case (test1, result1 [, test2, result2, default result]...) . . . . .Logical   Text

Case returns one of any number of results from a supplied list of tests.
When true, it returns the result of that test. If no expressions evaluate to
true, Case returns the "default result". If no "default result" is supplied,
Case returns an "empty" result. Case will use the very first value that evaluates as true. Case can be used in place of the If statement.

Example 1:   `Case(Status = "Active", "OK",Status = "Inactive",`
            `"EXPIRED","No Status Setting") = EXPIRED`
            presuming the field Status is set to be Inactive

Example 2:   `Case(IsEmpty(First Name), "You need to enter`
            `a first name.")`

Choose (test, result0 [, result1, result2]...) . . . . .Logical   Text

The test result must be a number indexing the list. The function index is a
0 based index, if the result = 0 result0 is used. Brackets indicate optional
parameters. Data returned can be text, number, date, time, or container.

Example 1:   `Choose(Variable,"Active","Inactive","Standby") =`
            `Standby`
            presuming the field Variable contains the value of 2

Example 2:   `Choose(Status(CurrentPlatform),"Windows User",`
            `"Mac User")`

If (test, result one, result two) . . . . .Logical   Text

If "test" evaluates as true (any non zero result), returns result one; if test is
false (0), returns result two.

Example 1:   `If(Breed = "Golden Lab","Best Dog","Nice Dog") =`
            `Best Dog`
            presuming the field Breed contains the value Golden Lab

Example 2:   `If(Status(CurrentUserCount) > 15, "You've maxed`
            `out on users","")`

IsEmpty (field) . . . . .Logical   Text

Returns true (1) if the supplied value is an empty (null); otherwise returns
false (0). IsEmpty ("text") returns 0. IsEmpty(Num) returns 1 if the field
"Number" is empty.

Example 1:   `IsEmpty(Paid Field) = 1`
            presuming the field Paid Field contains no values

Example 2:   `If(IsEmpty(Paid Field),"We need to collect from`
            `this person.","")`

IsValid (field) ....Logical   Text

Returns false (0) if the named related field is missing from the file or if the
related field contains an invalid value; otherwise it returns true(1). An alpha
character is not valid for a numerical field.

Example 1: IsValid(Number Field) = 0
            presuming field Number Field contained a letter "A"
Example 2: If(not IsValid(Number Field),"You need at least one
            number in this field.","")

Status (CurrentAppVersion) ....Status   Status

Returns the current version of FileMaker Pro being used.

Example 1:   Status(CurrentAppVersion) = "Pro 4.0v1"
            presuming version of FileMaker Pro being run is 4.0v1
Usefulness: When used in a script that is run on startup it is possible to check the version
            of FileMaker Pro that is being used.

Status (CurrentDate) ....Status   Status

Returns the current date.

Example 1:   Status(CurrentDate)
Usefulness: When it's necessary to compare a date field to the current date, to set
            the current date to a field, or for creating a complex time based relational key.

Status (CurrentError) ....Status   Status

Returns the current error. See the reference database called ERROR.FP3
that ships with Scriptology for a reference of error codes that you can trap.

Example 1:   If ["Status(CurrentError)=401"]
            Show Message
            ["No records match specified criteria."]
            End If
Usefulness: When you need to control the results of catching an error during a
            script being run or some other function of the database operations.

Status (CurrentFieldName) . . . . .Status   Status
Returns the current field name when that field is the active field in the current layout.

Example 1: If ["Status(CurrentFieldName) <> "Notes""]
        Show Message ["You must select the notes field
        for me to paste the date."]
    Else
        Paste Current Date []
    End If

Usefulness: Used when necessary to determine if the user is in a particular field.

Status (CurrentFileName) . . . . .Status   Status
Returns the current file name.

Example 1:   If ["Customers = Status(CurrentFileName)"]
        Perform Script [Sub-scripts,
        "Generate Invoice"]
    Else
        Open ["Customer.FP3"]
    End If

Usefulness: Determines what file the user is in within a set of multiple files. Performed by comparing a setting to a global field.

Status (CurrentFileSize) . . . . .Status   Status
Returns the current file size in bytes.

Example 1:   If(Status(CurrentFileSize) > 20480000,
        "This file is over 20 Mb", "")

Usefulness: For determining the actual size of a FileMaker Pro file. Could be used to monitor the size of files for web hosting purposes.

Status (CurrentFoundCount) . . . . .Status   Status
Returns the current count of all found records in the found set.

Example 1:   Status(CurrentFoundCount) = 216
        presuming the database returned 216 records from a find

Usefulness: Determine which layout to go to based on the found count. If 1 record found go to a layout in form view. If more than one record, go to a layout that shows a list view. Also useful to show the number of items displaying in list view.

Status (CurrentGroups) ....Status   Status

Returns the group name for the current password being used. If the password has access to more than one group then the group names are returned as a return separated list.

`4.0 Only`

Example 1:
```
If ["PatternCount(Status(CurrentGroups),
      "Accounting" or "Sales")"]
    Go to Layout ["Financial Main"]
Else
    Go to Layout ["Data Entry Layout"]
End If
```
Usefulness: Presenting different data or layouts based on the password access of the user.

Status (CurrentHostName) ....Status   Status

Returns the current host. Result is the current host as set in the control panel of computer using the database. Typically the name of the computer.

Example 1:
```
If["PatternCount(Status(CurrentHostName),"Server")
    <> 1"]
    Show Message ["This database cannot be
                   run on this machine."]
    Close []
Else
    Perform Script [Sub-scripts,
                     "Startup Processes"]
End If
```
Usefulness: For determining which computer is opening the database. By checking to see that the host name matches certain criteria you can limit where a FileMaker Pro database is hosted from.

Status (CurrentLanguage) ....Status   Status

Returns the current language setting on the computer being used.

Example 1:   `Status(CurrentLanguage) = English`
presuming the current language is set to English in the Application Preferences.
Usefulness: When commercializing a database you can check for localities of use.

Status (CurrentLayoutCount) . . . . .Status   Status
Returns the count of all layouts in the current database.

Example 1:   Status(CurrentLayoutCount) = 5
          presuming the database contained 5 total layouts, including hidden layouts
Usefulness: Can be used with a script that navigates from layout to layout to determine
          that the last layout has been reached.

Status (CurrentLayoutName) . . . . .Status   Status
Returns the name of the current layout.

Example 1:   Status(CurrentLayoutName) = Customer
          presuming the database is currently on a layout named "Customer"
Usefulness: For using the layout name as part of the actual layout. Merging in the name
          provides users with locational reference. Also useful to check what layout
          the user is on when a script is initiated.

Status (CurrentLayoutNumber) . . . . .Status   Status
Returns the current layout number which is being viewed in the current
database.

Example 1:   Status(CurrentLayoutNumber) = 3
          presuming the database is currently on the third layout of the file
Usefulness: By storing the Status(CurrentLayoutNumber) in a global field it is possible
          to navigate back to that layout using the
          Go To Layout [layout number from field...].

Status (CurrentMessageChoice) . . . . .Status   Status
Returns the button selected from a message dialog box using the
ScriptMaker script step, Show Message. Result is determined by the button clicked in a message dialog box. The rightmost value is one (1) and left-
most is three (3).

Example 1:   Show Message ["First = 1, Second = 2, Third = 3.
          What button please?"]
          If ["Status(CurrentMessageChoice) = 1"]
             Comment ["do script steps here..."]
          End If
Usefulness: One of the most powerful Status functions, it allows you to offer users
          dialog boxes and then make decisions based on the buttons that users click.

Status (CurrentMode) . . . . .Status   Status

Returns the mode that FileMaker Pro is in. Browse = 0, Find = 1, Preview
= 2. There is no result for Layout Mode.

Example 1:   If ["Status(CurrentMode) = 1"]
           Enter Browse Mode []
     End If

Usefulness: When the user clicks a button while in find mode FileMaker Pro can be
            defaulted to Browse mode before continuing.

Status (CurrentModifierKeys) . . . . .Status   Status

Returns the value of the modifier key that is held down while clicking a   **4.0 Only**
button or choosing a script from the ScriptMaker menu. If multiple modifier keys are used, the total of those keys is returned. See Chapter 23.

Usefulness: Interactive help systems and power user keys can be used with buttons.

Status (CurrentMultiUserStatus) . . . . .Status   Status

Returns the network status setting for the current database in use. Single
User = 0, Shared as Host = 1, Shared as Guest = 2.

Example 1:   If ["Status(CurrentMultiUserStatus) <> 0"]
           Show Message ["This solution is not
                        network savvy."]
           Set Multi-User [Off]
     End If

Usefulness: For determining if the database was opened as a guest or if
            the network status has been changed from single user to multi-user. Good
            for commercial solutions that want to limit network usage through licensing.

Status (CurrentNetworkChoice) . . . . .Status   Status

Returns the name of the network protocol currently being used. If no pro-   **4.0 Only**
tocol is selected then "" is returned.

Example 1:   If ["Status(CurrentNetworkChoice)<> "TCP/IP""]
           Show Message ["You need to set your
           network protocol to TCP/IP for this solution
           to work properly."]
           Open Application Preferences
     End If

Usefulness: For determining if the copy of FileMaker Pro being used has the proper network protocol set or if it is using one at all. Can be combined with the Status(CurrentPlatform) to check that the correct protocol is set.

Status (CurrentPageNumber) . . . . .Status   Status

Returns the current page being previewed or printed. Results are shown when in Preview mode. If mode is not Preview then the result is zero (0).

Example 1:
```
Enter Preview Mode []
Go to Record/Request/Page [Last]
Set Field ["Total Pages",
          "Status(CurrentPageNumber)"]
Enter Browse Mode []
```
Usefulness: Can be used to generate page footer text that reads "Page X of X". Performed by entering Preview mode, navigating to the last page and setting a global to contain the total number of pages.

Status (CurrentPlatform) . . . . .Status   Status

Returns the current computer platform being used. Result is one (1) if the platform is Macintosh and a two (2) if the platform is Windows.

Example 1:
```
If ["Status(CurrentPlatform) = 1"]
     Go to Layout ["Macintosh Main Interface"]
Else
     Go to Layout ["Windows Main Interface"]
End If
```
Usefulness: For making decisions on platform specific scripts, layouts and data operations.

Status (CurrentPortalRow) . . . . .Status   Status

Returns the number of the current row in a selected portal. Result is determined by the number of the portal row that is currently active and selected. Only works with portals and will return a zero (0) if no portal is selected.

Example 1:
```
Set Field ["Last Portal Row",
          "Status(CurrentPortalRow)"]
```
Usefulness: For determining if a user is in a portal or for returning to the last visited portal row.

Status (CurrentPrinterName) . . . . .Status　　Status

Returns a text string identifying the default printer name. Result is a
comma delimited list of items specific to the printer as set up by the computer.

Example 1:　If ["Status(CurrentPrinterName) <>
　　　　　　　　　　"Laser Printer 600""]
　　　　　　　　Show Message ["You must change
　　　　　　　　　　　　　　　　your printer setting
　　　　　　　　　　　　　　　　before printing from this
　　　　　　　　　　　　　　　　layout."]
　　　　　　　End If

Usefulness:　Used in conjunction with Status(CurrentLayoutName) you can determine
if a certain report is supposed to go to the target printer or not.

Status (CurrentRecordCount) . . . . .Status　　Status

Returns the total number of records in the current database being
viewed/used.

Example 1:　Status(CurrentRecordCount) = 3405

Usefulness:　Calculations and scripts that need to know how many total records there
are in the database file.

Status (CurrentRecordID) . . . . .Status　　Status

Returns the record ID for the current record. The record ID for each
record is much like a serial number that's incremented for each new record
created. Unlike a serial number, the record ID cannot be changed since it's
stored internally within each FileMaker file. The CurrentRecordID is a
constant value and does not change.

4.0 Only

Example 1:　Status(CurrentRecordID)

Usefulness:　Any time a constant reference is needed for a particular record the
CurrentRecordID can be used because it will never change.

Status (CurrentRecordNumber) . . . . .Status   Status

Returns the current record number out of the total records in the found set.

Example 1:   `If ["Status(CurrentRecordNumber) =`
`Status(CurrentFoundCount)"]`

          `Show Message ["This is the last record in`
          `the found set."]`
     `Else`
        `Go to Record/Request/Page [Next]`
     `End If`

Usefulness: Provides the current record number position that can be used in relation to the first and last records.

Status (CurrentRepetitionNumber) . . . . .Status   Status

Returns the current repetition in a repeating field.

Example 1:   `Status(CurrentRepetitionNumber)`
Usefulness: Determine if the user is in any repetition of a repeating field.

Status (CurrentRequestCount) . . . . .Status   Status

Returns the number of requests in a FileMaker Pro find.

Example 1:   `If ["Status(CurrentRequestCount) > 3"]`
          `Show Message ["This is your third find`
                         `request. Did you know you were`
                         `still in find mode?."]`
     `End If`

Usefulness: When in Find mode it is possible to check the number of requests. Allows prevention of incorrect data entry into a find.

Status (CurrentScreenDepth) . . . . .Status   Status

Returns the bit value of the current screen depth . Works with multiple monitors. Result is the monitor bit depth. (e.g 1 = black/white 4 = 16 colors 8 = 256 colors, 16 = thousands, 24 = millions).

Example 1:　　If ["Status(CurrentScreenDepth) = 4"]
　　　　　　　　Go to Layout ["Windows VGA"]
　　　　　　Else
　　　　　　　　Go to Layout ["Standard 256"]
　　　　　　End If

Usefulness:　　Can be used to check the color depth of the current screen. Allows a
　　　　　　　　database to default to black and white or 16 color screen for older displays.

Status (CurrentScreenHeight) . . . . .Status　　　Status

Returns the current screen height . Works with multiple monitors. Result is
the monitor height in pixels (e.g. 480).

Example 1:　　If ["Status(CurrentScreenHeight) > 480"]
　　　　　　　　Go to Layout ["Larger Monitor"]
　　　　　　Else
　　　　　　　　Go to Layout ["Standard 15" monitor"]
　　　　　　End If

Usefulness:　　Can be used to check the resolution height of the current screen. Allows a
　　　　　　　　database to default to a layout with different proportions on start up.

Status (CurrentScreenWidth) . . . . .Status　　　Status

Returns the current screen width . Works with multiple monitors. Result is
the monitor width in pixels (e.g. 640).

Script
Example 1: If ["Status(CurrentScreenWidth) > 640"]
　　　　　　　　Go to Layout ["Larger Monitor"]
　　　　　　Else
　　　　　　　　Go to Layout ["Standard 15" monitor"]
　　　　　　End If

Usefulness:　　Can be used to check the resolution width of the current screen. Allows a
　　　　　　　　database to default to a layout with different proportions on start up.

Status (CurrentScriptName) ....Status   Status
Returns the current script that is being run or is paused.

Example 1:   If ["Status(CurrentScriptName) = "My Custom
                    Find Script""]
                Halt Script
            Else
                Perform Script [Sub-scripts, "Initiate
                                    Find Process"]
            End If

Usefulness: Determines what portion of a sub-script is being run from within a
                script that runs other scripts. Useful for branching scripts.

Status (CurrentSortStatus) ....Status   Status
Returns the current sort status for the database being used. Zero (0) if
records are unsorted, one (1) if sorted, two (2) if semi-sorted.

Example 1:   If(Status(CurrentSortStatus) = 1,
                Green Light Icon,"")

Usefulness: Determining whether the database is sorted or not. Good for providing on
                screen indicators of the sort status of the database if the status area is hidden.

Status (CurrentSystemVersion) ....Status   Status
Returns the current system version being used on the computer. Result is
determined by the operating system on the computer.

Example 1:   If(Status(CurrentSystemVersion) = "7.5" or
                "7.6" or "7.6.1",
                "You should upgrade to Mac OS 8!","")

Usefulness: Determining whether the user is using an operating system that supports
                features in your solution (e.g. Open URL does not work on Windows 3.1)

Status (CurrentTime) ....Status   Status
Returns the current time on the computer being used. Result is determined
by the clock setting on the computer.

Example 1:   Int(Status(CurrentTime)/60) &
                " minutes since 12 midnight."

Usefulness: Can be incorporated with Set Field, with scripts, and calculations that are time
                sensitive.

Status (CurrentUserCount) . . . . .Status   Status

Returns the number of users accessing the current file. Result is the number of computers using the database and is inclusive of the computer which opened the database.

Example 1:   If ["Status(CurrentUserCount) > 6"]
                    Show Message ["There is a maximum of
                                    5 connections allowed to this
                                    database at any given time."]

               Close []
            End If

Usefulness: Determines how many users are connected to a shared FileMaker Pro database. Can be used in a login script to log the usage of a particular file.

Status (CurrentUserName) . . . . .Status   Status

Returns the current user name as set by the computer or FileMaker Pro preferences. FileMaker Pro preferences take precedence.

Example 1:   If ["PatternCount(Users::User Name,
Status(CurrentUserName)) <> 1"]
                    Show Message ["You do not seem to be in the users
                    file.
                    Please check with the administrator."]
            End If

Usefulness: Allows a script that performs a login process to watch for users that exist in a Users file. This provides administrative user control as to who logs in. (Using this function you can also check frequency of logins of users.)

Design Functions   **Type**   **Result**
DatabaseNames . . . . .Design   List

Results in a return separated list of all the databases running (e.g. DatabaseNames returns Customer.FP3, Invoice.FP3, Items.FP3, etc.).

4.0 Only

Example 1:   Set Field ["File List", "DatabaseNames"]
               presuming the field File List is a global to store the open files
Usefulness: Can be used in conjunction with the Open script command to present users with options for which file to open. Also used in web serving with FileMaker Pro.

FieldBounds (dbname, layoutname, fieldname) . . . . .Design   List

Returns the location in pixels of a field on a layout in a particular database.
Five values refer to the field boundaries of the top and left edges in the layout, separated by spaces: the first value is the left edge, the second is the
top edge, the third is the right edge, the fourth is the bottom edge and the
last is the rotation degrees.

4.0 Only

Example 1:   `FieldBounds("Customer.FP3","LayoutX","Field") =`
              `114 21 260 37 0`

Usefulness: Serving FileMaker Pro databases on the web.

FieldNames (dbname, [layoutname]) . . . . .Design   List

Lists all the fields for the database listed. The result is a return separated
list of the fields in the specified database.

4.0 Only

Example 1:   `FieldNames("Customer.FP3","LayoutX") =`
              `a list of field names`

Usefulness: Serving FileMaker Pro databases on the web.

FieldRepetitions (dbname, layoutname, fieldname) . . . . .Design   Text

Returns field format information about a repeating field. Parameters
include the database name, layout name and field name.

4.0 Only

Example 1:   `FieldRepetitions ("Customer.FP3", "LayoutX",`
              `"Repeating Field")`

Usefulness: Serving FileMaker Pro databases on the web.

FieldStyle (dbname, layoutname, fieldname) . . . . .Design   List

Returns information about a field from the Field Format dialog. That
information includes whether the field is set to standard or a value list or
scrolling. If more than one Field Format option applies, the values are
returned separated by spaces.

4.0 Only

Example 1:   `FieldStyle("Customer.FP3","LayoutX","Field")`
Usefulness: Serving FileMaker Pro databases on the web.

FieldType (dbname, fieldname) . . . . .Design   List

Returns information about the field from Define Fields. Four pieces of information are returned separated by spaces in the following order: stored vs. unstored, field type, indexed vs. unindexed and number of repetitions.

4.0 Only

Example 1:　`FieldType("Customer.FP3","Field") =`
　　　　　　　`Standard Text Unindexed 1`
Usefulness:　Serving FileMaker Pro databases on the web.

LayoutNames (dbname) . . . . .Design　　List
Returns a list of all the layouts in the specified database separated by returns.

4.0 Only

Example 1:　`LayoutNames("Customer.FP3")`
Usefulness:　Serving FileMaker Pro databases on the web. Can also be used for documentation.

RelationInfo (dbname, relationname) . . . . .Design　　List
Returns four values separated by returns in the following order: name of the related database, match field in the master file, match field in the related file and relationship options.

4.0 Only

Example 1:　`RelationInfo("Customer.FP3","Relationship")`
Usefulness:　Serving FileMaker Pro databases on the web.
　　　　　　　Can also be used for documentation.

RelationNames (dbname) . . . . .Design　　List
Returns a carriage return separated list of all the names of the relationships in the database designated.

4.0 Only

Example 1:　`RelationNames("Customer.FP3")`
Usefulness:　Serving FileMaker Pro databases on the web.
　　　　　　　Can also be used for documentation.

ScriptNames (dbname) . . . . .Design　　List
Shows a return separated list of all the scripts in a particular database.

Example 1:   RelationNames ("Customer.FP3")   **4.0 Only**
Usefulness: Serving FileMaker Pro databases on the web.
Can also be used for documentation.

ValueListItems (dbname, valuelist) . . . . .Design   List

Returns the contents of a value list. If the value list is based on the values found in another field then the entire index of that field is returned.

Example 1:   ValueListItems ("Customer.FP3","Value List")   **4.0 Only**
Usefulness: Serving FileMaker Pro databases on the web.
Can also be used for documentation.

ValueListNames (dbname) . . . . .Design   List

Displays the names of all the value lists in a particular database, separated by returns.

Example 1:   ValueListNames ("Customer.FP3")   **4.0 Only**
Usefulness: Serving FileMaker Pro databases on the web.
Can also be used for documentation.

External Functions   **Type**   **Result**

Allows communication between FileMaker Pro and any plug-in external functions that might be installed. One plug-in ships with FileMaker Pro 4.0 named Web Companion. Other third party developers will release plug-ins over time.   **4.0 Only**

Glossary
of Terms

Technical terms used in this publication

Many of the techniques and processes described in Scriptology reference terms that may be unfamiliar. Becoming familiar with the following terms and how they apply to FileMaker Pro will provide a more fluid learning experience.

aggregate: A term for an operation or function that uses information across a range of records.

array: In conventional programming an array is a data structure that store multiple pieces of data but is considered a single object. In FileMaker Pro an array can be represented by a repeating field.

ascending counter: A value stored in either a standard field or global number field that starts at an initial value and counts up by incrementing itself until it hits a target value.

break field: The field used as a basis for creating a division between data (e.g. given a database of a population, the characteristic of race could be used as a break field to create a division between the various races in the population). Break fields are used with summary and sub-summary functions. The database must be sorted for the break field to work properly.

child file: The FileMaker Pro file related to a parent or master file. The child file is always on the right hand side of a relationship. Also referred to as secondary, daughter or related file.

concatenation: Combining two or more strings into a single, longer string using a calculation. FileMaker Pro utilizes the ampersand (&) character to concatenate two or more objects.

constant: A value stored in a field that's always the same on every record.

control value: A value most often stored in a global field. It is a variable piece of data that controls the direction of an operation. For example, if a conditional statement were to look at the control value named "Delete without dialog" and the control value was set to true, the Delete Record script would delete a record without showing the dialog box confirming deletion. A control value can be a dynamically changing value such as a counter.

counter: A value used to determine the position at which a repetitive process is occurring. Most often it is a global number field in FileMaker Pro.

cycle: A cycle is a sequence of ScriptMaker steps that occur between a set of Loop steps. One cycle equals one completion of each of the steps within the loop.

data channel: A data channel is a connection (relationship) between two files that is generalized to the whole database system (multiple files). The relationship is not specific or unique and most often uses a constant value to create the channel (e.g. when a constant relationship is in place, using a Set Field allows data to be pushed through the channel).

data normalization: A technical term used in relational theory and database design. The theory stipulates that data not be duplicated, but rather optimized by the relational structure.

data path: A data path is the method through which information is passed from one field to another via a relationship. Most often it is the Set Field script step that uses a data path. See "data channel" for more information.

delimiter: A value or character that separates two or more pieces of data. Examples include tabs, commas and returns.

descending counter: A value stored in either a standard field or a global number field that starts at an initial value and counts down by decrementing itself until it hits a target value.

developer layout: A layout created in a file for the purpose of storing developer information and fields not visible to the user. Usually it's the first layout and is associated to a script that will toggle between it and the layout that is currently being viewed.

field filter: In FileMaker Pro, a calculation field that formats data in a specific format. Examples are phone numbers, ID numbers, etc.

filter: A filter "narrows" down a set or subset of data presented to the user. In FileMaker Pro there is a process of using a combination of a global field and a relationship to show a defined subset of records. This is accomplished using a portal based on a selection made in the global field.

flag: A flag is a piece of data, numerical or text, used to indicate, warn or notify of a particular setting. For example you would set a "Duplicate" flag with a Boolean value of (1) for true if there was a duplicate email address for a particular record.

foreign key: The field in the related (child) file that is used to create a match between the parent file and child file. Another term used is secondary key.

found set: A set of data that represents a portion or smaller group of data than the whole of the database, usually the result of a search. A found set of all records is the whole database.

global: A global field stores the same value or values for the entire range of records within a single database file.

index: The index of a database stores a single occurrence of each unique value that exists in a field. Stored fields have individual field indices which comprise the entire index for the database file. The index is used to improve search times within a database. In FileMaker Pro only the first 20 characters of each word are indexed.

loop: The process of performing a set sequence of repetitive steps on a found set of records, the whole database file, a field or multiple fields.

lookup: A term specific to FileMaker Pro wherein one of the files duplicates data stored in the other, based on a match between two database files.

many-to-many relationship: This type of relationship is defined where multiple records in a file are related to more than one record in a related file. While this structure cannot be directly created, there are two known methods to create many-to-many relationships. The primary method uses a third file called a join file that is related between two files.

master file: The FileMaker Pro file that relates to the child or secondary file. The master file is always on the left hand side of a relationship. Also referred to as primary or parent file.

match field: This term is used by FileMaker, Inc. to designate a "primary" or "foreign" key used in a relationship. It is the link that connects two files together when the values stored in the match fields are the same. There are different terms for the match field based on where it is used. If it is used in a lookup then it may be referred to as a trigger.

merge field: A mechanism used to display the values of a field with a text block in a FileMaker Pro layout. Since the merge field is a text block it will adjust its size according to the length of the value being displayed. Using Command-M or Control-M presents a dialog box of the fields that can be merged.

modal dialog box: This graphical user interface (GUI) term describes a screen element, window or dialog box. Modal means that the window is in a mode and no other computer interaction is possible. The opposite of modal is non-modal meaning movable screen objects.

nesting: The process of placing one FileMaker function within another FileMaker Pro function or placing a Perform Script [sub-script] within a script. Commonly refers to conditional statements such as the If statement and If script step.

network protocol: This term represents technical computer language used by FileMaker Pro to communicate when database files are shared (AppleTalk is for Macintosh networks, IPX/SPX for Windows and TCP/IP for the Internet).

one-to-many relationship: This relationship type is defined by the fact that one record in a file relates to more than one record in a related file.

one-to-one relationship: This relationship type is defined where one record in a file relates to a single record in a related file.

parent file: The FileMaker Pro file that relates to the child or secondary file. It is the main FileMaker Pro database from which a relationship originates. The parent, is the file on the left hand side of a FileMaker Pro relationship; also referred to as the primary file.

Portal: A portal is a FileMaker Pro term that describes a layout object with which related data from another FileMaker Pro file is presented to the user. A portal can be scrolling, have multiple rows and alternating colors. It is how the user interacts with data in a related file.

preference: A general setting that controls how a software environment presents the user with the information being manipulated. In a FileMaker Pro database system a preference is a value stored in a global field that determines how the database reacts to certain scripts running, how the database will perform a certain operation or how the database will display certain data.

primary file: The FileMaker Pro file that relates to the child or secondary file. It is the main FileMaker Pro database from which a relationship originates. The primary file is the file on the left hand side of a FileMaker Pro relationship; also referred to as the parent file.

primary key: Also referred to as a master key, the primary key is the field that drives a relationship from the Primary file to the Child file.

query: A common term for a search or find. The FileMaker Pro find mode supports multiple queries, called requests.

record: A record is a group of fields containing data. It's similar to the row of a spreadsheet. A database is comprised of many records.

record level locking: This mechanism is used in a database file to prevent multiple people from making changes to the same record at the same time while a FileMaker Pro file is being shared.

referential integrity: A mechanism used by databases to ensure that any related data, based on a match, is updated when the key for that relationship is changed or modified. Any data referenced because of the key change will maintain its integrity. FileMaker Pro does not directly support a referential integrity feature but it can be incorporated via scripting.

related file: Also known as the Child file, it is the file that contains data related to a main or primary file based on a matching key.

related field: A related field originates from a related file. In FileMaker Pro a related field can be present on any layout and is indicated with two colons preceding the field name.

relationship: A relationship is defined by common data matching between two separate FileMaker Pro files via a key field. A relationship is established using a match field, otherwise known as a master and foreign key or primary and secondary key.

request: A request is the set of criteria provided to FileMaker Pro while in find mode. Requests can use special characters to find a range (…), duplicates (!), less than (<), greater than (>), less than or equal (≤), greater than or equal (≥), exact match (=), today's date (//), invalid date or time (?), one character (@), zero or more characters (*), literal text ("") or a field content match (==). Multiple requests create an "or" search query.

reverse-relationship: A relationship that starts in a related file and relates back to the primary file using the same match key as was used in a relationship from the primary file to the related file. The purpose is to gain access to primary file data from a related file.

same-file relationship: This term is also know as a self-join relationship or self-related relationship. It's a process in which one FileMaker Pro database is used to create a relationship to itself in order to see other records within that database. Caution: Do not set a same-file relationship to allow deletion of related records. The reason is that the master records and the related records are in the same file. If you delete a record, it will delete all the related records as well. This is known as cascading deletes.

script: A script is a linear sequence of steps structured to automate a database process. In FileMaker Pro, a script is similar to a macro function but provides conditional branching.

SDK: (Runtime) Solutions Development Kit is a runtime FileMaker Pro engine that can be permanently attached to a file or files. This allows FileMaker Pro developers to distribute their solutions without requiring users to own FileMaker Pro. The SDK is only provided through FileMaker, Inc.

secondary key: A field in the related (child) file that is used to create a match between the parent file and child file. Also referred to as a secondary or foreign key.

self-join relationship: See same-file relationship.

Status Area: The status area is found at the left of a FileMaker Pro window. It contains the navigational card and bookmark metaphor as well as the record count, found count (after a search is performed) and the sort status. When in Layout Mode it contains the layout tools.

stored field/calculation: The stored field/calculation is an attribute of each field found in FileMaker Pro. The storage setting dictates whether an index is created for the field. See index for more information.

subset: A subset of data represents a smaller group of records within the database. A subset can represent a found set of data, the result of a search or a range of records. In FileMaker the most common reference to a subset of data is called a Found Set.

table: A table is a common database term defined as an array of data stored in horizontal rows and vertical columns. In essence, a table is a spreadsheet that stores data.

unique key: A value stored in a field that is unique to the record. Common methods used to create unique keys in FileMaker Pro involved a concatenated calculation.

value list: An associated list of data provided to a FileMaker Pro field through the Field Format dialog. It may either be static or dynamic. A static list derives its values from the value list dialog box. A dynamic list references the index values of another field either from the same file, or a separate FileMaker Pro file.

variable: Any piece of data that may change throughout the use of the database during on session. A field can be considered a local variable where a global is a global variable.

FileMaker Pro Specifications

Technical capabilities and limitations of FileMaker Pro

There are many times when knowing the capabilties and limitations of an environment help you create solutions. Contained in this appendix are the technical specifications about FileMaker Pro as provided by FileMaker, Inc.

Field Specifications

Date Field
Up to 255 characters per field, usually fewer are needed.

Date Range
Up to 255 characters in the format specified in the Date and Time control panel.

Field Types
Text; Number; Date; Time; Container (for OLE objects, sound, picture, or movie); Summary; Global.

Length of Field Name
Up to 60 characters.

Indexed (Key) Fields per File
Any field may be specified to index as an option, except: Container, Summary, Global, or unstored calculation fields. Only the first 20 characters of each word in a key field up to a total of 60 characters are used for matching in a relationship.

Number Field
Up to 255 characters per field. The first 120 characters are indexed.

Number of Field Repetitions (Sub Records)
Up to 1,000 for each field.

Number of Fields per Record
Limited only by disk space or maximum file size.

Number of Summary Functions
12

Number Precision

All numbers are converted to 64 bit extended floating point with precision of 15 decimal positions.

Numeric Range and Precision

Number fields can contain up to 255 characters including text. Only the first 120 numeric characters are indexed.

Summary

Depends on result type. See Text Field, Number Field, Date Field and Time Field for more information regarding field size limits.

Text Field

Number of characters limited only by memory (Up to 64,000 characters). Only the first 20 characters of each word are indexed. In addition, only lower ASCII characters are indexed so characters like "@" and "#" are not indexed. If you want higher ASCII characters to be indexed then you need to enter Define Fields and change the Storage Options to use a default language of ASCII rather than English or whatever language is selected.

Time Field

Up to 255 characters per field, usually fewer are needed.

Time Range

Times are not limited to 24-hour format to allow for calculations spanning multiple days. If the minutes or seconds exceed 60, the excess is carried over to minutes or hours as appropriate.

Calculation Specifications

Calculation Formula

Depends on result type. See Text Field, Number Field, Date Field and Time Field for more information regarding field size limits.

Calculation Operators

+, -, *, /, ^, =, ≠, <, >, ≤, ≥, AND, OR, NOT, XOR, ¶ (paragraph), " " (text literal), & (concatenation).

Number of Calculation Functions

109 logical, text, numeric, date, time, conversion, status, aggregate, financial, and trigonometric functions.

Size of Calculation Formula

Maximum of 32,767 characters, including text and numbers, any referenced fields, operators, functions and parentheses. If you ever need to make a calculation this large and you come up against this limitation, make the names of your fields shorter and you'll save characters.

Maximum Record Size

Limited by disk space or maximum file size.

Number of Records per File

Limited only by disk space or maximum file size.

Layout Size

Up to 110 inches wide by 110 inches long; may be limited by currently selected printer and page setup. Objects beyond current page width do not print.

Number of Columns Across the Page

Up to 99 columns.

Number of Labels Across the Page

Up to 99 labels.

Number of Layout Objects

Maximum of 32,767 objects on each layout.

Number of Layouts per File

Limited by disk space or maximum file size.

Import and Export filters are stored in the Claris folder within the System folder (Macintosh) and in the Claris folder, typically found within the Program Files folder, in the same directory as the FileMaker Pro folder (Windows).

File Formats for Import	**File Formats for Export**
FileMaker Pro, Tab-Separated Text, Comma-Separated Text, SYLK, DBF (dBASE), DIF, WKS, BASIC, Merge, Excel, ClarisWorks database.	Tab-Separated Text, Comma-Separated Text, SYLK, DBF (dBASE), DIF, WKS, BASIC, Merge, HTML, Edition File and FileMaker Pro.

BASIC (Import/Export – .BAS extension)

The preferred format to exchange data with Microsoft BASIC programs.

ClarisWorks 2.0/3.0/4.0 (Import only – .CWK or .CWS extension)

FileMaker can import data from ClarisWorks 2.0, 3.0 and 4.0 databases. Make sure to use the most current updater or version of FileMaker Pro 3.0 or higher. The ClarisWorks 4.0 import extension did not ship with the initial release.

Comma-Separated (Import/Export – .CSV or .TXT extension)

Comma-Separated text inserts quotes around each field, puts commas between each field and carriage returns (ASCII 13) between each record in an ASCII text file. Returns within fields are exported as soft returns or ASCII 11. FileMaker does not have the ability to adjust the delimiters. Changing all soft returns to hard returns requires a find and replace feature found in most word processing programs.

Data Access Manager (Import only)

Will import data from remote data sources like an SQL Server. Here is the information regarding 3 query building tools since FileMaker cannot communicate directly with a SQL Server: ClearAccess (Macintosh and Windows) Fairfield Software 800-522-4252 or 515-472-7077, DataPrism (Macintosh and Windows) Brio Technology, Inc. 800-486-2746 and GQL (Macintosh) Andyne Computing 800-267-0665 or 613-548-4355

DBF (Import/Export – .DBF extension)

The format used for exchanging data with dBASE.

DIF (Import/Export – .DIF extension)

This format attempts to pass along data type and formatting information in addition to the text. One of the pieces of information that DIF format retains is the names of fields. This could save a lot of time when transferring data from one database to another. If the receiving database understands DIF format then all the field names will be retained.

Edition File (Export only)

This Macintosh only export format is used for Publish and Subscribe. FileMaker does not support subscribing but it does support publishing via export. Each time an Edition file needs to be updated, a new export has to be done. The best way to facilitate this process is to create a script that restores an export.

Excel (Import only — .XLS extension)
Import data from Microsoft Excel (Mac OS versions 4.0 and 5.0, Windows versions 4.0 through 7.0 as well as Microsoft Excel for Office 97).

FileMaker Pro (Import/Export — .FP3 extension)
FileMaker Pro can import directly from FileMaker Pro 2.0 through 4.0, and export to FileMaker Pro 3.0 or 4.0. Only the current found set will be imported when importing from a FileMaker Pro database.

HTML Table (Export Only — .HTM extension)
Export data as an HTML table for use on a Web page. Rows are records and columns are fields.

Merge (Import/Export — .MER extension)
Exports data in a format that most word processors will be able to use as merge documents for a form letter. The first line exported contains the names of the fields which allows the word processor to match the fields with the data.

Picture Formats (Import Only)
GIF, JPEG, EPS, TIFF, PICT, MacPaint, QuickTime movies. Others via XTND and DataViz translators. Don't forget to check the Preference option for storing Macintosh compatible graphics if you design cross-platform databases on a Windows machine.

File format	Windows OS	Macintosh OS
Computer graphics metafile (.cgm)	Yes	No
Windows bitmap (.bmp)	Yes	No
Tag image file format, TIFF (.tif)	Yes	Yes
Graphics interchange format, GIF (.gif) (transparent and animated GIF files are not supported)	Yes	Yes
Joint Photographic Experts Group, JPEG (.jpg)	Yes	Yes
ZSoft Paintbrush (.pcx)	Yes	No
Aldus/Windows metafile (.wmf)	Yes	No
Micrografx Designer (.drw)	Yes	No
Lotus Picture (.pic)	Yes	No
Autocad Slide (.sld)	Yes	No
Mac OS PICT (.pct)	Yes	Yes
Claris MacPaint (.mac)	Yes	Yes
Encapsulated PostScript, EPSF (.eps)	Yes	Yes
QuickTime movie (.mov)	Yes (but not with Windows 3.1)	Yes

SYLK (Import/Export – .SLK extension)

The preferred format for exchanging data with spreadsheets, but Tab-Separated format works just as well. This format attempts to pass along data type and formatting information in addition to the text.

Tab-Separated (Import/Export –.TAB or .TXT extension)

This format is the most commonly used since it can exchange information with spreadsheets, other databases and word processors. Tab-Separated Text puts tabs (ASCII 9) between each field and carriage returns (ASCII 13) between each record in an ASCII text file. Returns within fields are exported as soft returns or ASCII 11. FileMaker does not have the ability to change the delimiters so in order to change all of the soft returns to hard returns, it will be necessary to use the find and replace feature of your word processing program.

WKS (Import/Export – .WK1 or .WKS extension)

The preferred format for Lotus 1-2-3 spreadsheet.

File Specifications

Number of Files Open Simultaneously

Up to 50 files. This number is limited by the number of users connected. For instance, you cannot have the maximum number of files networked to the maximum number of guests. FileMaker Pro Server allows a maximum of 100 files with 100 users.

Number of Files per Disk

Limited only by disk space.

File Size

Limited only by disk space, to a maximum of 2 GB (gigabytes) on a hard disk. If you ever reach the file size limit, the file will begin to overwrite itself.

Number of Scripts

Limited by disk space; up to 52 displayed in menu.

Number of Sort Levels

Ten fields in a sort specification.

Networking Protocols

AppleTalk, TCP/IP and IPX. Only TCP/IP and IPX are available for cross-platform database sharing. FileMaker Pro 2.0 used to support AppleTalk cross-platform but support was dropped in FileMaker Pro 3.0. FileMaker Pro 3.0 for Macintosh comes with MacIPX as a custom install option. TCP/IP networking under Windows 3.11 requires Windows for Workgroups. FileMaker is only certified with Microsoft implementations of these protocols.

Number of Network Users per File

Maximum of 25 guests. Other network applications may limit this number since there are only so many network connections FileMaker can handle. In addition, the number of files may also limit the number of users. FileMaker Pro Server allows a maximum of 100 files with 100 users.

Index

A

ABORT.FP3, 42, 137
Access Privileges, 265
Allow User Abort, 42
Alt Key, 369
AND, 169-170
ANIMATE.FP3, 357
animations, 356
appending, 270
array, 358
array, 358
arrow keys, 375
ascending counter, 155
ASCII, 223, 337
ASCII.FP3, 223
auto-enter calculation, 235
auto-enter serial number, 392
AutoGrid, 375

B

Beep, 43
bitmap fonts, 339
BOOKMARK.FP3, 391
Boolean, 165, 229, 230, 242
branching, 35
buttons
  active, 362
  dimmed, 362
  Exit, 31
  Halt, 31
  inactive, 362
  Pause, 31
  Perform Script, 31
  portals, 308
  Resume, 31
  states, 362

C

calculated relationship, 295
calculated replace, 263
calculation result, 217, 325
calculation functions
  (see Appendix B)
Case, 14, 168, 177, 180, 205, 231, 264, 361, 368
Change Password, 44
check boxes, 246, 248
Check Found Set, 45
Check Record, 45
Check Selection, 46
child file, 287
CLAIRVOY.FP3, 296
Clear, 46, 193
client, 275
clone, 355
Close, 47
CLOSE.FP3, 139
color palette, 343
color, 343
COLORS.FP3, 343, 345
comma delimited, 268
command key, 369
Comment, 48
COMMENT.FP3, 21, 48, 205
concatenate, 240, 270, 272
concatenated key, 297
COND.FP3, 254
COND2.FP3, 255
Conditional branching, 166
conditional menus, 251
conditional, 14
constant relationship, 151
constant, 149, 151, 393
contains, 82

suffix, 23
support
  books, 387
  magazines, 386
  mailing lists, 383
  training, 385
  training courses, 383
  user groups, 386
SYNCH.FP3, 86, 118

variables, 358, 394
View As, 141
View Index dialog, 220
window dialog box, 371
WordCount, 272
XOR, 167, 169, 172

T

tab delimited, 268
tab order, 258-259
TCP/IP, 332
temporary calculations, 191
TextToDate, 218
TextToNum, 218
TextToTime, 218
time-based key, 299
TimeToText, 218
Toggle Status Area, 136
Toggle Text Ruler, 137
Toggle Window, 138, 374
toolbox scripts, 396
trigger field, 284

U – Z

Undo, 139
unique key, 295
UNIQ_VAL.FP3, 240
Unsort, 140
unstored, 153
Update Link, 141
user interface, 354
validation•calculated, 229•cross-field,
  236•duplicates, 239•globals, 233•multi-
  ple criteria, 230
value lists, 246, 251-252